health
magazine

SuperFoods

The Essential Guide to
Boosting Energy, Fighting Disease,
and Losing Weight

TIME
LIFE
BOOKS

Alexandria, Virginia

Time-Life Books is a division of Time Life Inc.
Time-Life is a trademark of Time Warner Inc. and affiliated companies.

TIME LIFE INC.
Chairman and Chief Executive Officer: Jim Nelson
President and Chief Operating Officer: Steven Janas
Senior Executive Vice President and Chief Operations Officer: Mary Davis Holt
Senior Vice President and Chief Financial Officer: Christopher Hearing

TIME-LIFE BOOKS
President: Larry Jellen
Senior Vice President, New Markets: Bridget Boel
Vice President, Home and Hearth Markets: Nicholas M. DiMarco
Vice President, Content Development: Jennifer L. Pearce

TIME-LIFE TRADE PUBLISHING
Vice President and Publisher: Neil S. Levin
Senior Sales Director: Richard J. Vreeland
Director, Marketing and Publicity: Inger Forland
Director of Trade Sales: Dana Hobson
Director of Custom Publishing: John Lalor
Director of Rights and Licensing: Olga Vezeris

SUPER FOODS—TIME LIFE
Director of New Product Development: Carolyn M. Clark
New Product Development Manager: Lori A. Woehrle
Executive Editor: Robert Somerville
Director of Design: Tina Taylor
Project Manager: Jennifer L. Ward
Technical Specialist: Monika Lynde
Page Makeup Specialist: Jennifer Gearhart
Production Manager: Virginia Reardon
Quality Assurance: Jim King and Stacy L. Eddy

Front cover: Renée Comet Photography, Inc.
Back cover (l-r): Amy Neunsinger (photo), Carol Applegate (styling); Stuart Watson; Rita Maas

SUPER FOODS—HEALTH MAGAZINE
Food and Nutrition Editor, Health magazine: Sheridan Warrick
Editor-in-Chief, Time Inc Health Custom Publishing: John Poppy
Art Director: Robin Terra
Associate Art Director: Margery Cantor
Executive Editor: Eric Olsen
Senior Editor: Annie Stine
Associate Editor: Beatrice Motamedi
Copy Editors: Cheryl Olsen, Ellen Rush, Lorrie Voigt
Researchers: Katie Isenberg, Kristen Philipkoski, Kimberly Wong
Photo Editors: Caren Alpert, Caroline Cory
Designers: Tom Burleigh, Amy Feldman, Shannon Laskey

TIME INC HEALTH
Editor-in-Chief, Health magazine: Barbara Paulsen
Vice President/Publisher, Health magazine: Mary E. Morgan
Chief Operating Officer: Martha A. Lorini

Copyright © 1999, 2000 by Time Inc Health
A division of Time Health Media Inc.

Editorial offices:
Two Embarcadero Center, Suite 600
San Francisco, CA 94111
(415) 248-2700

First printing.
Printed in the U.S.A.
10 9 8 7 6 5 4 3 2 1
ISBN 0-7370-1628-0

CIP data available upon request:
Librarian, Time-Life Books
2000 Duke Street
Alexandria, VA 22314

This book is not intended to replace common sense or a doctor's advice. Given the differences of age, gender, and medical history, only your doctor can render a definitive diagnosis and recommend treatment for you and your family. Super Foods is as accurate as its publishers and authors can make it; nevertheless, they disclaim all liability and cannot be held responsible for any problems that may arise from its use.

CONTENTS

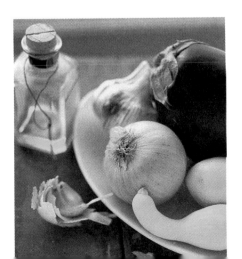

Eat Like the Devil, Feel Like a Saint

There is no love sincerer than the love of food," quipped George Bernard Shaw, and I guess I'd have to agree. As HEALTH magazine's Mr. Food, I spend all day every day consulting with chefs and growers, tasting new products, envisioning delectable dishes, dialing up nutrition experts, poring over journal articles, thinking food, talking food, all but breathing food. And yet I still love to go home, cook up a storm, then sit down to a great dinner and a glass of wine.

Best of all, I've made a fantastic discovery in the process. Cynics insist that keeping up on the latest nutrition news takes the joy out of dining, that you can't be a food-lover and a smart eater at the same time. That's just sour grapes. My nightly smile of contentment has only widened as I've learned that salmon, olive oil, garlic, hot peppers, avocados, pizza, asparagus, tomatoes, raspberries, almonds, and even dark chocolate not only taste wonderful but actually help shield me from heart disease, cancer, diabetes, osteoporosis, obesity, and many other maladies I'm quite happy to avoid.

Super foods is what I call these miracle workers, and it's no exaggeration. By identifying hundreds of protective compounds in many of the items you can find in the supermarket, the nation's nutritionists have launched a health revolution—and you're the one who stands to benefit.

But don't take my word for it. Dig into this book. Inside you'll find a rundown on which foods appear most effective in cutting your risk of several diseases (page 10); the best advice on losing weight (pages 36 and 62); surprising news about good and bad fats (page 70); plus an essential update on vitamins and minerals (page 88). Oh—and a huge batch of fully tested recipes that make it easy to put these powerful health promoters on your table at every meal (page 108).

Don't worry for a second that the recipes might be, you know, a bit *too* healthy. We cut the calories and the artery-clogging fat you hate but kept the flavor and the richness you love. Of course, that's the whole idea behind this book: With the facts at your fingertips, you really can eat like the devil—and feel like a saint.

Sheridan Warrick

SHERIDAN WARRICK
Food and Nutrition Editor,
HEALTH *magazine*

Eat to Fight Disease

The Top 50 Healing Foods

It's one of the greatest discoveries of the 20th century: Through diet alone, you can dramatically cut your risk of heart disease, cancer, diabetes, and more.

What a sweet prescription: Grace your plate with the right foods and you'll increase your chances of living a long, healthy life. Intrigued by the evidence that diet is key to guarding against disease, scientists are looking into what makes certain ingredients so vital. Chances are you've heard of what they've found: phytochemicals and antioxidants, powerful compounds that maintain sound blood vessels and thwart carcinogens.

The foods in this chapter are rich in these and other substances that help keep you well. So get to know the fabulous 50 and their talented relatives. They're among the most welcome guests you could have at your table.

Fight cancer

Often it seems to strike at random, but cancer isn't always mysterious. Smoking and chewing tobacco, avoiding exercise, and tanning are to blame for a big share of the more than 1 million new cases of cancer that will be diagnosed in the United States this year.

But of all the things you do that can tip the odds in your favor or tilt them against you, what you eat is among the most important. A panel appointed by the World Cancer Research Fund and the American Institute for Cancer Research has concluded that good nutrition can reduce the incidence of many types of cancer by up to 40 percent.

The following foods carry no guarantees, but slice a tomato, dice a pepper, chop some garlic, and you'll almost certainly cut your risk.

Beets After years of being an often-overlooked regular at the salad bar, beets are beginning to get the respect they deserve. In a 1994 study of more than 60 fruits and vegetables, researchers in Germany found that beets contain some of the most powerful cancer-fighting agents around. One of them, an antioxidant called betacyanin, gives red beets their particularly rich hue. Canned beets retain their native sweetness, but fresh will give you a lot more folic acid (also known as folate), a B vitamin that may protect against heart disease and colon cancer.

To roast: Place beets in a pan with a sprinkle of water, cover tightly with foil, and bake at 375° for about an hour, until they're soft enough to pierce easily with a fork. When they're cool, slip them out of their skins.

Blueberries This member of the fiber-filled berry family is extraordinarily rich in antioxidants, topping all other foods in the ability to neutralize free radicals, unstable molecules that can damage DNA. The color's the secret; blue pigments called anthocyanins, also found in cherries,

Gold beta-carotene, red lycopene, and purple anthocyanins are among the disease-fighting compounds that give fruits and vegetables their delicious colors.

plums, and other blue-red fruits, have been shown to inactivate a number of common carcinogens.

Broccoli & cabbage One of the first vegetables found to have anticancer properties, broccoli is still considered among the most potent. Its cruciferous cousins—cabbage, cauliflower, and brussels sprouts—aren't far behind.

Research has shown that a substance in broccoli called sulforaphane stimulates the body to produce an enzyme that defuses potential carcinogens. In one study, rats fed an extract of broccoli and then exposed to a strong carcinogen were far less likely to develop cancer than were rats on a standard diet. And when the broccoli eaters did get cancer, their tumors were smaller and took longer to grow than those in the other rats.

Garlic & onions The distinctive tang that characterizes garlic and onions comes from chemicals called organosulfurs. But these compounds do more than give the bulbs their buzz. Like the sulforaphane in crucifers, they boost levels of enzymes that detoxify potential carcinogens.

Research shows that substances in garlic can significantly slow the development of prostate cancer cells. Studies also suggest that garlic's organosulfurs may block carcinogens in foods eaten with it. Garlic extract has slowed the growth of breast, skin, and colon cancers in mice.

Although you have to eat onions raw to get the benefit of their sulfurs, the yellow and red varieties also contain quercetin, an antioxidant that can survive cooking.

Green tea A few years ago researchers at Rutgers University replaced the drinking water of some lab mice with green tea and then exposed the whole group to chemicals that normally cause tumors. The mice that went on drinking plain water developed cancer; most of the tea sippers remained cancer-free.

The credit goes to polyphenols, antioxidants that are plentiful in green tea (black tea contains significantly lower levels, herbal tea none). Further studies of tea have shown that when malignant cells do form, one group of polyphenols

---

HEALTH NOTE

Apricot kernels, source of the **BOGUS CANCER DRUG** laetrile, are back, sold on the Internet and in health marts. Beware: They can be toxic. A woman in Arizona was hospitalized with cyanide poisoning after eating about 30 kernels. Skip them, doctors say.

---

seems to prevent the cancerous cells from multiplying—and may even kill them while leaving healthy cells unharmed.

Two tips for tea drinkers: Let it cool a little (boiling-hot beverages may damage the esophagus), and go easy on the milk (its proteins bind with the polyphenols, possibly canceling their effect). For more on the benefits of tea, see "Wake Up to Tea," page 52.

Hot peppers In salsas and sauces, stir-fries and spicy drinks, red-hot chile peppers are growing more popular than ever. Now researchers suspect that capsaicin, the stuff in peppers that sets your tongue on fire, may extinguish carcinogens before they cause trouble.

A potent antioxidant, capsaicin obstructs the deadly union of nitrites and amines. When researchers mixed pure capsaicin into a brew of nitrosamines, those cancer-causing substances were almost completely neutralized.

In addition, capsaicin may keep carcinogens in cigarette smoke from locking onto DNA, possibly preventing genetic damage that can lead to lung and other cancers.

Oranges, lemons, & limes These fruits contain an abundance of limonene, a substance that boosts levels of naturally occurring enzymes thought to break down carcinogens and stimulate cancer-killing immune cells. Citrus fruits also contain glucarase, which inactivates carcinogens and speeds them out of the body.

Pure limonene reduces and prevents tumors in mice, but one study suggests that orange juice may work just as well. When mice exposed to a potent carcinogen downed the juice (an amount equivalent to about a gallon a day for humans), they developed 40 percent fewer early signs of cancer than did mice on a juiceless diet.

Soybeans Poor, nondescript soybeans. Ground into flour or shaped into cubes of tofu, they haven't played a big part in the American diet. But that's changing as scientists continue to report that soy is rich in genistein, a substance that appears to protect against cancer in several ways.

Estrogen stimulates cancer cells in the breasts

and ovaries, a process genistein interrupts by plugging up receptors for the hormone. Genistein may also prevent small blood vessels from forming around cancer cells, depriving them of oxygen and nutrients. One study found that a diet rich in soy protein lengthens the menstrual cycle by roughly a day and a half, reducing a woman's exposure to estrogen. That could help explain why Japanese women are a fourth as likely to get breast cancer as women in the United States.

Tofu need not merely be tolerated. Marinate and then grill, bake, or sauté it; puree it into a dip, dressing, or fruit shake. It will virtually disappear into your favorite stir-fry, soup, or casserole.

Spinach, chard, collards, & kale In the kitchen these humble leafy greens need little attention. Drop them into a pot of boiling water, sauté them with garlic and olive oil—voilà, you have a soup or a side dish that's almost as good as a sprightly carrot or a cantaloupe when it comes to supplying

a cancer-fighting antioxidant called beta-carotene.

The chlorophyll in the leaves of these veggies does more than mask the beta-carotene's orange color. Researchers suspect that when chlorophyll is broken down during digestion, it too becomes a powerful defense against cancer. According to one study, animals fed a compound much like digested chlorophyll while they were exposed to carcinogens showed a significantly lower risk of developing cancers of the stomach, colon, and liver. More amazing, when mice were fed the green pigment and then exposed to a potent skin cancer–causing substance, they developed far fewer tumors than did untreated mice.

Leafy greens are also rich in compounds called indole-3 carbonals, which may protect against breast and endometrial cancers.

Tomatoes Epidemiologist Edward Giovannucci of Harvard University recently analyzed 72 studies in which scientists had compared cancer rates

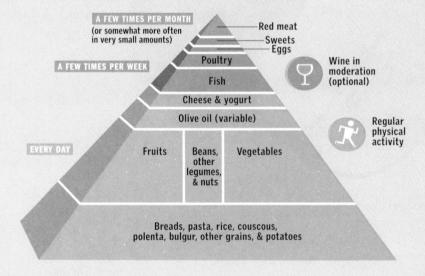

THE Best Diet FOR A LONG LIFE

For the ideal mix of foods, some experts favor a change from the well-known U.S. Department of Agriculture Food Pyramid. They like the Traditional Healthy Mediterranean Diet Pyramid, developed in 1994 by researchers at the Harvard School of Public Health. Based on the eating habits found in southern Italy and Greece—where people tend to live long, healthy lives—it calls for big helpings of starches and other complex carbohydrates every day in the form of pasta, grains, fresh fruits, beans, and other vegetables, along with protein from small portions of cheese or yogurt. Modest amounts of fish and poultry are okay, but they're not for every day. Red meat is only a once-in-a-while treat.

among people according to the amount of tomatoes and tomato-rich foods they ate. Giovannuci found that tomato eaters had a 40 percent lower incidence of cancer.

They also tended to have high blood levels of lycopene, an antioxidant that infuses tomatoes with their luscious redness. Tomatoes supply as much as 90 percent of the lycopene many of us get.

There's strong evidence that tomatoes need to be cooked and combined with fat—such as olive oil or cheese—to release their lycopene in a form your body can absorb.

Winter squashes Nineteenth century French painter and gourmand Henri de Toulouse-Lautrec loved winter squashes for their brilliant color,

which is also the source of their nutritional beauty. Winter squashes are full of carotenoids, the pigments that color autumn leaves as well as many fruits and vegetables.

The most famous carotenoid is beta-carotene, the orange pigment named after carrots but also found in butternut, hubbard, and turban squashes, not to mention their jocular cousin, pumpkin.

The potential of beta-carotene has sparked significant scientific interest during the last decade. In the late 1980s a study in Great Britain showed that men who ate fruits and vegetables rich in beta-carotene nearly every day had about half the

cancer risk of those who ate almost none. Still another study found that cigarette smokers were less likely to get lung cancer if they ate foods high in beta-carotene. (Beware of supplements, however; research shows that megadoses of beta-carotene could *raise* your lung cancer risk.)

Spoon up half a baked butternut and your body converts it into all the vitamin A you need for a day plus half the vitamin C; a healthy dose of potassium, calcium, and iron; and a nice hit of fiber. It's a hearty dish that's so creamy it seems almost decadent—and it's only 82 calories.

Defend your heart

Good cholesterol, bad cholesterol, good fat, bad fat. The heart disease puzzle is definitely complicated, but you hold quite a few pieces in your own hands. Study after study confirms it: You can reduce your risk of falling victim to America's number one killer by eating certain foods and avoiding others.

As you cruise the supermarket, search out foods with fiber: It prevents cholesterol from being absorbed into your bloodstream, where it can clog your arteries. You also want foods high in folic acid, the B vitamin that helps protect blood vessels from damage. Finally, mind the fats: Steer away from saturated (the kind in butter and meats) and look for monounsaturated (found in olive and canola oils). And if you're there for just a quick shop, turn toward the produce section, the most heart-friendly place in the store.

Apples & pears An apple—or a pear—a day may keep the doctor away after all. Both are packed with pectin, a water-soluble fiber that can help lower the risk of heart disease.

In one study a group of healthy men and women added two or three apples a day to their diet; four out of five saw a drop in their levels of artery-clogging cholesterol. In another study, research subjects with high cholesterol who ate cookies loaded with apple fiber reduced their cholesterol by 7 percent. And in animal studies a diet rich in pectin has been shown to diminish by half the narrowing of arteries caused by atherosclerosis. If you grow tired of crunching your pectin, try prunes, apricots, and bananas; they're also rich in the fiber.

Avocados Once shunned along with cheddar and ground beef, the buttery avocado is now considered an ideal stand-in for meat and cheese in a sandwich, burrito, or salad. How did the rough-skinned fruit turn its reputation around? As studies rolled in on the pros and cons of various fats and oils, it became clear that avocados are actually good for you: They are high in monounsaturated fat, which may slightly raise HDL (the good cholesterol) and slightly lower LDL (the bad).

Of course heart disease isn't the only health problem related to fat intake. While avocados may be cast in a new light, they're still loaded with calories, so don't get bogged down in the guacamole.

Beans From common kidneys and limas to exotic appaloosas and pinquitos, beans are a feast for the eyes and the taste buds.

Like all fiber-rich foods, beans help your heart by reducing total cholesterol levels. A half-cup serving provides between five and seven grams of fiber, depending on the variety. One study has shown that eating a cup of cooked beans per day can lower blood cholesterol by an average of 10 percent.

Beans are also full of folic acid, which controls the body's level of an amino acid called homocysteine. Some experts say that high amounts,

of homocysteine are as risky to the heart as smoking and perhaps more consequential than cholesterol. Some scientists speculate that if this amino acid didn't damage cells first, cholesterol couldn't collect in the arteries. Folic acid, together with vitamins B-6 and B-12, acts as a kind of chemical broom, sweeping excess homocysteine from the body.

Blackberries & raspberries Few fruits deliver a thrill as sweet, messy, and primal as a blackberry or raspberry plucked ripe from the bramble. Luckily, we can now add healthy to those delights. These berries may guard against cancer, but their best-kept secret lies in the tiny seeds that get stuck between your teeth: Blackberries are among the richest sources of fruit-borne fiber you can find.

Many studies have shown that soluble fiber (the easily digestible kind found in vegetables, fruits, and whole grains) lowers cholesterol. But a recent study at the Harvard School of Public Health offers powerful evidence that insoluble fiber (the kind found in a food's peel, stalk, or husk—and in many berries' seeds) also plays a part in protecting against heart disease. After tracking

High in fiber, folic acid, vitamins E and A, and heart-friendly fats, avocados are among the healthiest foods you can eat.

51,000 men for more than a decade, researchers theorized that each ten-gram increase in insoluble fiber reduces the risk of heart disease by 20 percent. Blackberries, with nearly four grams per cup, deliver more insoluble fiber than most other fruits, including apples and pears.

Cantaloupe, carrots, & sweet potatoes The widely praised beta-carotene gets its name from carrots, but it colors a range of orange and yellow fruits and vegetables. (It's also hiding behind the chlorophyll in broccoli and dark leafy greens.) As well as having anticancer properties, beta-carotene is a gift for the heart.

The higher the levels of beta-carotene in the bloodstream, research shows, the lower the risk of heart attacks. In studies conducted by the U.S. Department of Agriculture, volunteers who ate two to three carrots a day saw their cholesterol levels fall an average of 11 percent. In a Harvard study that followed 80,000 nurses for more than a decade, those who ate at least five servings of carrots a week had a 68 percent lower risk of stroke than those who ate no more than one serving a month.

While you're most likely to munch a carrot for your afternoon snack, don't overlook the sweet potato, another great source of everybody's favorite antioxidant. And you'll also do well to bet on cantaloupe, the winning fruit in the beta-carotene derby.

Celery Prized for its crunch and scanty calories, celery is mostly water, which makes it a terrific light snack. And some scientists believe that a compound in celery stalks called 3-n-butyl phthalide may help keep blood pressure in check. The compound, which gives celery its aroma, seems to work by lowering the blood's concentration of stress hormones that typically cause blood vessels to contract. Research also shows that eating four stalks a day can lower blood cholesterol levels by as much as 14 percent.

Fish According to folklore, fish is brain food. But the latest findings say its real benefit is a healthy heart. Because the fat in fish consists of omega-3 fatty acids—one kind of fat that's actually good for you—

physicians around the country are urging their patients to eat fish twice a week. Many species provide omega-3s, but the best sources are rich, oily types like salmon, sardines, bluefin tuna, and mackerel.

An ocean of evidence shows the various ways that omega-3s trigger changes within the heart, blood vessels, and blood. This type of fat fends off arterial blockages, helps relax narrowed arteries so blood can flow more freely, reduces blood levels of a low-density lipoprotein associated with heart disease, and promotes healing of arterial walls.

Does an occasional serving of salmon counteract a lifetime of visits to the local burger joint? As a matter of fact, it may. In 1995 researchers found that heart attack patients who added fatty fish to their diets just once a week slashed their risk of a second attack in half. For more details, see "A Food Lover's Guide to Fats," page 70.

Grapes One of the oldest cultivated fruits, grapes date all the way back to Neolithic times. Today scientists are discovering new reasons to savor these juicy globes. Researchers say that grapes, which may destroy certain cancer-causing compounds, are also packed with flavonoids, antioxidants that may prevent blood clots. One heart researcher found that the flavonoids in purple grape juice were as effective as aspirin in preventing the kind of blood clotting that can lead to heart attacks.

Olives & olive oil Health gurus now agree that the total amount of fat you eat is far less important than the types. Saturated fats, found in meat and dairy foods, lead to heart problems when you eat a lot of them, as do trans fatty acids, which lurk in margarine, shortening, and that doughnut you indulged in on the way to work.

But research shows that if the fat you consume is polyunsaturated (the type in corn and soybean oils) and monounsaturated (olive and canola oils), it actually protects you from heart disease. Monounsaturated fats appear to reduce total cholesterol without lowering the HDL that helps keep arteries plaque-free. (See "A Food Lover's Guide to Fats," page 70.)

HEALTH NOTE

30
Percentage of children who eat the recommended two to four daily servings of fruit

36
Percentage who eat the recommended three to five daily servings of vegetables

How Well Do You Know Your Carbs?

The carbohydrates in fruits, vegetables, beans, pasta, and grains fall into two groups: starches, or complex carbs, and sugars, or simple carbs. Test your carb-smarts with this quiz.

1 A complex carbohydrate is always better than a simple one.

TRUE OR FALSE

2 Eating pasta can ease stress.

TRUE OR FALSE

3 Brown bread is, by definition, better for you than white.

TRUE OR FALSE

4 Apple juice is just as good for you as the whole fruit.

TRUE OR FALSE

5 When you're faint with hunger, a chocolate bar will revive you as quickly as a soft drink.

TRUE OR FALSE

6 Eating mashed potatoes can have the same effect on your blood sugar as drinking a cup of juice.

TRUE OR FALSE

ANSWERS

1 **False**. When starches contain little or no fiber—as in white bread, white rice, and potatoes—your body converts them promptly to glucose, spurring a blood sugar surge. Regularly overloading on these (or on sweets) can raise your risk of Type 2 diabetes.

2 **True**. A starch like pasta can boost serotonin, the body's feel-good chemical. But you must eat it on an empty stomach, without oil or cheese.

3 **False**. Unless brown bread is mainly whole grains (thus high in fiber), it's the same as white.

4 **False**. The juice is essentially sugar dissolved in water, with a few nutrients—but no fiber.

5 **False**. Both are full of sugar. But the candy bar contains fat, which slows the energizing effect.

6 **True**. Without fiber, many complex and simple carbs act the same in your body.

This information has elevated the olive's status in the grocery store, where the drab green balls (with a bit of red peeking out) used to be crammed into jars and positioned between the hamburger relish and sweet gherkins. Now, usually enthroned in their very own display case, they come in all varieties: wrinkly black dry-cureds and glossy green brine-cureds, Greek kalamatas, French niçoise, Italian frantoios—some stuffed with garlic and hot peppers.

Despite their new acclaim, olives and their oil are high in fat. Olive oil is an ideal replacement for butter and margarine, but not something to splash onto your food with abandon.

Shrimp Although they're low in fat and have a hint of heart-friendly fish oils, shrimp were for many years a guilty pleasure. But bring out the cocktail sauce: Researchers have found that the much-maligned crustaceans generally do no harm and concluded there's no reason to avoid the high-cholesterol treat.

In one study, scientists had 18 healthy adults spend three weeks on a low-fat diet that included ten ounces of steamed shrimp a day (much more than most folks eat). The shellfish did boost the study subjects' levels of low-density lipoprotein—bad cholesterol—but that increase was offset by a rise in high-density lipoprotein, the

HEALTH NOTE

Studies show that omega-3 fatty acids may block the body's production of certain substances linked to joint inflammation and damage. Some **ARTHRITIS** sufferers have found relief by eating fish rich in these good fats. Any fish with more than five grams of fat per serving is a good choice.

good stuff. So the LDL-to-HDL ratio stayed the same.

The cardiologist who led the study says that when served occasionally and healthfully—in pasta or salad, not batter-fried or butter-soaked—shrimp is a fine choice even for people with high cholesterol.

Get rough on diabetes

Scientists predict that by 2007 more than 21 million Americans—about one of every ten adults—will have Type 2 diabetes, the kind that people in their forties and older may develop. A chronic illness without a cure, diabetes is the fourth leading cause of death by disease in the United States.

Some research suggests that a diet heavy in high-carbohydrate, low-fiber foods that are digested quickly, such as white bread and white-flour pasta, could set you up for this illness. A Harvard study reported that

women whose meals are chock-full of fiber-rich foods significantly lower their chances of developing Type 2 diabetes.

Most of us take in less than half the 25 to 30 grams of fiber that nutritionists recommend we get each day. Consuming that much requires some effort, but it doesn't mean that every meal has to begin and end with oat bran. Other foods, including many fruits, vegetables, and grains, are great sources too.

Artichokes The thistly artichoke may appear formidable, but it's worth peeling every poker-faced leaf to reach the soft fiber-filled heart. Brussels sprouts, squash, and chard are also high in fiber, but downing a cup of those veggies doesn't match the fun of deconstructing the globe of an artichoke. The bit of heart at the bottom of each leaf is delicious plain, but if you need to dip, don't go diving into butter or mayonnaise. Try lemon juice, yogurt, or a low-fat salad dressing.

Beans No respectable high-fiber plan can ignore beans, which supply more per cup than almost any fruit or vegetable in town. And don't get stuck in a chili rut; beans are bountiful in their variety. When you tire of pinto and navy, there are adzuki and cannellini, ivory rice and jacob's cattle. As versatile as potatoes, beans can take on the earthiness of southern cooking or the sophisticated airs of French cuisine.

Whole grains Research shows you can improve your health merely by switching to whole grain cereal at breakfast. But don't stop there. Brown rice has nearly four grams of fiber in a cup while the same amount of white rice has only one gram. A cup of whole wheat macaroni has more than twice the fiber of the refined white kind. A piece of

What's in a SERVING?

You know you're supposed to get five servings of fruits and vegetables a day, but just how much is one?

One serving of fruit is
- a whole fruit such as a medium apple, banana, or orange
- a grapefruit half or a melon wedge
- $3/4$ cup (6 ounces) 100 percent fruit juice
- $1/2$ cup of berries
- $1/2$ cup of cooked or canned fruit
- $1/4$ cup of dried fruit

One serving of vegetables is
- a medium-size carrot, potato, artichoke, ear of corn, etc.
- $1/2$ cup chopped vegetables, raw or cooked
- 1 cup raw leafy vegetables such as spinach or lettuce
- $3/4$ cup (6 ounces) 100 percent vegetable juice
- $1/2$ cup cooked dry peas or beans

How Healthy Is Your Diet?

Evaluating your eating habits takes more than tallying up daily servings of fruits and vegetables. Circle one answer to each question, then see how you score at the end.

1 A typical weekday breakfast for me is
a) bacon and eggs or a big muffin
b) pancakes, french toast, or a bagel with cream cheese
c) a bowl of whole grain cereal with berries or banana slices

2 My midmorning snack is most often a
a) doughnut or croissant
b) granola bar or low-fat muffin
c) orange, apple, or other fruit

3 When I have a sandwich for lunch, it's likely to be
a) ham and cheese or tuna salad on white bread
b) roast beef with mayo on whole wheat
c) turkey or chicken breast on multigrain bread, hold the mayo

4 At salad bars my plate usually ends up heavy with
a) sliced meat, chopped egg, and cheese
b) lettuce, creamy dressing, and croutons
c) leafy greens, beans, and veggies

5 If I eat lunch at a fast-food restaurant, I usually order
a) a burger or deep-fried fish sandwich with soda and fries
b) a chef's salad
c) a chicken breast sandwich, no sauce

6 My midafternoon snack is typically
a) a candy bar, cookies, or chips
b) crackers with cheese or peanut butter
c) celery, carrot sticks, unsalted nuts, or a piece of fruit

7 The biggest portion of my dinner is most likely to be
a) pot roast, fried chicken, or sausage
b) chicken or turkey breast, or lean cuts of pork or beef
c) fish, beans, or vegetables

8 My dinner vegetable usually is something like
a) french fries
b) salad made with iceberg lettuce
c) broccoli, green beans, carrots, corn, or tomatoes

9 When sautéing, I use
a) butter or stick margarine
b) corn or soy oil
c) olive or canola oil

10 With lunch or dinner, I like to drink
a) a soft drink
b) coffee, tea, or water
c) 1 percent or nonfat milk

11 When dining out, I like to order
a) a thick juicy steak
b) pasta with meat sauce
c) grilled fish or shrimp

12 The pizza toppings I ask for most are
a) sausage and pepperoni, extra cheese
b) chicken or beef and cheese
c) peppers and onions, light on the cheese

13 If a restaurant serves large portions, I
a) eat everything on my plate
b) take my leftovers home for a late snack
c) order an appetizer and a salad

14 Desserts are usually
a) ice cream, cake, or pie
b) fruit sorbet or frozen yogurt
c) berries or other fresh fruit

S C O R I N G

If you answered C most often, congratulations! You're eating better than most Americans.
If you circled mostly Bs, you'd be smart to trade some meat and cheese for fruits and veggies.
If you circled mostly As, you might want to do a few things to tune up your diet.

whole wheat bread gives you at least one gram of fiber, a slice of white just half a gram. Weary of the grains you grew up with? Go exotic with quinoa or amaranth.

When scanning labels in the bread aisle, look for the word *whole*. Whether you're after wheat, oat, rye, or pumpernickel, it should be the first word in the ingredient list.

Wheat germ & wheat bran When refined, all grains are divided into three parts: germ, bran, and endosperm. White flour is made of ground wheat endosperm, even though most of the nutrients are in the bran and the germ. To make whole wheat flour, the three constituents are reunited after milling.

In addition to being a top-notch source of folic acid and vitamin E, wheat germ carries a considerable load of fiber—nearly four grams in a quarter of a cup. Wheat bran, of course, takes the fiber cake with an impressive six grams per quarter cup.

GETTING YOUR Fill of Fiber

Some researchers believe that people who don't eat enough fiber may be endangering their health just as much as do people who smoke or let their high blood pressure go untreated. And that's a lot of us: Although most nutritionists recommend consuming 25 to 30 grams of fiber a day, the average American manages to get only half that much.

If you're among the fiber-deprived, try putting more of the rough stuff into your diet starting first thing in the morning. A high-fiber cereal topped with berries will get you halfway to your goal. Snack on an apple midmorning, then have some beans for lunch or dinner.

Still short? With five grams of fiber, a 5 1/2-cup serving of air-popped popcorn is likely to put you over the top.

But don't expect to become a fiber convert overnight. Because it isn't broken down by the body's enzymes, fiber can ferment in the intestine, sometimes causing bloating and gas. You can avoid discomfort by adding grams gradually—an extra five a day for a few days, then another five.

FOOD	FIBER (G)
Fruits	
Blackberries, 1 cup	7
Figs, 3 dried	7
Apple	4
Pear	4
Orange	3
Vegetables	
Acorn squash, 1 cup cooked	9
Artichoke, globe	6
Brussels sprouts, 1 cup	6
Potato, 1 large with skin	5
Broccoli, 1 cup	4

FOOD	FIBER (G)
Corn, 1 cup	4
Swiss chard, 1 cup cooked	4
Cauliflower, 1 cup raw	3
Grains	
Kellogg's All Bran Cereal, 1/2 cup	10
Cornmeal, yellow, 1 cup	9
Brown rice, 1 cup cooked	4
Bulgur, 1/2 cup cooked	4
Oatmeal, 1 cup cooked	4
Whole wheat bread, 2 slices	4
Barley, 1/2 cup cooked	3
Cheerios, 1 cup	3
Beans, 1/2 cup cooked	
Kidney, red	8
Lentil	8
Black	7
Navy	7
Pinto	7
White	6
Garbanzo	5

There's plenty you can do with the nutty-tasting crumbs of germ and bran. Sprinkle some on hot or cold cereal or on a scoop of nonfat frozen yogurt. Slip some into a casserole or use them to coat a piece of fish or chicken. Substitute half a cup for an equal amount of flour when making bread, muffins, or pancakes.

Breathe easier

Enjoy a diet rich in vegetables and fruits and your lungs will thank you. Research suggests that these foods may protect you from asthma, chronic bronchitis, and emphysema. In a recent study investigators measured the lung function of nearly 18,000 adults. The difference between those with the most antioxidants in their diets and those with the least was equal to that between nonsmokers and people who have smoked a pack a day for ten years.

What you eat plays a role on the common cold front, too. Can't see past your plugged-up nose? Decongestants and antihistamines have their place, but they are not your only recourse when your airways feel blocked. Before you sniffle your way to the medicine cabinet, try stopping in the kitchen and cooking up something hot—really hot. Whether it's soup, sauce, or salsa, make it as fiery as you can stand. Pepper, curry powder, and garlic stimulate the release of a wave of watery fluids in the mouth, throat, and lungs, helping to thin out the stuff that's got you stuffed up.

Chicken soup It may be good for the soul, but Mom was right, too: A piping hot bowl of chicken soup actually relieves the symptoms of a cold. Researchers have found that just leaning over a bowl of warm soup seems to help break up nasal congestion, and chicken soup may do the job best. Why? Chicken contains an amino acid called cysteine, which bears a striking chemical resemblance to acetylcysteine, a drug that doctors prescribe for patients with bronchitis and respiratory infections.

Hot peppers Chiles are nature's decongestant. Ancient Mayans used them to calm asthma and coughs, and they're still considered standard

> **KITCHEN TIP**
>
> Cut the sodium when you cook dried beans by adding salt at the start, instead of at the end as most cookbooks suggest. The beans incorporate the seasoning while cooking, allowing you to bring out their flavor with less. It's a myth that adding salt early will toughen beans.

therapy in India and Mexico. Medical textbooks in Asia and Europe frequently mention chiles and other hot spices as treatments for the common cold.

The credit goes to capsaicin, the chemical that heats up hot peppers. In addition to stimulating the nerve fibers that control saliva, capsaicin puts a match to nearby nasal glands, triggering a sudden outpouring of fluids. This process helps drain clogged sinuses; it also relieves the pain and pressure that accompany allergies or that follow infection with a cold virus.

The next time you're so stuffed up you have to breathe through your mouth, just fill it with some hot salsa. Within minutes you'll be dabbing at your runny nose, having started the decongesting process that can end your misery.

Onions & leeks "Wel loved he garleek, oynons, and eek lekes," Geoffrey Chaucer wrote in *The Canterbury Tales*. Studies suggest there's more to love about onions than their savory tang. The same sulfur compounds that bring us to tears when we chop an onion lessen swelling, redness, and allergic reactions.

What's more, the anti-inflammatory substances in onions appear to control asthma. In one test a German researcher found that when people drank onion juice before being exposed to irritants, their bronchial asthma attacks were reduced by half. Yellow and red onions contain quercetin, an antioxidant and anti-inflammatory that may spell relief for hay fever sufferers.

Worried that the onion lingering on your breath will discourage visitors? Try nibbling a sprig of fresh parsley; it'll neutralize the odor of the sulfur compounds.

Soothe your stomach

It's to be expected that our stomachs will, from time to time, rebel against the repeated indignities we subject them to.

Some bellyaches call for immediate medical attention; sudden acute abdominal pain and fever may signal appendicitis, for example, and vomiting with blurred vision is a symptom of serious food poisoning. But many other stomach upsets may require little more than pampering your digestive tract with the right foods.

Bananas Troubled by an acid stomach? Peel a banana. The unassuming fruit appears to shield the stomach's lining from ulcers by stimulating an increase in the cells and mucus that form a protective barrier. In animal studies conducted by Australian researchers, bananas reduced ulceration by 75 percent.

Creamy yet virtually fat-free, bananas are also famous for befriending irritable intestines, thus alleviating both diarrhea and constipation.

Ginger Whether you're suffering from motion sickness or morning sickness, a cup of ginger tea, a glass of ginger ale, or a simple gingersnap may calm your roiling stomach.

When 80 Danish naval cadets took powdered gingerroot before hitting the high seas, they reported remarkably less nausea and vertigo than did their shipmates who took a placebo. In another study British researchers found that powdered ginger was more effective than an anti-nausea drug commonly prescribed for patients recovering from surgery.

Prunes The wrinkled plum is probably the best-known natural laxative around. For starters, prunes are high in fiber; ounce for ounce, they contain more fiber than dried beans and most fruits and vegetables. And a single prune contains more than a gram of sorbitol, a sugar alcohol that the body has trouble digesting, further speeding excretion.

Most of the fruit's nutrients make their way into the juice, so if the thought of chewing your prunes is unappealing, you can always drink them. Prune juice retains a significantly higher proportion of the whole fruit's nutrients than do juices from other fruits.

Rice The Japanese erect shrines to honor it. The Chinese pay homage to the grain just by eating up to eight cups a day. Now there's evidence that rice and other starchy foods—including corn, wheat, and potatoes—can be potent antidotes to diarrhea.

Several studies have shown that children given a porridge containing rice, wheat flour, corn, or potatoes recover more rapidly from bouts of diarrhea than do children given a lactose-free

A Pharmacy in your

You've probably heard garlic can lower cholesterol and soy may relieve hot flashes. But the latest wave in the medicinal munchies craze is products made with an *added* nutrient, herb, or other ingredient thought to improve health. These are the new "functional foods."

Stop by your local health food store, for example, and pick up a bag of Robert's American Gourmet tortilla chips, which are dosed with Saint-John's-wort, an herb used to treat depression. Or check out Kellogg's new Ensemble line, foods packed with extra soluble fiber to lower blood cholesterol. Ensemble includes everything from potato chips to frozen pasta entrées. The items are currently available in a handful of midwestern cities and should go nationwide by year's end.

Many natural food stores already stock Hain's split pea soup made with Saint-John's-wort. Yes, if you're feeling down you can warm up to a bowl of velvety green soup laced with the blues-buster herb. Got the sniffles? How about some Hain's chicken broth seasoned with the immunity-boosting herb echinacea?

Some of today's functional foods, of course, aren't so different from old-style fortified products like iodized salt. They're simply foods loaded up with certain nutrients in order to prevent illness. The high-fiber Ensemble items are obvious examples, as is orange juice enriched with calcium—a bonus for women trying to keep their bones strong.

But other types of functional chow take the concept further, with makers adding not just nutrients but compounds used to treat disease. Foods spiked with herbal extracts fall into this category. And while scientists around the world are studying the therapeutic value of medicinal herbs in pill form, most have trouble with the notion of getting, say, your daily dose of Saint-John's-wort from a can of soup or a bag of chips.

"How many chips are you going to eat?" asks Allen Kratz, a clinical pharmacist and coeditor of the Journal of the American Nutraceutical Association. "Some people will eat a whole bag, others just one. Where is your standardization of dose?"

The minimum recommended daily dose of Saint-John's-wort for the treatment of depression is 300 milligrams, and many people take three times that. A serving of Hain's soup contains just 98 mg of the herb. Do the math and you'll see that sipping your way to sanguinity could leave you bloated.

That's not the idea, says Andrew H. Jacobson, president of Hain's natural food division. The soups, he explains, were created for consumers who already use the herbs. "We're not telling people to

throw away their Saint-John's-wort or echinacea," says Jacobson. "It's another way for people who will normally take this product to get it into their diet."

This irks Kratz. "You don't go around eating Saint-John's-wort as part of your diet," he says. "If you're going to take it, take it in a therapeutic dose." And don't use it casually, either, he says. Medicinal herbs can have side effects and even interact with drugs. Saint-John's-wort, for instance, may make some users sunburn more easily, and a recent study suggests it could interfere with fertility.

Kratz does applaud Hain for listing the amount of herbal extract per serving on its labels; he recom-

mends avoiding the many products that don't announce how much of an herb is inside.

On the other hand, there are products like Benecol. In May 1999, McNeil Consumer Healthcare got the go-ahead from the Food and Drug Administration to sell Benecol, a margarine-like spread that can bring down cholesterol. The heart-friendly spread seems at first glance to be much like the foods made functional with herbs. It, too, contains a powerful medicine-like additive, stanol ester, an extract of pine tree bark that limits the intestine's ability to absorb cholesterol. But unlike most of the herbified foods hitting the market, this product has solid research behind it. Studies show that people with high cholesterol who have the spread a few times daily can lower their total cholesterol by 10 percent.

Some of the foods revved up with extra nutrients also have science on their side. Kellogg's, for instance, has marshaled enough data to convince the FDA that its Ensemble foods lower cholesterol and generally promote heart health. The HeartBar, now available in drugstores nationwide, contains the amino acid arginine and has been shown to dilate arteries and improve blood flow in people with heart disease. A company called OmegaTech is test-marketing bio-engineered eggs containing a type of fish oil that may help prevent heart attack.

Some nutrition experts would remind us that while functional foods can help people with specific dietary needs, they aren't the only solution. Nor necessarily the best. Alice Lichtenstein of Tufts University says fiber-enhanced lasagna may be a reasonable alternative for a person with high cholesterol who can't or won't eat a lot of fruits, vegetables, and whole grains. But these natural foods supply more than fiber, she's quick to add, and you'll be missing important vitamins and minerals if you skip them.

As for those faddish products with arbitrary doses of questionable ingredients, well, there's one thing the world doesn't need more of: dysfunctional food. —*Timothy Gower*

infant formula. Researchers suspect that the magic ingredient is indigestible starch.

Yogurt When traveler's diarrhea strikes, try a cup of yogurt (but make sure it's been refrigerated properly). Researchers have found that the benign organisms in yogurt—the same ones responsible for yogurt's creamy texture and sour taste—can destroy strains of E. coli, the ubiquitous bacteria responsible for many cases of turista. Pasteurized yogurts won't work, however, because the sterilization process destroys their beneficial bacteria.

Some doctors suggest that if you're on antibiotics, eating a cup of yogurt a day can help replace many of the good bugs that these drugs typically knock out along with the bad.

Rich flavors plus:
Shiitake and enoki mushrooms (below left and right) contain the immune booster lentinan.

Protect your eyes

Sooner or later most of us will have to pull out the reading glasses before we can order a meal in a dimly lit restaurant. But two of the chief causes of more serious vision loss among older people may not be inevitable.

As we age, we face an increasing risk of cataracts, a clouding of the lens of the eye, and of macular degeneration, a form of damage to the retina. Although some cases of cataracts can be treated surgically, either condition can lead to blindness.

While we can't keep our eyes forever young, it is possible to reduce the odds of developing these life-altering problems. Studies show that antioxidants protect the lens and retina from injury; the more fruits and vegetables we eat, the less likely we are to develop either cataracts or macular degeneration. When you're at the market, focus on the greens and reds, the oranges and yellows. You'll like what you see.

Spinach While Popeye's passion doesn't live up to its reputation as a great source of iron (a cup provides just 10 percent of what a woman needs each day), spinach does significantly lower the risk of developing macular degeneration, a study at the Massachusetts Eye and Ear Infirmary found. Spinach is rich in lutein and zeaxanthin, substances that serve to block out blue light in the eye, which might otherwise damage the retina. A couple of servings a week, the lead researcher says, are enough to reduce your risk.

Corn It's not as lutein-loaded as spinach, but yellow corn has its share of this antioxidant. In fact, lutein gives the yellow type (there are more than 200 varieties) its sunny color.

Most people prepare sweet corn by throwing it into a pot of boiling water. However, many of the nutrients are lost with that method; try steaming it instead. And though corn on the cob evokes memories of picnics and who-cares-about-butter days, there's another easy, age-old way to enjoy fresh summer corn: Cut the kernels off the cob. Sweet, crunchy, and essentially fat-free, the kernels are instantly ready for use in everything from salsa to soup, salad to soufflé.

Red bell peppers If you're seeing red, chances are you're seeing well. While green bell peppers deliver a decent dose of antioxidants, a sweet pepper left to ripen and redden on the bush offers more than twice as much vitamin C and nine times the beta-carotene. That's a powerful mix that fends off many conditions, including cataracts. Excessive heat destroys vitamin C, so don't let red peppers cook so long that they lose their crunch.

Ward off infection

There's no escape. Fly across the country and you could soon have the same virus that gave the guy across the aisle such a nasty cough. Walk barefoot in the sand and one of the millions of microbes living on the beach might set up shop in the little cut on your toe. Sample that street vendor's kabob and you may not feel like leaving your hotel room for a few days. Whether you become infected by a specific microorganism depends on the nature of the bug and the state of your immune system. You have no power over the former but you can influence the latter. A well-balanced diet dramatically increases your ability to fight off an infection.

Cranberries The tart juice of the cranberry has long been a popular treatment for bladder infections. A researcher at Harvard Medical School put it to the test in a study of 153 elderly women. Half of them drank ten ounces of sweetened cranberry juice a day; the others drank a taste-alike beverage. The cranberry juice drinkers cut their risk of developing bacterial urinary tract infec-

tions by 40 percent compared with the control group—suggesting that women who drink a tall glass every day have the advantage. The secret to the berry's success? In 1989 scientists identified two unique compounds in cranberries that block the ability of bacteria to attach to the surface cells of the bladder.

Mushrooms According to tradition, mushrooms cleanse the body, defend against illness, even speed recovery. These may seem tall orders for a lowly fungus, but scientists are uncovering new evidence that some mushrooms, at least, really do have special properties.

Shiitake and enoki, for example, are rich in lentinan, a complex molecule that may stimulate the immune system. In studies in Japan, animals fed one milligram of lentinan a day showed significant increases in their levels of T cells, the immune cells that help fend off bacteria and viruses.

But the main reason mushrooms are popular is that they're extremely low in calories and fat and exceedingly high in flavor. That means they add heft and pizzazz to all sorts of dishes, from stews to stir-fries, without adding pounds to your body or stress to your heart.

Oysters "He was a bold man who first swallowed an oyster," King James I of England declared. A healthy man as well, it turns out. Far and away the richest source of zinc around, oysters may help keep the immune system in peak condition.

Immunologists have long known that strong immunity depends on zinc, which is crucial to the production of antibodies and the growth of disease-fighting T cells. Studies show that when zinc levels fall, animals become more susceptible to many bacterial and viral infections.

When Italian researchers gave a small group of older people 15 milligrams of zinc a day—a little less than what you'd get in one ounce of oysters—T cell activity and levels of immune hormones in the blood shot up dramatically.

If you're not quite as bold as that first oyster eater, try the shellfish steamed, baked, or grilled.
—*Peter Jaret, David Sharp, & Dorothy Foltz-Gray*

New Age Nutrition: Foods in a Pill

Nutraceuticals, as these supplements are called, have begun to crowd the shelves in health food stores. Are tomatoes in a capsule as good for you as the real thing?

No sooner do scientists announce the discovery of some cholesterol-lowering or cancer-fighting substance in a fruit or vegetable than there it is in a bottle. And not only at health food stores. In more and more markets these days, just around the corner from the grapes and greens, a parallel universe has emerged. Here, instead of stalks of broccoli, you'll find jars of broccoli extract, 500 milligrams per pill. Instead of garlic bulbs in their papery sheaths, garlic extract. And to go with your virtual meal, green tea—the encapsulated equivalent of four steaming cups.

Welcome to the age of nutraceuticals, a time when anything that's healthy in fruits and vegetables is ground up, extracted, and otherwise packed into easy-to-swallow capsules. But where supplement makers see a straight line from the health benefits of a vegetable to a pill that contains its essence, food scientists see a twisting path full of pitfalls. Much lower rates of breast cancer and heart disease among Asian women compared with American women, for instance, have sent scientists scurrying. Is it soybeans? Green tea? A little of both? Or could it be that Asian diets are rich in all sorts of vegetables?

Food chemists try to solve such puzzles by isolating the compounds that seem to prevent disease. But that leaves plenty of guesswork, says Paul Lachance, director of the Nutraceuticals Institute at Rutgers, the State University of New Jersey. "For one thing, we don't always know whether the substances we're identifying are the most important ones."

For another, it's sometimes hard to tell whether the active ingredient survives processing. Even if it does, scientists aren't sure what it means to swallow a lone chemical that normally comes mixed with many others. "Until we know all those things," says Lachance, "turning a food into a pill represents a giant leap of faith."

A few years back, remember, evidence pegged beta-carotene as the reason diets rich in plant foods help fend off heart disease and cancer. Then came the discouraging crash. Volunteers who downed a supplement every day fared no better than those who didn't. Worse yet, some of the pill takers ended up at higher risk for certain cancers, including lung cancer in smokers.

"Beta-carotene taught us that we still have a lot to learn about these substances and how they work together," says Edward Giovannucci, an assistant professor at Harvard Medical School.

Yet many food scientists are excited by the research on nutraceuticals, despite all the ambiguities. Some chemicals have been tested thoroughly enough to establish that they *do* help keep us healthier. Besides, even the glad tidings that broccoli and brussels sprouts contain half a dozen potent cancer inhibitors don't seem to be enough to entice most Americans to dish them up. Should

Cayenne pills are loaded with capsaicin, a chemical found in hot peppers that may protect you from cancer and stomach ulcers.

you give nutraceuticals a try? That depends entirely on the supplement. Some have been shown to yield measurable health benefits. Others look promising but are still more or less a gamble.

Broccoli

Broccoli may be one of the most powerful cancer-fighting vegetables around. Sulforaphane, a substance in broccoli (and broccoli sprouts), can fend off tumors by protecting DNA from damage.

Should you pop a pill? One supplement claims to provide 500 milligrams of broccoli extract, including 200 micrograms of sulforaphane. That's about what you get from a standard serving of broccoli.

But a pill won't give you broccoli's fiber or most of its vitamins. For now, eating crucifers (broccoli, cauliflower, and other members of the cabbage family) is the best way to get the goods.

Cayenne

There's a logic to spooning salsa onto your steak fajitas. The hot substance in chile peppers, called capsaicin, appears to disarm carcinogens in some foods you eat. Capsaicin may also deactivate carcinogens in cigarette smoke. Evidence from tests on lab animals suggests that hot pepper can reduce herpes outbreaks and protect against ulcers, too.

Should you pop a pill? Cayenne pills are simply gel caps filled with powdered red pepper. Taking them might make sense if you don't like spicy food. But if you're not afraid of a little zing, sparking a chili with jalapeños or a stir-fry with cayenne is both flavorful and economical. A bottle of 100 cayenne capsules runs about $8, five times what you'd pay for the same amount of ground red pepper.

Tomatoes

A few years back tomatoes hit the headlines when Harvard Medical School researcher Edward Giovannucci announced that a diet rich in spaghetti sauce, pizza, and stewed tomatoes may reduce the risks of several kinds of cancer,

HEALTH NOTE

In the first thorough U.S. study of Cholestin, a supplement made from Chinese rice yeast, those who took a daily dose for eight weeks saw their **CHOLESTEROL LEVELS DROP** an average of 18 percent. But because it has potentially serious side effects, you should try Cholestin only under a doctor's supervision.

particularly cancer of the prostate. Most research points to lycopene, a brilliant red antioxidant particularly abundant in tomatoes.

Should you pop a pill? One lycopene supplement claims to contain 5,000 micrograms extracted from tomato seeds. That's easily as much as the heartiest tomato eaters got in the Harvard study. But don't plunk down your cash yet.

The problem, Giovannucci says, is that the Harvard researchers were looking at tomatoes and tomato-based foods in the diet, not lycopene.

True, lycopene is the likely reason tomatoes cut cancer risk, but other chemicals could be interacting with it in ways scientists don't yet understand. Besides, a bottle of just 30 capsules costs more than $20. For that amount you could buy yourself half a dozen jars of primo pasta sauce.

Garlic

It's hard to believe that any one food might be able to lower cholesterol, bring down high blood pressure, bolster the immune system, and diminish the risk of cancer. Yet respected scientists see promise of all those benefits in garlic.

Should you pop a pill? Much of what's known about the pungent bulb's medicinal powers comes from research on extracts like those on store shelves. However, the anticancer benefits have been documented mainly in lab animals that were fed a lot of garlic—2.5 percent of their food by weight. For hopeful humans, that translates to a large handful of garlic cloves every day. In that light, even ardent garlic lovers might find reason to reach for a supplement.

Grapes

Fresh, juiced, dried, or fermented, grapes are a source of potent antioxidants called flavonoids, which may partly explain why regular wine drinkers are less likely to die of heart disease than are teetotalers. (All varieties of grapes contain flavonoids, but reds are richest.)

Should you pop a pill? The nearest thing to wine or grape juice in the supplement section is grape seed extract, which is high in a flavonoid abundant in grapes. Pill makers tout the extract as an alternative to wine. But grapes and grape juice are also fine options for nondrinkers, and they're almost certain to pack a richer antioxidant mix than the extract.

No one yet has the faintest idea what an ideal dose would be, nor has anyone shown that antioxidants in the extracts even make it into the bloodstream, where they must go to do any good. So help yourself to the fruit or the juice. Or pour yourself a glass of red wine with dinner.

Soy

More than three dozen studies have shown that, taken daily, soy protein powder lowers cholesterol levels by as much as 34 percent. And many researchers suspect that isoflavones (estrogen-like chemicals in soybeans) may reduce breast cancer risk. These same chemicals appear to keep bones strong and ease hot flashes, and may impede the growth of malignant tumors.

Should you pop a pill? Few Americans eat soy foods, so capsules might seem like a fine idea. But scientists still aren't sure which elements are the active ones. The cholesterol benefits were found in studies of soy protein isolate, but most pills contain only refined isoflavones. Still, supplement makers confidently propose taking two or three pills a day.

Try giving soy foods another chance. A few handfuls of soy nuts are likely to deliver the same amount of isoflavones you'd get in a standard capsule. Many markets sell soy protein powder; although it lacks the bean's fiber and carbohydrates, you can easily mix it into smoothies, scramble it with eggs, and bake it in bread.

Green Tea

Tea leaves are loaded with catechins, compounds that may be especially skilled at subduing the kind of cell damage thought to trigger cancer and heart disease.

Should you pop a pill? At least three green tea supplements have been carefully studied. A University of Kansas researcher found that the extracted catechins in one product were 100 times better than vitamin C at blocking genetic damage in bacteria and 25 times better than vitamin E. That's not proof that tea pills will protect you, but it's a strong hint. —*Peter Jaret*

Feed Your HEAD

Many nutraceuticals claim to heal your body; other pills promise to improve your mind. Of course, there's no substitute for lots of physical and mental activity (hiking, biking, learning new things) to help you hold on to your marbles. But you might also benefit from one of these supplements.

GINKGO POPULAR BUT PROBLEMATIC
Many people think this herb, the best-selling brain pill in the country, will prevent a still-bright memory from clouding over. Not so. Only in cases of some mental decline has ginkgo proved effective. On the other hand, if you're forgetting the names of good friends, ginkgo's antioxidant and anticoagulant effects might make a difference. If you're using any blood thinner—even aspirin, vitamin E, or garlic—check with your doctor before trying this supplement.

PS A PROMISING UPSTART
Phosphatidylserine, or PS for short, is a natural substance that helps neurons communicate. It also protects brain cells from free radicals, and it may stimulate production of acetylcholine, a key neurotransmitter. When you're young, your body makes enough PS. But if you're over 40 and your mind feels sluggish, a supplement is worth considering. A number of studies have shown that PS can help people with memory problems (including early-stage Alzheimer's) improve their concentration and recall of names, faces, and phone numbers. One researcher suggests starting with 300 milligrams a day for a month, then cutting back to 100 mg a day.

ESTROGEN THE BEST CHOICE—FOR SOME
If you're entering menopause and have no family history of breast cancer, estrogen may be the smartest pill you can swallow—and not just for your heart and bones. Some studies suggest the hormone helps women with Alzheimer's. And healthy women who start replacement therapy early do better on tests of recall than women who postpone or forgo it. Estrogen appears to reduce brain cell inflammation and damage from free radicals, says Sally Shumaker, director of the Women's Health Initiative Memory Study. It also seems to increase the density of dendrites, the branches of brain cells that make communication possible. —*Beth Wolfensberger Singer*

The Freshest Foods You Can Eat

Millions of Americans are harvesting their own vegetables, shopping at farmers' markets, and buying organic produce. Here's how you, too, can reap the benefits.

It's a warm afternoon in New York State, and Joan Gussow is outside tending her garden. Sunlight washes over tidy rows of vegetables that march from her back porch down to the banks of the Hudson River. The beans and corn have been harvested, the broccoli is ready to eat, and the zucchini are threatening a takeover. Sturdy five-foot-tall tomato plants are dripping with ripe, red fruit. "Have a tomato," she says. Just one? There are too many, in hues from rosy pink to dark purple with stripes. A fat cherry tomato tugged from the vine is warm and tangy with a robust sweetness that explodes in the mouth. This is how a tomato is supposed to taste.

And this is how more backyards should look, says Gussow, professor emeritus of nutrition at Columbia University Teachers College in New York City. For decades she has served as an agriculture-policy gadfly, advocating a return to the small-scale farming and organic methods she believes are crucial to the long-term health of our food system and our communities.

Then, five years ago, she applied the slogan "Think globally, act locally" to her own life, and with her late husband, Alan, transformed the yard. "We wanted, as much as we possibly could, to eat what the garden provided," she says.

Inspired, the Gussows laid brick walkways and built raised beds, double-digging the soil, adding compost, and deciding which vegetables to plant side by side to help ward off damaging insects and diseases.

Since she and her husband planted their garden, Gussow has not bought a single onion, potato, head of lettuce, or any other piece of produce from a grocery store. With the exception of a few basics—grains, locally baked bread, dairy products, organic coffee, and some Hershey's Kisses—she has succeeded in eating almost entirely from her own garden.

"People think I'm depriving myself," says Gussow, picking a handful of strawberries. "But everyone who comes to the house enjoys what they eat." From early spring to late fall, something is always ripe.

No sooner does the asparagus bolt than the beans and peppers become plentiful and the pear tree grows heavy with sun-burnished fruit. During winter Gussow digs into the potatoes, carrots, onions, sweet potatoes, and squash she's stored, or the homemade sauces and blanched vegetables she's stacked in marked containers in the freezer.

That doesn't mean she always dines on exactly what she desires. There was the year, for instance, that a third of her potatoes and onions rotted. "I suppose I could have bought them anywhere," Gussow says. "But I'm trying to prove that if you're willing to take what nature hands out, you can feed yourself year-round."

The next summer she ate tomatoes virtually

Work we love: A fourth of all American households now have vegetable gardens.

nonstop. "My god, I had tomato sauce 12 nights in a row," she says. She wasn't short on dinner ideas, it turned out. The abundant tomato crop led to pasta with raw tomatoes, basil, garlic, and olive oil; tomato soup with tiny new potatoes and coriander; tomato and lettuce sandwiches on crusty country bread; and chunky tomato salsa with black beans and fresh tortillas.

"At 70," Gussow says, "I'm healthier than I've been for most of my life." No matter where Gussow gets her food, her philosophy is as simple as it is old-fashioned. "I just eat food—real, whole food." How do you put that into practice? Well, she says, "Don't eat anything your ancestors wouldn't have recognized." That means lots of greens and beans, loads of fruit, modest amounts of meat and cheese. She keeps an eye on the fat in her diet but thinks the art of eating has become far too complicated.

"You can eat 'healthy' foods from the grocery store—like a fat-free, fudge-rolled granola bar that has all the appropriate amounts of protein, vitamins, and minerals—and have a horrible diet," she says.

You don't have to have a huge yard to bring in a crop, Gussow insists; in fact, you don't have to have any yard at all. "Apartment dwellers can have two or three window boxes and grow tomatoes, or continually sow salad mix and keep themselves in greens," she says. No time? Enroll in one of the nation's community-supported agriculture programs. From spring through fall, you can have boxes of organic, locally grown fruits and vegetables delivered to your home, office, or a site nearby. (For a list of programs in your state, call the Bio-Dynamic Farming and Gardening Association at 800/516-7797.)

Gussow promotes foods grown

Fresh is best: A vegetable's folic acid and vitamin C begin to fade within minutes of harvest.

without pesticides and chemical fertilizers not simply because she believes that they're safer or more nourishing. "It's a persistent hope that we'll prove organic foods are more nutritious. But after 30 years of looking, I have to say the scientific evidence is lacking." Nutrients vary greatly with the weather and seed and soil types, she says. Organic soil is healthier, so the plants ought to be healthier. No one really knows, though, if that's the case. As for safety, she says, "You can't assume organic produce is necessarily lower in pesticides." Spray drift from other farms and contaminated water can leave significant residues.

"The main argument for eating organically, seasonally, and locally is environmental," she says. Buying produce from nearby organic farmers helps ensure that more farmland isn't commercially developed and that fewer chemicals taint the water supply and harm wildlife. "We have to be aware of the impact that what we eat has on the world," Gussow says.

The true health benefit of homegrown produce, says Gussow, is that you'll eat more of it, period. "There's just no comparison between vegetables you get in the store and ones you pick from a garden. Real vegetables are so intensely flavored when they're fresh that you don't need all the salt, sugar, and fat that are loaded into our food. When you get used to the flavors of fresh vegetables, you don't want anything else."

And if what you crave is not available? Wait, advises Gussow. "I don't like to eat things out of season. They don't taste right. It's so much better to build up the anticipation of that first fat blueberry or the first red pepper when the season finally comes."

— *Laura Fraser*

HEALTH NOTE

More than 2,500 **FARMERS' MARKETS** are now open for your tasting pleasure. For the one nearest you, log on to the U.S. Department of Agriculture's Web site at *ams.usda.gov/ farmersmarkets/map.htm.* Or consult the *National Farmers' Market Directory,* available free from the USDA, Box 96456, Washington, D.C. 20090; 202/720-8317.

Playing the MARKET

Green beans again? For many of us, the known universe of vegetable matter is largely defined by what our parents served. At the supermarket, our imaginations fail us and we reach for the familiar and convenient. Shopping—and eating—can get pretty darn boring.

A world beyond carrot sticks and applesauce awaits us, though, down at the city square on Saturday morning, or on the waterfront Wednesday afternoons, or wherever your community hosts its farmers' market. A late 20th century rebirth of an idea as old as the city itself, farmers' markets are sprouting up across the country. (You'll even find three in Alaska.)

The routine couldn't be simpler. A farmer rises early, picks what's ripe and most beautiful, drives to the market, sets up an attractive stall, and waits for you to stroll by. At the phenomenal Saturday market in Madison, Wisconsin, flaxen-haired young women hawk shining ears of corn: "Untouched by human hands! Picked by Norwegian goddesses!" Unless you have your own garden, you won't find anything fresher.

Freshness is a culinary virtue that has been so commercialized that many of us are tempted to lose interest in it. To do so would be a mistake; you might well learn that your distaste for brussels sprouts was only for *old* brussels sprouts. Buy them pert and firm on their comical Christmas-tree stalk, slice them fine, sauté them lightly, stir in a little chicken broth with some toasted walnuts, and finish off with a squeeze of lemon—you'll never take their name in vain again.

Don't worry, you'll also find green beans and carrots, although perhaps in varieties you've never had the pleasure of tasting. And you will always find some brand-new treat as well. The farmers at these events tend to be enthusiasts; they come here because a supermarket chain doesn't know what to do with their green almonds or the hybrid citrus that's a cross between a grapefruit and a pomelo—and here, would you like a taste?

Tasting is the essence of the farmers' market, especially during tomato season. Those who don't mind tomatoes that taste like Nerf balls are already shopping at the corner store, but at the farmers' market in late summer, when the vines are burdened with sun-filled globes in a hundred varieties, you ultimately have to choose between one grower's marvel striped and the next stall's moskvich. Sellers chop samples as fast as passersby will pop them in their mouths.

It seems almost crazy sometimes how much food is given away, especially to voracious kids who are obviously not doing the family shopping. But these children are forming their tastes—and once they've sampled a ripe blenheim apricot, they may not reach for Sugar Bombs for dessert. Why not nature's own sugar bombs?

And that is the genius of the farmers' market. These growers know you probably never saw a lot of this stuff before, and they're ready to win you over. We used to buy roses from a gentle guy named Robin, who also had bins full of oddities:

purslane, hot asian mustard greens, neat bundles of sorrel.

"So Robin," I asked one day, "what do you do with sorrel, anyway?" I obviously wasn't the first to ask the question. He produced a slip of paper with a recipe for a sorrel soup so fabulous that he eventually lost some of our business; because we always want some handy, we now grow sorrel in our own garden.

Shopping at the farmers' market does require a readjustment in both cooking strategy and state of mind. If you go with a list in hand you might well be disappointed. Better to go and see what life hands you: a basketful of tiny artichokes (strip off the outer leaves and sauté in olive oil, garlic, and thyme), a bunch of perfect turnips (cook, tightly covered, with onions and a little butter; add boiling water; pass through a food mill; add cream and croutons), some fresh berries for the morning smoothie.

The produce may cost a little more, but it's well worth it. "We're supporting the people who take care of the land for all of us," says the great restaurateur Alice Waters. "I'm always willing to pay extra money for that."

Did I mention that it's fun? You might be serenaded by a strolling violinist as you ponder the purple potatoes or take a break near the rare orchids. The growers are always happy to chat, as are your fellow shoppers. In fact, your neighbor standing over there holding the mystery vegetable is probably waiting for the chance to tell someone all about it. —*Paul Rauber*

Lose Weight & Gain Energy

Six Easy Ways to Cut Calories

Want to eat less? Here's how—and you won't feel the least bit deprived. The secret's in choosing foods that help your stomach and your brain tell you when you've had enough.

When I reached my early forties, my hunger for experience suddenly surged: I wanted to read more books, visit more countries, know more people. Unfortunately, my appetite for food grew, too.

How could this happen? After age 25, people gradually begin to lose muscle mass. As a result, the rate at which we burn calories slows by about 5 percent each decade. So the sad truth is that even if we eat what we've always eaten and exercise as much as ever, the extra pounds are likely to creep up on us.

In my case the weight didn't creep. Because I gave up cigarettes shortly after I turned 40, the pounds came galloping after me and piled on like linebackers. In a scant five months I gained almost two dress sizes.

For the next five years I struggled—unsuccessfully—to lose the weight. That's when hunger set in. A nutritionist put me on a 1,200-calorie-a-day plan that left me so tired I could barely walk down the hall. Boosting my intake to 1,600 calories gave me more energy but didn't dispel the hollow feeling that inspired dreams of buttery croissants and cheesy quiches. In daylight hours my meals became joyless refueling stops.

Then I made a discovery that was to transform both my body and my relationship to food. Doing research one day in the musty library of the New York Academy of Medicine, I came across a scientific publication called *Appetite*. A journal with my name on it! Leafing through the volumes, I learned that a group of scientists had been studying just the problem I was living with. Or, to be more precise, they'd been examining the mechanics of satiation, trying to figure out what makes people feel that they've had enough to eat.

Most of us, if we think about it at all, assume the physical mechanism that causes people to feel full is a simple one. We eat, after ten minutes or so our food gets broken down and begins to reach the bloodstream, our blood sugar rises, and voilà, we've had as much as we want.

Recently, however, researchers have determined that feeling satisfied is the result of a more complicated sequence of events. Blood sugar is only part of the story. The weight, volume, fiber content, and nutrient makeup of food all play parts in triggering physiological processes that contribute to the agreeable "ah" sensation that follows a sumptuous meal.

Cutting calories, I realized that day in the library, doesn't mean a person has to walk around famished all the time. Researchers have identified multiple ways of tricking the body into feeling happily satiated. Armed with this knowledge, I vowed—like Scarlett O'Hara in *Gone With the Wind*—never to go hungry again.

For most of the past year I've put the research to work in my own kitchen by making the foods

Munching on crunchy vegetables cuts your craving for fattier treats by filling you up with carbohydrates and fiber.

that scientists have found to be most physically satisfying—fruits, vegetables, legumes, nuts, grains, and fish—the stars of my table. So far I've lost ten of the 15 pounds I want to drop. True, I'll never have Scarlett O'Hara's waist. But now that I'm not hungry all the time, frankly I don't give a damn.

Here are the six simple strategies that help me keep hunger at bay.

Sip soup

Starting dinner with a golden bowlful of squash soup gratifies more than just your taste buds. Research shows that soup is among the most physically satisfying of all foods. The reason? It weighs a lot.

A first course of soup will soothe your soul, please your palate—and satisfy your appetite. Try a puree of winter squash, tomatoes, or broccoli.

Just a few minutes after you eat them, soups and other foods heavy with liquid trigger receptors in the stomach that tell the brain you're sufficiently fed, says Allan Geliebter, a psychologist at the Obesity Research Center of St. Luke's–Roosevelt Hospital in New York City. One study, for instance, found that people given a first course of tomato soup ate less during subsequent courses than did people who started their meal with either melon or cheese and crackers.

Soups made from vegetables of any variety have another winning quality: They're packed with carbohydrates, which the body converts quickly to glucose, thus raising blood sugar levels and diminishing your hunger.

Other foods loaded with carbohydrates and liquid: vegetarian stews, pickles, potatoes.

Head for the hummus

The creamy richness of this Middle Eastern dip, whether spread on a rye cracker or a celery stick, may feel decadent. In fact, says John Blundell, a psychobiologist at the University of Leeds in England, it's one of many high-fiber foods that can fill you up fast without filling you out.

These foods, which include beans, fruits, vegetables, and whole grains, pack a lot of volume for their calories. While a three-ounce cheeseburger fits easily in your hand, you'd have to polish off a plate crowded with vegetables (say, a baked potato topped with salsa, a couple of ears of corn, a cup of carrots, and a cup of cooked spinach) to approach the burger's 470 calories. High-fiber, high-volume foods also fill the stomach quickly, stimulating receptors there that let the brain know you're full.

Other high-fiber foods that fill you up: bran muffins and cereals; artichokes and broccoli; grains like brown rice and quinoa; apples, bananas, and dried fruit.

Look to the sea

Smoked trout, grilled shrimp, raw oysters, broiled scallops, sushi, and other gifts of Neptune are not only delicacies but also terrific appetite quenchers. That's because they're rich in protein. When researchers at the University of Australia in Sydney evaluated 38 foods for their ability to satiate, high-protein items consistently scored well. And fish ranks among the most satisfying of these foods.

When protein leaves the stomach, it stimulates the small intestine to release a hormone called cholecystokinin. This chemical travels via the bloodstream to the brain, where it signals the hypothalamus that the meal is ending.

Researchers aren't sure why protein sets off this process. But they point out that the body has a limited ability to store protein. It's possible there was once an evolutionary advantage to a mechanism that told the body not to take in protein that it would just have to excrete, says Blundell.

Other high-protein foods: reduced-fat cottage cheese, milk, and yogurt.

Toss down some peanuts

Count peanuts and their nutty cousins among the few fatty foods that quickly trigger feelings of fullness. (For more good news about nuts, see "A Food Lover's Guide To Fats," page 70.)

"Nuts are highly satisfying," says Richard Mattes, a nutritionist at Purdue University in West Lafayette, Indiana. "If you snack on them you tend to eat less later to compensate for their high calories." The reason, Mattes suspects, is that nuts are rich in fiber and also contain protein.

Go easy on other fatty foods, though. "Of all the macronutrients, fat is the least effective at turning off eating," Mattes says. Fats are slow to trigger satiation signals because they are low in weight for the number of calories they deliver. Protein and carbohydrates both have only four calories per gram, while fat has nine. So you're likely to take in far more calories from high-fat foods before you start feeling full.

Other nuts that do the trick: almonds, walnuts, and cashews.

HEALTH NOTE

Wondering why your friend is slim and you're not? The answer may be on the tip of your tongue: According to researchers at Yale, **THIN PEOPLE** have thousands of taste buds, while heavier folks have mere hundreds. The more taste buds you have, the less likely you are to crave sweet or fatty foods.

Pour on the water

Call it the Perrier paradox: A glass of water has no calories, yet it can help you feel satisfied. The trick is in the timing.

Drink water on an empty stomach and it will pass through you too fast to cue a satiation signal. But sip it just before sitting down to eat or along with food, says Geliebter, and the volume and weight it adds to the meal will make you put down your knife and fork sooner. Consider adding an eight-ounce glass of water to each meal. You'll eat less and be that much closer to the recommended 64 ounces of water a day.

Other drinks that deliver: iced tea, flavored mineral water, and diet sodas.

Choose wine

For all the warmth and conviviality that a couple of drinks can bring, they exact a price. Though researchers don't fully understand why, the calories in alcohol don't register with your internal "I've had enough" gauge the way calories from food do. Studies have shown that after a drink or two, people eat just as much as they would have if they hadn't taken in calories from the liquor.

What's more, alcohol reduces inhibitions. For people who consistently eat less than they want to, this loosening of willpower can lead to a disastrous encounter with a buffet table or dessert tray, warns Geliebter.

Curiously, a few studies have suggested that at least some of the calories in alcohol seem to be "free"; that is, for some reason they don't translate to extra weight. This is a matter of debate, though, so for now it's probably safest to assume that the liquor passing your lips could indeed widen your hips.

If you want to imbibe, go for drinks that are low in calories. Wine is by far your best choice, with about 20 calories per ounce. Beer has just 12 calories per ounce, but a typical serving is 12 ounces, so you'll get many more calories than you would from a four-ounce glass of wine. Hard liquor has 74 calories per ounce—don't make martinis a habit.   —*Nancy Stedman*

Is Pasta Making You Fat?

Lately noodles have taken the rap for widening our waistlines. Don't you believe it. Here's what the Italians have known for centuries about building pasta into a perfect meal.

Few people are neutral about pasta these days. On one side are the nouveau noodle lovers, people who turned to the starch as a low-fat alternative to red meat. Americans prepare pasta at home 23 percent more often today than they did in 1984, according to the NPD Group, a firm that studies America's eating habits. No less an authority on weight management than Sophia Loren once said, "Everything you see, I owe to spaghetti."

That's madness, cry fans of popular weight-loss manuals such as *The Zone* and *Protein Power*. Pasta, they say, makes you pack on pounds because it rapidly breaks down into sugar during digestion, forcing your pancreas to make more insulin—the hormone that, among other things, tells your body to store fat. Many Zoners felt redeemed when a 1997 study showed that diets high in insulin-spiking carbohydrates can raise the risk of diabetes. Having a bowl of linguine for dinner? Why not just shoot up with table sugar?

In fact, pasta is neither as good nor as bad as either group claims. Yes, swapping a porterhouse steak for spaghetti with marinara sauce will spare you a lot of artery-clogging saturated fat. And the tomatoes in the sauce are loaded with a cancer-fighting pigment called lycopene. But while noodles are enriched with a healthy dose of folic acid, their nutritional profile is otherwise

limited—traces of iron, thiamine, and a few other minerals, and not much else.

In any case, it's not pasta that's the problem—it's how most Americans eat it. Consider weight loss, for example. While Zoneheads would have us think that pasta plumps us up because it unbalances our hormones, the truth is far simpler: We're wolfing down too much of it.

Lighten up

"If you eat too many calories, you're going to gain weight," says research nutritionist Linda Van Horn of Northwestern University Medical School. "And it doesn't matter where those calories are coming from."

The National Pasta Association's Web site notes with pride that half a cup of cooked spaghetti has "a mere 99 calories." Half a cup? Haven't these people ever been to an Olive Garden? I ordered the spaghetti entrée at one of these family-style Italian eateries recently. It was served on a platter the size of a hubcap—two cups of noodles easily, twice that much food if you consider the meatballs and sauce. My wife's lasagna, meanwhile, was as big as a brick. In Italy spaghetti is served in small portions, usually as a first course. When Americans eat pasta, we get caught up in the spirit of *abbondanza*: We eat with a license to splurge.

We also corrupt our noodles with cream- and

STUART WATSON

The party line on pasta: reasonably sized portions, a light sauce, and a side dish of vegetables.

Mediterranean cooks
have been pairing
pasta with beans for
hundreds of years.
At right, Pasta
Shells With Chickpeas
and Tomatoes (for
recipe, see page 154).

HEALTH NOTE.

Making your last meal
of the day a light
one can **IMPROVE
YOUR OVERALL DIET**.
A National Cancer
Institute survey of
women aged 19 to 50
found that those
who ate their largest
meal at dinner tended
to take in more fat
overall than women
who had bigger lunches
or breakfasts.

cheese-based sauces. When the food cops at the Center for Science in the Public Interest in Washington, D.C., surveyed the country's Italian restaurants, they found the typical plate of fettuccine alfredo contained an angioplastic 47 grams of saturated fat (a Big Mac has ten). And we don't do much better at home. A quarter cup of Contadina pesto has as much saturated fat as six strips of bacon. We may eat green salad with our pasta, but we still tend to heap on the noodles and forget about side dishes of healthier vegetables.

As for diabetes, carbophobes get carried away when they claim that eating macaroni can lead to the disease. Downing a reasonable portion of pasta does cause the glucose levels in your blood to rise. But according to David Jenkins, a professor of nutrition sciences at the University of Toronto who studies the effects of various foods on blood sugar, noodles are not in the same league as glucose boosters like white bread and potatoes.

What's more, you can prepare pasta in ways that will blunt the modest sugar spike, which is a good idea all the same, especially if you have a family history of diabetes. These culinary adjustments, in fact, will allow you to eat moderate servings of pasta several times a week while also keeping your weight in check and protecting your heart.

The magic combo

The trick? Boost the fiber content of your pasta dishes. Adding vegetables will help, or you could try using whole wheat noodles; they may look a bit woody, but they taste pretty much like the standard version, particularly if they're under a flavorful sauce. But the smartest way to re-vamp your tagliatelle is to mix in some beans and other legumes, which are far and away the best sources of fiber; a half-cup of most varieties provides eight grams.

That probably sounds weird: Add a starch to a starch? Yet the duo has a long and venerable history. You've heard of *pasta e fagioli,* the classic soup made with beans and shells? Well, Italian chefs have been pairing these types of foods since antiquity. The ancient Romans used fiber-rich chickpeas to make pasta sauce centuries before the first tomato appeared in Italy. Similarly, a dish reminiscent of couscous and chickpeas, a contemporary Middle Eastern mainstay, was served in Baghdad as early as 1226. And the tradition continues. Today legumes are a staple in Mediterranean kitchens, where chefs may combine white beans with linguine and herbs, match green beans with penne, or scatter fava beans into a farfalle salad.

So how does this inspired combination guard your health? For starters, tossing some lentils or beans into your pasta sauce can help you lose weight. "Fiber-rich foods hang around in your stomach longer, making you feel more satisfied," says Van Horn, who has been studying fiber for most of her career. "If you're eating pasta with beans, you're displacing some empty calories with a nutritious source of carbohydrates and protein. Chances are, you'll end up eating less pasta."

What's more, fiber is a powerful weapon against several diseases. It can help your heart, for example, by lowering blood cholesterol levels. A 1996 study at Harvard Medical School found that men who consumed 29 grams of fiber a day had a heart attack risk nearly 33 percent lower than those who took in the typical daily dose of 12 grams (experts advise getting 25 to 30 grams a day). As for diabetes, fiber may protect against it by turning gummy in your gut, thereby slowing the progress of glucose molecules as they pass through your intestines and into your blood. And as mothers have known for centuries, fibrous foods ease constipation.

Fortunately, beans and pasta complement one another in the kitchen, too. Just ask Dolores Riccio. She's the author of *366 Delicious Ways to Cook Pasta With Vegetables,* in which an entire chapter is devoted to the starchy twosome. Riccio has heard the common gripe: Who can be bothered with beans if you have to soak them the night before cooking? But while she feels dried beans provide superior taste, she says canned beans are a fine substitute.

One tip for cooking with beans is to spice them up with something pungent. When you combine just about any variety with sautéed fresh garlic and some chopped anchovies, black olives, or greens such as spinach, you've got a wonderful sauce.

Don't forget that green peas are legumes. For one of her favorite entrées, Riccio simply sautés peas in olive oil, then tosses them with chopped walnuts (which add texture and a small amount of fiber), herbs, and pasta. "Use tiny shells, so the peas can nest," she suggests. Other fiber-rich vegetables that will embellish pasta include artichokes, broccoli, and even pumpkin.

However you decide to add fiber to your pasta (or to the rest of your diet), be sure to do it gradually. Eat a hefty portion of beans every day after years of nonbean cuisine and your gut will surely rebel. That's because the bacteria in your intestines feast on the beans' indigestible sugars, producing gas. Taking it slow keeps excess gas to a minimum and gives your body time to get used to the new cast of characters. Try adding five grams of fiber a day for a few days, then another five. (A few drops of Beano will also help; this remedy contains an enzyme that attacks the sugar molecules before the intestines' bacteria can.)

When venturing from your own kitchen, you can safely dine at your favorite trattoria even if there's nary a bean on the menu. Just use your noodle. Eat reasonable portions, avoid high-fat sauces, and order a side dish of vegetables. Armed with a fork and the knowledge that a person should not live on linguine alone, you can have your pasta and enjoy it, too. — *Timothy Gower*

> **KITCHEN TIP**
>
> For a creamy, low-fat alfredo-like sauce, blend two ounces of gorgonzola or grated aged parmesan with one cup of nonfat cottage cheese. Thin the mixture with a spoonful or two of the pasta water.

What's Good on the Menu

We're buying more of our meals away from home—and getting extra fat and calories in the bargain. Try these strategies for staying on the light side without cheating your taste buds.

Eating more restaurant meals lately? Who isn't? Trapped in traffic after a hectic day, you remember that what's facing you at home is an empty fridge. Small wonder you throw up your hands when someone asks, "What's for dinner?"

More often than ever before, the answer is restaurant food. Granted, most Americans still fix their dinners the old-fashioned way, in their own kitchens. But more and more of us are dining out. On a typical day in 1997, almost half of all adults ate a meal at a restaurant. Takeout is increasingly popular, too: In the last dozen years, the number of meals eaten at home but prepared elsewhere has nearly doubled. More than 90 percent of family restaurants and 75 percent of white-tablecloth places now offer food to go, according to the National Restaurant Association.

The trend isn't bad, except for the fact that ordering out isn't always the same as eating sensibly. Restaurant portions, for example, are almost always bigger and heavier than the ones we cook ourselves. Chinese tonight? Kung pao chicken with rice—what many consider one helping, two at most—delivers upward of 1,600 calories, according to the Center for Science in the Public Interest. That's nearly three dinners' worth of calories for a typical American woman. Even a modest helping of lasagna from a supermarket deli runs some 1,000 calories.

Still, you don't have to sweat over a hot stove to eat a light, healthful meal. You just have to know what to look for.

"Don't be afraid to ask for what you want," says Elaine Kvitka-Nevins, a nutritionist in Scottsdale, Arizona, who's known as the "no-oil lady" at her local Chinese restaurant. Kvitka-Nevins is a consultant to Heart Smart International, an organization based in Scottsdale that advises restaurateurs nationwide on how to turn out dishes that meet federal health guidelines. She concedes that dodging loads of artery-clogging saturated fat can be a tough assignment.

"You walk in, you're tired and hungry, and everything smells so good. It's easy to succumb," Kvitka-Nevins says. Still, a few simple tactics can help you navigate a restaurant without leaving with a whale of a meal.

Hand back the menu

It happens to everyone: You head into a restaurant, intending to order just a light salad or maybe a piece of broiled fish. But then you open the menu and your resolve melts. Suddenly you're thinking pizza, double-decker sandwich, maybe even the seafood crepes bathed in béchamel. That simple piece of fish? Heck, you're so distracted by the smell of garlic bread that you forgot to look for it.

What should you do? If you're hungry and

Take-out meals can ruin an otherwise great diet. One serving of fried rice, which many people consider a side dish, might run up 600 calories.

you already have a good idea about what's best for you, don't consult the menu. Ask up front for the catch of the day—broiled sans butter, please—and a side salad. Most chefs will be happy to comply with special requests as long as they're simple. If you do open the menu, discipline yourself to look only at what you really want to eat—the salads, for example, and not the dinner entrées or desserts. Pass up the meaty dishes and go for ones packed with fiber and other disease-fighting compounds, says Kvitka-Nevins. You might just leave the restaurant having gotten the healthy meal you came in for.

Grill your server

Waiters and counterpeople are more than just the folks who refill your water glass or throw extra napkins into your bag. Think of them as a font of information about the chef's skills and the contents of his refrigerator. So go ahead and ask: What's good today? What's the lightest entrée? How about the fruit "garnish"—what's in it, and can you have it on the side?

While you're at it, be honest about your special needs. Before ordering, tell your waiter that you're watching your fat (or butter or salt); he can make suggestions or consult the chef. Special requests can be tricky when you're ordering takeout; many items are already prepared or even prepackaged. Still, there are many selections that may meet your requirements. Just let your server know what those needs are.

Boost your food IQ

So what's a béarnaise, anyway? How do you make a meringue? Is there any difference between broiling and grilling? The more you know about food, the better you'll be at making intelligent choices about what you eat. A béarnaise sauce, for example, is a blend of egg yolks and vinegar, finished with a dollop of butter. Rich? You bet. But if the chef is making a heavy sauce to go with your chicken breast, chances are good he can skip the sauce and coat that breast with the meat juices instead. He'll save time and you'll save fat—without sacrificing flavor.

Cookbooks and restaurant reviews can also help you boost your food IQ. For instance, smart diners know without asking that an Italian *(continued on page 49)*

(continued on page 49)

LIGHTEN Your Lunch

A light lunch, my father likes to say, is one with no gravy. Such a kidder. Truth be told, I'm not sure he's ever had a lunch without gravy. He's a southerner who likes nothing more than a noontime meal of chicken-fried steak or some other lard-laden regional favorite.

But geography isn't destiny. Although I proudly share my father's southern roots, I don't want his waistline. My tastes run more toward sandwiches or salads at lunchtime. After all, you can't get much leaner than a turkey sandwich or a caesar salad . . . can you?

In fact, deli sandwiches and salads—even the ones we think are the healthiest—are some of the worst offenders undermining a healthful diet, says Jayne Hurley, a senior nutritionist at the Center for Science in the Public Interest in Washington, D.C. Hurley lifted the bread off deli sandwiches and found layers of meats, cheeses, and fillings that often added up to half a day's worth of fat and calories. "You think it's 'just a sandwich,'" says Hurley, "but what you're really getting is an entire meal between two slices of bread." A turkey club, for example, can be as artery-clogging as my father's beloved chicken-fried steak. And a caesar salad can match calories with a hamburger and fries.

Assuming you still want to eat dinner, how can you control calories at lunchtime without giving up the corner deli? Here's what Hurley suggests.

Don't pile it on. The average deli sandwich contains about five ounces of meat—twice the serving size recommended by government food experts. Some overstuffed deli favorites contain seven or eight ounces, more meat than you should eat in an entire day. The solution? Ask the sandwich maker for just half the normal amount of meat. And while you're at it, ask him to give you extra sprouts, greens, and other veggies that add nutrients without boosting fat.

Spread yourself thin. Think twice before you answer "yes" to mayonnaise and other fatty spreads. A single tablespoon of mayonnaise has 12 grams of fat, enough to triple the amount in an otherwise lean turkey breast sandwich. Replace mayonnaise with mustard—you'll get one-fourth the fat but just as much flavor. And consider abandoning that old dieter's standby, the tuna salad sandwich. A deli-sized scoop contains nearly a quarter cup of mayonnaise—that's a whopping 43 grams of fat and 716 calories.

Go easy on cheese. A helpful rule of thumb is to layer your sandwich with just one source of fat. If you've always ordered ham-and-cheese sandwiches, try skipping the cheese. The average slice packs about 100 calories, most of which is fat. Or order a simple swiss-cheese sandwich. Either way, you'll halve the fat.

Study your salad. Who would have thought that a simple caesar salad with chicken could add 660 calories and 46 grams of fat to your day? The fact is that some dressings can turn a sensible salad into a fat bomb. Each tablespoon of regular dressing contains 75 calories, says American Dietetic Association spokesperson Pamela Savage-Marr, and most salad

bar ladles are four tablespoons. The alternative? Ask for half the usual amount of dressing on your caesar; at the salad bar, opt for vinegar or a low-calorie dressing. And load up on the veggies and beans instead of fatty toppings like cheese and bacon.

If all else fails and you find you just can't resist the siren call of roast beef with everything on it, consider brown-bagging. In ten minutes you can make a low-cal version of nearly any deli standard using a few slices of lean meat, whole grain bread, tomato, lettuce, and mustard. And you'll save cash as well as calories: A homemade sandwich and a piece of fruit cost about two bucks compared with the four or five dollars you'll drop at a deli. That's a saving of nearly $500 a year. Just think of what you might do with that. I have. I'm going to fly home—and take my father out to lunch. —*Alex Gramling*

THE Lunch COUNTER

What'll it be? Ham or turkey? Caesar or spinach? Check the list below to compare standard deli fare on white bread* with some healthy alternatives.** The figures for fats and fiber are in grams per serving.

	PORTION	CALORIES	FAT	SATURATED FAT	FIBER
Ham sandwich	9 oz	666	40	12	1
Roast beef on whole wheat	7 oz	293	7	3	5
THE LEANEST LUNCH MEATS ARE TURKEY, CHICKEN BREAST, AND ROAST BEEF.					
Tuna salad sandwich	11 oz	716	43	8	1
Chicken breast on multigrain	8 oz	284	7	2	5
TUNA SALAD IS 6 TIMES FATTIER THAN CHICKEN BREAST.					
Turkey club (with bacon)	13 oz	737	34	10	2
Turkey breast on pumpernickel	7 oz	262	5	1.5	5
FOR A THIRD OF THE FAT, CHOOSE TURKEY BREAST INSTEAD OF OTHER TURKEY MEAT.					
Chicken caesar salad	4 cups	660	46	11	2
Spinach salad (with one chopped egg and ½ cup of croutons)	4 cups	304	14	4	4
SPINACH HAS 2.5 TIMES THE BETA-CAROTENE OF ROMAINE LETTUCE.					
Chef's salad	5 cups	930	71	18	2
Garden salad (with ¼ cup each of bell peppers, carrots, tomatoes, and garbanzo beans, and 1 tablespoon sunflower seeds)	4 cups	280	14	2	9
LETTUCE MAY BE A VEGETABLE, BUT IT HAS ALMOST NO FIBER.					

*Analyzed by the Center for Science in the Public Interest **The healthy sandwiches each have 2 ounces of meat, 2 teaspoons of mustard, 4 slices of tomato, 2 pieces of romaine lettuce, and 1 slice of onion. Healthy salads have 4 tablespoons of low-fat dressing.

THE New Rules of ORDERING

Every cuisine has its grease traps: Thai curries made with rich coconut milk, for example, or buttery French béarnaise. Even a dish of Chinese broccoli and red peppers gets stir-fried in so much oil that a double cheeseburger is light by comparison. To find foods with an emphasis on flavorings instead of fat, here's what to look for on a menu—and what to look out for.

CHINESE

Pick: Wonton or hot-and-sour soup; stir-fried vegetables on their own or with lean sliced meats or shrimp (ask the cook to cut back on the oil or to use broth instead); steamed vegetables or fish.

Pass: Any "batter-coated" or "crispy" items (both terms mean deep-fried); egg-based dishes; moo shu pork (ask for moo shu vegetables with no egg); fried rice (help yourself to steamed).

FRENCH

Pick: Spinach salad (hold the bacon); grilled lean meat in wine-based sauce; steamed, grilled, or poached fish; stews like bouillabaisse or ratatouille; fresh fruit or sorbet.

Pass: Beurre blanc, hollandaise, and other sauces based on cream, butter, eggs, or cheese; fatty meats such as duck legs (skinless breasts are fine), sweetbreads, foie gras, and pâté; high-fat desserts.

JAPANESE

Pick: Miso soup or salads for starters. For entrées, teriyaki, boiled dishes (nabemono), or raw fish dishes like sashimi or sushi.

Pass: Tempura or anything else under the heading of agemono (literally "deep-fried things"); fried pot stickers or gyoza; dishes made with eggs.

HOMESTYLE

Pick: Skinless chicken or turkey breast; grilled fish; steamed vegetables; new or baked potatoes (hold the butter and sour cream); chicken soup; green salad (light dressing); fresh fruit.

Pass: Poultry with skin or other fatty meats; meat or chicken potpie; deep-fried fish; mashed potatoes with gravy; home fries or fried potatoes; creamed vegetables; rich desserts.

INDIAN

Pick: Yogurt-based curries; marinated and roasted fish or chicken (tikka or tandoori); baked breads like nan or chapati with no butter or oil; low-oil vegetable dishes (ask your server).

Pass: Korma or other dishes that use a lot of cream or coconut oil; fried appetizers like samosas and chicken or cheese pakoras; fried breads such as poori or paratha; dishes cooked with ghee (clarified butter).

ITALIAN

Pick: Green salads; minestrone; grilled vegetables; pasta with tomato- or wine-based sauces; grilled meats or fish; plain bread or breadsticks.

Pass: Eggplant parmigiana, fettuccine alfredo, lasagna, and other dishes or sauces that are heavy on cream, butter, eggs, or cheese; breaded or deep-fried entrées; fatty meats like pancetta, prosciutto, and salami; garlic bread made with butter or oil.

MEXICAN

Pick: Bean and vegetable burrito (without cheese); chicken fajitas; grilled seafood or chicken; soft tortillas with salsa; beans prepared without lard or fat.

Pass: Burrito with meat, cheese, and refried beans; chimichangas; chiles rellenos; quesadilla; guacamole and chips.

SEAFOOD

Pick: Fish, shrimp, or scallops broiled, baked, grilled, or steamed—not pan-fried or sautéed—with lemon; oysters; grilled or steamed vegetables.

Pass: Deep-fried fish; seafood alfredo and other dishes with creamy or buttery sauces; french fries and onion rings; tartar sauce.

THAI

Pick: Hot-and-sour soup; chicken satay; stir-fried vegetables alone or with shrimp or lean meats (easy on the oil); steamed fish; steamed rice.

Pass: Coconut-based soups and curries; "crispy" or deep-fried appetizers or tofu; peanut sauce.

kitchen can produce a special order of pasta with just garlic and olive oil—it's a staple of Italian cuisine, and the preparation is simple. The same goes for steamed greens at most Asian restaurants.

Demand low-fat desserts

Dessert is the one time of your meal when it really pays to ask about the daily specials. Most restaurants make an effort to provide at least one low-fat, low-calorie choice. Often, chefs will prepare sugarless fruit- and gelatin-based desserts for diners who have diabetes. Other innovations depend on the cuisine; at a traditional French restaurant, for example, you might see a nonfat *fromage blanc,* or soft cheese, with fresh berries.

Indeed, seasonal fruits are always a good bet. Check the menu for fruit cups, or fresh fruits with crème fraîche or liqueur-based sauces. Request toppings on the side so that you can spoon them on at the table or later at home.

Or consider desserts that rely on egg whites, such as angel food cake or meringues. They're

very low in cholesterol and saturated fat. And look for a nonfat fruit sorbet or low- or nonfat frozen yogurt, with as few as 90 calories per serving. You won't even miss ice cream—but your body will benefit. If you're in the mood for something more hefty, choose a cobbler or a crisp instead of a cake, pie, or torte; the latter usually have frostings or crusts laden with butter or lard and are often crowned with rich creams or custards.

Remember to tip

For each special request, your waiter or counterperson must make an earnest plea to a harried chef. Make it worth the effort by tipping generously—to the tune of 20 percent or more.

Tipping the chef to your preferences is another way to improve your dining experience. If you frequent a particular restaurant, consider asking to speak with the chef or proprietor. Let her know how often you eat there and what you like about the place—and what you'd like to see more of. A good chef is always open to suggestions, particularly from someone who really appreciates well-prepared food.

Take it home

When dining out, think of the doggie bag as your best friend. It does for you what you often can't: helps you eat less. Say you're eating at one of those chain restaurants where the entrées aim to please lumberjacks. You *could* ask for less, but you'll pay just as much. So you might as well get it to go: Ask your server to bag half of the huge salad you're about to order. Even at more elegant restaurants, don't be shy about asking to take your uneaten portions home. If you're taking out, it's easy to divide and conquer: Ask the kitchen to place your food in two bags or boxes. When you get home, enjoy one and stash the other for tomorrow. Don't make your body pay if you're served more than you need.

—Susan V. Seligson &
Suzanne Schlosberg

Poached Pears With Raspberry Coulis and Mint (for recipe, see page 182).

Secrets of a Great Breakfast

Of course you watch what you eat at lunch and dinner. But don't expect to reap any benefits unless you're just as smart about the crucial first meal of the day.

Morning isn't my best time. My routine, if you can call it that, consists of addled mumbling, groaning, and staring into space. Until ten o'clock or so the world has a decidedly gray tinge. I have always been this way. Ironically, my most colorful morning memories are the vibrant boxes of cold breakfast cereals.

Every morning my younger brother and I wordlessly crunched our way through bowls of Cheerios or Raisin Bran, all the while staring, transfixed, at the back of the cereal box. Why these packages fascinated us eludes me now, and I cannot recall a single thing I read on them. I must have been in training for the morning paper.

My mother, who left for work before my brother and I ate breakfast, regarded those bright, cheerful boxes of cereal with profound, unspoken guilt. Not until I was a teenager did she admit that she wished she could send us off to school with what we all thought was a good breakfast: eggs and toast and juice.

Little did she know that her morning guilt was misplaced. Her breakfast of necessity is exactly what many nutritionists now recommend. New research anoints cold cereal—long the stuff of Saturday morning commercials and, for adults, a sign of delayed maturity—the healthiest breakfast of all.

"It's a very exciting finding," says Won Song, a professor of human nutrition at Michigan State University. "Cereal eaters overall have a better nutritional intake than others."

Spoon it up

Why? For the answer, you might as well listen to what your mother always told you: Breakfast really is the most important meal of the day. While a low-fat, high-fiber breakfast is best, the real benefit comes from eating some kind of morning food—cereal, a bagel with low-fat cream cheese, or some toast, yogurt, and fruit. Simply eating this morning meal may keep you from falling into a nutritional deficit that you might not be able to make up at lunch and dinner.

Unfortunately, a quarter of us don't eat any breakfast at all these days, and nearly half don't eat it regularly. What we *do* eat for breakfast is more healthful fare than what we ate 30 years ago; still, we don't seem to have made equally sensible changes at our other meals. Calorie-conscious eaters who aren't hungry early in the morning might think it's safe to ignore breakfast, but studies show that people who forgo it eat more food—often less-healthy food—later in the day and never get the nutrients they really need.

"Skipping breakfast essentially means you won't get enough fruit, fiber, or calcium for the day," says Barry Popkin, a nutrition professor at the University of North Carolina at Chapel Hill.

Looking for a big helping of vitamins, fiber, and calcium? Nothing beats a bowl of cereal with milk.

Wake Up to TEA

Here's one way to really shake up your morning: Stash your coffeepot and brew a cup of tea instead. At pennies per cup, with less than half the caffeine of coffee and more than 3,000 varieties to choose from, tea could be the perfect drink. There is one more reason to think so, and it's a biggie: Sipping just a cup or two a day may lower your risk of heart disease and cancer.

This isn't the case with herbal teas. They may have a wholesome aura, but there's surprisingly little scientific evidence that the flowery potions offer much more than tasty refreshment. Green tea, on the other hand, has been the subject of researchers' scrutiny for the last few decades. Interest in black tea is beginning to reach a boil, too.

It makes sense that black and green teas would show similar promise; they're both made with leaves from the same type of tree, an evergreen known as *Camellia sinensis*. Green tea is produced from leaves that are handled gently and heated soon after harvesting. Leaves destined for black tea are vigorously rolled to make them release an enzyme that interacts with oxygen, causing the leaves to develop a heartier flavor and darker hue.

Scientists think green tea gets much of its disease-fighting punch from compounds called polyphenols, particularly one named epigallocatechin gallate (abbreviated, fortunately, as EGCG). Acting as an antioxidant in the body, EGCG neutralizes free radicals (unstable molecules that can damage cells).

Plenty of foods contain antioxidants, but EGCG is the champion, says chemist Les Mitscher of the University of Kansas. In laboratory analyses he found that resveratrol—the antioxidant in wine, which some scientists credit with helping prevent heart disease—is about two-thirds as potent as EGCG. Vitamin C, he determined, is only half as powerful a free-radical fighter. Experts are also encouraged by studies on lab animals. When rats slurp tea, they develop fewer lung, stomach, colon, and other cancers.

As far as studies on humans go, the results have been mixed. Some surveys of tea-fancying populations show benefits; others do not. But Jeffrey Blumberg, an antioxidant expert at Tufts University, says that these studies typically ask people only whether they drink tea, not what kind, so you can't draw definitive conclusions from the data. And like many scientists who read tea leaves for a living, he's excited about a new wave of clinical trials that offer some of the first solid evidence of tea's potential.

At a symposium in Washington, D.C., last fall, a team of Chinese scientists described this experiment: Each day they served three cups of a mixture of green and black teas to people with a type of mouth sore that often turns into oral cancer. Researchers also painted the mixture directly onto the sores. At the end of six months the sores of more than one-third of the subjects had shrunk significantly.

At the same conference, Japanese scientists reported on a small study showing that early-stage breast cancer spreads less rapidly in women who drink a lot of green tea. And Indiana University researchers presented evidence suggesting that smokers who can't kick the habit should at least swap their morning coffee for tea. Toxicologist James Klaunig found that when cigarette users drank the equivalent of six cups of tea a day, their bodies suffered 40 to 50 percent less damage from the toxins in smoke. That could lower their risks of cancer, emphysema, heart disease, and other illnesses. Both black and green teas soaked up dangerous free radicals, although green was more

SCOGIN MAYO

effective. A number of cosmetic companies are even adding green tea extract to skin care products; preliminary studies imply it blocks some of the ultraviolet rays that can cause skin cancer.

Is it worth switching to green tea if you're simply devoted to black? There have been few head-to-head comparisons, but Blumberg believes that even though black tea loses much of its EGCG during processing, it contains other beneficial compounds that green tea lacks. When healthy people drink black tea, Blumberg's research shows, their levels of antioxidants rise.

And if you're avoiding caffeine? No problem, says John Weisburger, a tea expert at the American Health Foundation. Decaffeinated tea, he says, has virtually the same quantity of anticancer compounds as its more stimulating counterpart.

It's not clear, however, whether powdered or premade teas deliver the therapeutic oomph of the fresh-brewed product. A U.S. Department of Agriculture analysis of several bottled and instant iced teas failed to turn up significant levels of antioxidants. Weisburger suggests you hedge your bets by brewing tea yourself. One teaspoon steeped in two cups of boiling-hot water for three to five minutes is plenty.

And what about herbal teas? Though they don't have all those antioxidants, herbalists and other drinkers still swear they can help a variety of ailments. For example, some sources report that chamomile oil, widely used in Europe, calms the central nervous system, aids digestion, and soothes minor aches and pains. Ginger tea is sometimes used to relieve indigestion, menstrual cramps, and motion sickness. And raspberry tea reportedly allays morning sickness, prevents miscarriage, and eases labor pains.

The many varieties of fine tea are as different from one another as chardonnay is from merlot. Whether you prefer the smokiness of lapsang souchong, the subtle grassiness of green tea, or the tart zing of raspberry, find one you like and brew until your teacup runneth over. —*Timothy Gower*

Going without a morning meal also means that we don't break the fast that begins when our heads hit the pillow at bedtime. Most of us wouldn't consider going 12 hours without food during the day, yet we routinely do so after dinner. The body's blood sugar level drops during the night, which isn't problematic because not much energy is expended in sleep. In the morning, though, those low levels need to be brought up again so that we can meet the physical and mental demands of the day.

Studies show that children are mentally sharper and can solve problems better when they've eaten breakfast. "If you have wheat products—which the body quickly converts to glucose—in the morning, your cognitive functions are significantly improved," Popkin says. "We've seen it in the lab and in schools."

Add-ons that add up

Cereal's most significant power lies in the good company it keeps. In her study, Song surveyed more than 11,000 men and women about their morning-meal habits. The ones who had cereal got far more nutrients than those who ate other kinds of breakfasts and derived fewer of their daily calories from fat. Why? Along with cereal, people ate fruit and drank low-fat milk.

By choosing cereal, women picked up 20 percent more calcium, a helpful boost for those at risk for osteoporosis, Song notes. When you add a banana to your cereal flakes, you get an extra two and a half grams of fiber, plus about a fifth of the potassium, vitamin B-6, and vitamin C you need for the day. (Fruit juice, in contrast, has all the calories but none of the fiber of whole fruit.)

Just as important as eating cereal, fruit, and milk is what you're not eating—eggs, butter, full-fat cream cheese, and the like. By avoiding fatty breakfasts, the cereal eaters in Song's study got just 33 percent of their entire day's calories from fat—which is closer than most of us get to the 30 percent goal set by the American Heart Association.

The truth about flakes

You probably remember the ad copy from the back of the cereal boxes that you read as a kid: Fortified with a zillion vitamins and minerals, cereal is a good start to a good day. Well, brace

Are You Drinking Too Much Coffee?

If you're like many Americans, that cup of coffee is equal parts pick-me-up and guilt. Sure, it gets you going, but maybe you wonder about its effect on your health. Should you cut back? Forsake caffeine altogether? Take this quiz to find out if your coffee consumption is a problem.

1 Once you start drinking coffee, you become addicted to it and it's extremely hard to quit.

TRUE OR FALSE

2 Pregnant women should cut down on caffeinated coffee.

TRUE OR FALSE

3 You don't have to avoid caffeine if you're at risk for high blood pressure.

TRUE OR FALSE

4 Drip coffee will hit you harder than an espresso.

TRUE OR FALSE

5 A latte is always better for you than a glazed doughnut.

TRUE OR FALSE

6 Decaf coffee is healthier than the caffeinated kind.

TRUE OR FALSE

| ANSWERS

1 **False.** Addiction is marked by the need for increasing doses of a drug, the drive to have it at all costs, and severe symptoms if use stops. Fewer than 5 percent of people who quit coffee suffer any serious longterm effects.

However, that doesn't mean that quitting or even cutting back is easy for the rest of us. Going cold turkey can result in mild headache, fatigue, or drowsiness, according to the National Coffee Association. You're better off decreasing your consumption over several days.

2 **True.** No links have been found between coffee consumption and birth defects or miscarriage, but one recent study finds that women who drink caffeinated coffee during pregnancy have an increased risk of preterm delivery. If you're pregnant, lean toward caution by switching to decaf or cutting back on caffeinated coffee.

3 **False.** It does appear that people who regularly drink caffeinated coffee have a higher risk of developing high blood pressure. In a study of male medical students who were followed to age 60, researchers found that those who drank three or more cups of coffee a day were three times more likely to have problems with blood pressure than those who didn't indulge. Other studies indicate that the caffeine in coffee can boost your blood pressure *and* your risk of heart disease and stroke.

4 **True.** An eight-ounce cup of drip coffee contains 175 milligrams of caffeine, versus 74 for a single one-ounce shot of espresso.

5 **False.** If you're watching your weight, a doughnut (190 calories, ten grams of fat) beats a 16-ounce whole-milk latte (220 calories, 11 grams of fat). Still better is to choose a latte that won't fill you up with unnecessary calories. A 16-ounce latte made with low-fat milk is 170 calories, while a nonfat milk latte is 130 calories. As long as you don't shovel on the sugar, a latte can also be a marvelous way to get the calcium you need to keep your bones strong. A "grande" latte—two shots of espresso poured into 14 ounces of steamed milk—delivers 500 mg of calcium, fully half your daily needs.

6 **False.** Researchers have concluded that except for those with certain conditions, regular coffee poses no more problems than decaf. Ask your doctor how much is okay for you.

yourself: That may actually be true. There are more than 200 brands of cereal on the market, and most provide about 25 percent of the recommended daily allowance of many essential vitamins and minerals.

One serving of the typical oat cereal gives you 2.6 grams of soluble fiber, nearly as much as you get from an orange. A homely bowl of cornflakes provides 45 percent of your daily iron needs. And thanks to fortification, cereal eaters also help themselves to a fourth of a day's recommended dose of folic acid, which lowers the odds of neurological birth defects in developing fetuses, protects against heart disease, and may even help prevent colon cancer.

Choosing the right crunch

If you want cereal in your life but haven't eaten it since your braces came off, what should you look for? The American Dietetic Association suggests choosing a brand with fewer than five grams of sugar per serving (Cheerios, for example, have only two grams of sugar; Frosted Cheerios have a whopping 13 grams).

Check out varieties of cereal with oat bran and wheat flakes. Try to get a cereal that provides you with at least five grams of fiber per serving.

Be wary of granola. Unlike flakes, many types of granola are coated with sugar and oil to glue the crunchy clumps of oats together. They're heartier, not healthier. You don't get more vitamins or fiber, but you do get a lot more fat.

So choose a nutritious cereal, pour on the milk, and dig in. Just remember that the serving size for most cereals is three-fourths of a cup. With skim milk, that comes to about 180 calories. Most of us eat twice the listed serving size, so you could be getting a heftier meal than you realize.

At least it would be a nutritious one. Maybe it's time for me to call my mother and tell her she can stop feeling guilty.   —*Wendy Marston*

HOW WAS YOUR Breakfast?

It's hard to know if your morning meal gives your health a boost. Many cereals are loaded with hidden calories. And while some baked goods are low in artery-clogging fat, they're often short on calcium and fiber. Check the list below for the standard fare and some surprisingly healthy alternatives.

	CALORIES	SATURATED FAT	FIBER	CALCIUM
CEREAL Lose the fat, slash the calories				
Granola with nuts and raisins (1 cup with ½ cup skim milk)	480	6 grams	8 grams	180 mg*
Raisin bran (1 cup with ½ cup skim milk)	230	0 g	8 g	180 mg
MUFFIN Double the fiber				
Blueberry muffin (3.5 ounces)	275	1.2 g	3.6 g	57 mg
Oat bran muffin (3.5 ounces)	270	0.9 g	7.4 g	63 mg
BAGEL Cut the fat, quadruple the fiber				
Plain with cream cheese (3.5-ounce bagel, 1 ounce cream cheese)	350	6 g	1.5 g	44 mg
Multigrain with strawberry jam (3.5-ounce bagel, 1 tablespoon jam)	300	0 g	6 g	4 mg
BREAKFAST SPECIAL Boost the calcium, lower the fat				
Ham and eggs (3 ounces ham, 2 eggs, 1 pat butter)	350	8.5 g	0 g	61 mg
Blueberry pancakes with syrup (3 small pancakes, 2 tablespoons syrup)	370	2 g	1.5 g	235 mg

*milligrams

Energy Boosters That Really Work

In a slump—day after day? The problem may lie in how you eat, move, and relax. Here are six simple ways to recharge yourself and put the spring back in your step.

It used to be that come rain, fog, or shine, by the time the clock rolled around to 3 p.m., I'd have sunk into a stupor. Oh, I had my tricks for warding off the inevitable. At one o'clock I'd reach for the coffeepot and a dose of after-lunch revival. I'd call someone—anyone—in the hope that conversation would perk me up. But as the afternoon wore on and the hands of the clock began to stall, I'd feel as though I needed toothpicks to prop up my eyelids. That was the signal to rip open a bag of pretzels or grab a handful of chocolate chips.

Alas, the coffee made me jittery, the pretzels left me hungry for real food, and the chocolate— well, I knew where that led: directly to my thighs.

It was small consolation to realize that others shared my predicament. In a nationwide Gallup Poll, 75 percent of those queried reported feeling sleepy sometime during the day. Fatigue is one of the most common complaints that send people to the doctor. And prolonged exhaustion can signal a medical problem. A thyroid on the blink, depression, an incipient case of diabetes: Any of these can leave you wrung out. About 20 million Americans suffer from a condition known as apnea, in which the upper airway collapses during sleep and leads to fitful slumber, drowsy days, and serious health problems, to boot.

But most of us can beat the blahs just by making some simple changes. Vitality is a matter of body, mind, and spirit, and experts in the fields of nutrition, exercise, sleep, and psychology offer tips that range from the commonsensical to the startling. Putting them into practice has given me a new spring in my step—even during those once-dismal afternoon hours.

Eat early and often

In this world of ever-expanding waistlines, says nutritionist Nancy Clark, it may seem surprising that most people don't eat enough—at the right time of the day, that is. They skip breakfast, grab a meager lunch on the run, and then chow down at dinner. Although many people on this meal plan hope it will help them lose weight, studies suggest it actually does the opposite by slowing down their metabolism.

Whatever it's doing to your girth, skimping on calories is clearly hard on your brain cells, which, unlike the cells in the rest of your body, have no banked blood sugar—no energy stores, in other words. "A lot of people are needlessly fatigued because they're not eating early in the day," says Clark, who works at SportsMedicine Brookline, a large athletic-injury clinic in the Boston area. "They forget that food is fuel."

In fact, many nutritionists all but disregard the idea of breakfast, lunch, and dinner; to them, the whole day looks like mealtime. The best way to keep your energy flowing is with frequent small

A burst of exercise around lunchtime will fend off the afternoon blahs.

meals, says David Jenkins, professor of nutritional sciences at the University of Toronto. Need a role model? Forget Cindy Crawford; think monkeys and apes. They munch all day, taking in nutrients slowly but continually. "I'm quite sure that's the way humans evolved to eat, too," Jenkins says.

Little meals every few hours keep your metabolism humming at a steady clip instead of surging in fits and starts. A feast sends blood sugar levels soaring, increasing the energy available to cells. But it also triggers the release of large amounts of insulin, which can shove so much of this blood sugar into muscle cells for storage that you wind up feeling droopy and spent. More numerous but lighter meals produce a smaller but more enduring lift. As a bonus, this eating pattern seems to help lower cholesterol.

Go nuts with snacks

Five or ten small meals a day may sound like heaven, but let's face it: They can take more planning than is practical here on earth. Even Jenkins admitted one recent midafternoon that the last meal he'd eaten was breakfast. Snacks—the right kind, that is—are the answer.

Forget about my old favorite, those chocolate chips. Sugary foods like candy or even fruit juices are digested quickly, producing a blood sugar peak followed by an energy valley. Instead, try snacks that contain moderate amounts of protein, fiber, even fat. The body takes longer to break these down, and that smooths out the roller-coaster effect. Nuts make a particularly good choice, Jenkins says, because they're loaded with protein, fiber, and vitamins. And though they're high in fat, it's almost entirely the heart-healthy monounsaturated and polyunsaturated kinds. (For more about nuts, see "A Food Lover's Guide to Fats," page 70.) Or try fresh or dried fruits, which wrap their sweetness in a package of fiber that slows sugar absorption.

As for my other standby, pretzels, remember that not all breads are created equal. White flour, whether in a pretzel or a baguette, is digested rapidly, so it leaves you with almost the same energy shortfall you'd get from a candy bar. Dense, coarse, whole grain breads provide longer-lasting fuel. So instead of a sesame bagel, pick pumpernickel; instead of pretzels made from white flour, pick whole wheat.

Snacks You'll LOVE

Forget baseball, television, and even sex: The true American pastime is one that we know all too well, the comfy game of hand-to-mouth.

Virtually all of us snack at least once a day, says Columbia University researcher Audrey Cross; half of us snack two to four times a day, according to her survey of more than 1,800 adults and children.

Our favorite snack time is afternoon, when we tend to reach for something salty. Next in popularity comes the cozy hour before bed, when we might dish up ice cream. There's also the midmorning nosh, typically something sweet.

In 1997 these treats totaled 21.6 pounds per American, says the Snack Food Association, up more than two pounds from a decade ago. All told, snacks account for 20 percent of our daily calories. But don't feel *too* guilty: Many weight-loss experts actually encourage you to nibble. Snacking, it turns out, helps you control how much you eat at mealtimes. Snacks can also provide some of the five to seven fruit and veggie servings a day that experts recommend.

"Snacking is great," says John La Puma, a physician who runs a weight-management program at Alexian Brothers Medical Center outside Chicago. "A snack can keep you from bingeing when you get too hungry. And snacking is a good way to pay more attention to what your body is telling you—to recognize when you're hungry and to eat only as much as you need." One study found that snackers had lower total cholesterol, including artery-damaging LDL: Frequent small meals, it's believed, may reduce blood insulin levels, slowing the body's cholesterol output.

On the other hand, snacks do add up. A four-ounce package of honey buns? Oh, 450 calories. A six-ounce bag of nacho-flavored chips? A full 850 if you buy the fattiest brand.

Luckily, there are snacks out there that are good for you. Here are a few great options—delicious munchies that will set you back no more than 160 calories per serving. Who said a little knowledge is a dangerous thing?

FRUIT JUICE BARS

With chunks of actual peaches, oranges, pineapples, and other treasures, frozen fruit-and-juice bars are nibbling Nirvana. One good pick: Fruit*full* juice bars, with only 70 calories per bar and no fat. If frosty fruit doesn't wake up your taste buds, help yourself to an old-fashioned Fudgsicle. It'll satisfy your chocolate lust at a cost of just 90 calories, a mere ten of them from fat. What's more, one Fudgsicle delivers 8 percent of a woman's daily calcium needs.

LIGHT POPCORN

Watch your step when you prowl the market aisles for a package of microwave popcorn. Some kinds stick you with 11 or more grams of butter or hydrogenated vegetable oil per cup of popped kernels. Instead, try Orville Redenbacher's Light Natural Gourmet Popping Corn, which has less than half that amount of fat and all the flavor you could want. Each cupful delivers a whole gram of fiber yet sets you back a scant 20 calories, only a quarter of them from fat.

BAKED CHIPS

Who doesn't love a good chip? But let's face it, some baked versions leave too much to the imagination.

Here are two that actually taste good: Kettle Crisps are lightly salted and taste like real potatoes. Even better, only 15 of the 110 calories in a one-ounce serving come from fat. (Most leading brands get half their calories from fat.) Or try Mexi-Snax's Pico de Gallo Chips, made with plenty of south-of-the-border sizzle, and relatively little oil: One ounce has 140 calories, only 50 from fat.

FRUIT BARS AND BISCUITS

Mom was right: When it comes to cookies, you can't do better than Fig Newtons. Two bars deliver one gram of fiber and 110 calories—not quite as good as a piece of fruit, but low in fat and respectably endowed with potassium, iron, and calcium. Another good choice: Golden Fruit Raisin Biscuits. Unlike many cookies that stint on fruit, these put raisins first on the ingredient list, and fat makes up just 15 of the 80 calories in each biscuit.

DARK CHOCOLATE

Of course it's rich. And, you're thinking, permanently off-limits for the low-fat crowd. But wait. A third of the fat in a typical chocolate bar is from stearic acid, a form of saturated fat that doesn't raise blood cholesterol. Another third comes from mono-unsaturated oleic acid, which has been shown to lower cholesterol. Chocolate is also high in anti-oxidants called phenols, the same heart-friendly substances found in red wine. And in a study of more than 7,800 men, Harvard researchers discovered that those who regularly savored any kind of candy lived almost a year longer than those who rarely indulged. So have some dark chocolate. Just avoid brands that include hydrogenated vegetable oils.

RAISINS

Many of the disease-fighting antioxidants in grapes and wine are also found in raisins, according to nutrition expert Gene Spiller, who directs the Health Research and Studies Center in Los Altos, California. Raisins are fiber-rich and fat-free; and even though they're high in natural sugars, a generous handful tips the scales at just 100 calories. —*Peter Jaret*

Retool your machinery

People who exercise regularly have a number of energy advantages. For one thing, muscle cells that are repeatedly put through their paces respond by making more of the tiny internal factories, called mitochondria, that convert blood sugar into usable fuel. The more mitochondria you have, the more energy each cell has at its disposal. Regular exercise also prompts your body to sprout extra capillaries, the hairlike blood vessels that bring oxygen to cells. The more oxygen your cells get, the hotter your internal fires can burn, and the more efficient your energy production.

But exercise delivers a payoff even before it upgrades your cellular machinery. A workout makes you breathe deeply and gooses your heart rate, boosting blood flow and hence oxygen delivery to cells throughout your body. It also triggers the release of epinephrine and norepinephrine, the fight-or-flight hormones that in smaller amounts act as pep hormones.

So steer clear of an afternoon slump by going for a run or bike ride around lunchtime. (We have a natural urge to doze in the afternoon, when much of the world takes a siesta.) Or if the mere thought of working out exhausts you, try light strength training: It gets your muscles in shape while giving you a lift. In a 1997 Tufts University study, people recuperating from serious heart problems lifted weights twice a week. As their strength increased, the men and women reported feeling only about half as tired in their daily lives as before.

Don't get comfortable

If you find ennui building and you have no time to exercise, don't panic: Emergency measures can be easy.

"Stand up and walk around," says exercise physiologist Garth Fisher, retired director of the Human Performance Research Center at Brigham Young University in Provo, Utah.

Movement sends an important message to your brain, where a cluster of neurons called the reticular formation controls vital functions such as breathing, blood pressure, and heart rate while constantly monitoring the body. If you remain still for too long, the control center takes that as a signal that it's time for sleep and further slows all systems in preparation.

So if you tend to be fidgety, great. If not, set the phone out of reach so you have to stretch to answer it. At the office move the wastebasket far enough away that you can't use it without getting out of your chair. Walk over to a colleague's desk for a brief chat or go down the hall for a sip of water. Even a short stroll will help revive you. When you feel particularly lethargic, you may have to get up as often as every 15 minutes.

Turn in and tune out

Of course, food and exercise aren't the only factors you need to consider. A good night's sleep is crucial. After all, the best diet in the world isn't going to help you be more energetic during the day if you've spent the previous night gazing at the red glow of your alarm clock.

In the days before electric lights were common, a typical night's sleep lasted ten hours, according to William Dement, the director of Stanford University's sleep disorders clinic. These days we're lucky to average seven. Sleep researchers estimate that at least 30 percent of healthy adults in this country suffer the effects of significant sleep deprivation, a debt typically amassed in increments of half an hour to an hour each day. "Sleep deprivation

---

HEALTH NOTE

Myth: Giving in to your cravings will make you gain weight. Reality: The more you resist, the more you crave, and the worse you feel when you finally cave in. What should you do? **ENJOY YOUR FAVORITES** in moderation. An occasional scoop of double-chocolate fudge won't destroy your diet, and it may actually prevent you from bingeing.

is a humongous problem," Dement says. "The sleepy brain makes lots of mistakes. The sleepy brain cannot perform."

Studies show that if you shortchange your body of sleep by an hour and a half, you can lose up to a third of your normal alertness the next day. Most people require about eight hours of sleep each night, though individual needs can vary widely. To find out how much sleep your body demands, experiment with your bedtime and see how you feel the next day. Just 30 minutes more can make a remarkable difference. You might also consider taking a 30-minute nap during the day: More rest can measurably improve your mood and mental sharpness, Dement says.

Routines late in the day can also set the stage for an energetic tomorrow. An afternoon workout bumps up body temperature slightly, an increase that lasts a few hours before dropping back down. Studies indicate that this rise and fall triggers deeper sleep.

You might also spend some time analyzing what experts call your sleep hygiene—that is, where you sleep and how you prepare yourself for it. Is your bed littered with crumpled bills and papers from work? No wonder you toss and turn all night.

Experts say your bed should be a sanctuary: Use it for sleep and sex, not work, phone calls, or other chores. Do you space out with the remote control before bed, skipping from flick to flick until fatigue takes hold? Don't be surprised if your mind keeps changing channels after you've closed your eyes.

For a restful night, experts say, have a restful evening. Rituals that relax you, such as light reading, a hot bath, and deep breathing, help you wind down and signal your body that sleep is near.

As for a nightcap, you're probably better off without it: Alcohol may help you get to sleep, but you might wake up once the drink wears off. Experts suggest that you avoid drinking alcohol within three to six hours of bedtime.

Keep your balance

If you're serious about putting more zest back in your life, the first step is to get out of overload mode by finding ways to be less stressed out and tired.

Slowing down isn't easy. Chances are you juggle plenty: work, family, friends, and exercise. But if you're constantly zipping from aerobics class to dinner to a meeting to the symphony, you're treating life as if it were an emergency.

Your body responds to these constant demands by keeping levels of stress hormones like norepinephrine high. These hormones get you going in a real crisis; they start the heart pounding and interrupt digestion, moving blood away from the stomach and into the muscles to prepare them for action. But they also send signals to mobilize all your energy and to quit storing any, so that soon you're running on empty.

Some people overfill their lives just as others overeat, says psychologist Mihaly Csikszentmihalyi of the University of Chicago. And overstimulation of any kind will leave you feeling bloated and weary. The solution? Cut back. Stop trying to pursue every possibility. And while you're at it, be just a little less dependable. Women in particular tend to feel responsible for too many things in their lives.

"We need to ask ourselves if we're willing to pay the price for this type of commitment," Csikszentmihalyi says. "If you go to the well too often, it will run dry."

—*Sally Lehrman*

HEALTH NOTE

Which munchies are best for your lifestyle? *The American Dietetic Association's Snacking Habits for Healthy Living* (Chronimed, 1997, $7) lists **SNACKS** appropriate for athletes, office workers, kids, and others. For a copy, call 800/848-2793.

Lose Weight— Without Dieting

Forget the fad books, the daily affirmations, the herbs and drugs. For most people, the weight loss program that really works is as simple as taking a walk every day.

Home from a day packed with meetings and phone calls at her Boston office, Diana Pisciotta exchanges her work clothes for leggings, a turtleneck, and sneakers. After pausing for a snack of crackers and jam, the 23-year-old pulls on her windbreaker and heads back out the door. Let others grapple with costly commercial weight-loss programs, painstaking calorie counting, or the latest diet drug. Pisciotta has cut her weight from 145 pounds to 125 pounds and intends to keep it there by following one simple path. She walks 45 minutes every day.

Three thousand miles west, in Berkeley, California, Taly Rutenberg, 39, puts down her two-year-old daughter for a nap and switches on her motorized treadmill. After a five-minute warm-up, she adjusts the speed to four miles an hour. While walking she entertains herself watching television: Today it's a cooking show on PBS, followed by an "I Love Lucy" rerun.

As the credits roll for Desilu Productions, she knows her workout is over and, drenched with sweat, she dials down the treadmill. Like Pisciotta, Rutenberg loses no sleep strategizing about how to get thinner. She just walks an hour every day. It's a no-brainer, she says. She has dropped 35 pounds in a year and a half.

Figuring out how to slim down has become a source of endless conjecture. Book upon book shouts one answer or another: elaborate low-fat or high-protein diets, body-sculpting plans that virtually require a master's degree in physiology to understand, regimens of drugs from fen-phen wanna-bes to Prozac. The guides open to whole chapters of empty pages on which to record every emotion you feel, every gram of sustenance you consume, every side effect you encounter on the journey to a happier, thinner you.

To be sure, some of these exacting methods help some people lose weight. But like many women, Pisciotta and Rutenberg decided to skip the confusion and cut to an answer that's so clear it takes but six words to deliver: Walk briskly 45 minutes a day. Do that, say weight-loss experts, and you'll drop excess pounds and keep them off. Don't do it and you probably won't be able to keep weight off no matter what else you try.

Sound too easy? Well, it's the plain truth. And here is the evidence.

Why walking is best

Aside from the fact that walking is one activity that many people can easily do, the reason experts support it is that in real life, for real women, walking usually works. While millions of women lose millions of pounds every year, it's mainly walkers who keep the weight off.

This finding is the contribution of James Hill, a nutritionist at the University of Colorado at

Short on time? Breaking a daily 45-minute walk into three 15-minute sessions burns calories just as effectively.

Denver. Hill has studied more than 2,000 people who have lost at least 30 pounds and kept them off for a year or more. These people, he says, share a commitment to exercise.

What kind? Amazingly, 49 out of every 50 of Hill's study subjects walk regularly. "They do other forms of exercise, too," he says. "But walking is the prevalent thing."

Others back up Hill's discovery that however you drop pounds, walking is usually a key to staying slimmer. "It's highly unlikely you'll keep weight off if you don't increase your activity level," says James M. Rippe, a cardiologist at Tufts University School of Medicine who has coauthored 120 papers on fitness. "For 95-plus percent of people, that means walking. It's simple, convenient, and easy on the joints. And it burns lots of calories."

Why 45 minutes is key

By now every American over the age of ten has heard about the 1996 surgeon general's report that recommended 30 minutes of physical activity per day. People who get that amount, government researchers tell us, decrease their risk of every ailment from osteoporosis to heart disease.

It's been easy to assume that these 30 minutes a day will peel away the pounds as well. But neither the surgeon general nor the scientific community make that claim, and Rippe and Hill won't either. "I don't think 30 minutes is enough to lose weight and keep it off," Rippe says. Citing his registry of successful weight-losers, Hill agrees. "People who are avoiding weight regain do a lot more than that."

Still, no definitive study has set exactly how many minutes of walking a day will do the job. "From a science basis, we really don't know," Hill says. But ask him and other researchers for their best advice, and over and over you'll hear 45 minutes a day. That's about how much his registry members walk, Hill says. Adds Rippe, "That's a reasonable goal, and you will control your weight."

For aspiring exercisers who find three-quarters of an hour daunting, it helps to know that breaking up the time—say, into three 15-minute walks—burns calories just as effectively as does taking one 45-minute walk.

Why do it daily

Physiologically speaking, walking five days a week rather than seven gives you the same results if you make up for the no-exercise days with hour-long walks. Or you could enjoy a vigorous three-hour hike on Saturday and follow up with 45-minute walks on Monday, Wednesday, and Friday. How to reach the week's total of five hours and 15 minutes is up to you.

Emotionally, though, choice might not be what you need. Many women find that making the commitment to walk every day eliminates the decision making that can derail the best-intentioned exercise plans. "I'd never think of skipping brushing my teeth or washing my face," Pisciotta says. "I feel the same about walking. It's fundamental."

Why dieting isn't necessary

Sorry, taking up daily walking does not give you license to eat with abandon. "If you're not willing to pay any attention to what you eat, you won't lose weight," Rippe says. But as long as you generally eat well—favor low-fat meals of modest size, eat a variety of nutritious foods, drink plenty of water, and (the key for Pisciotta) cut out most junk food—walking can do the rest.

What's more, the regular exertion should make it easier for you to eat sensibly. Judith Stern, a professor of nutrition and internal medicine at the University of California at Davis, finds that a person's commitment to exercise often leads to dietary resolve. "If you're exercising for weight loss," she says, "it seems to put a psychological brake on how much you eat."

How fast you'll lose

A 150-pound man or woman walking at a pace of four miles per hour will burn about 300 calories during a three-mile, 45-minute walk, says Susan B. Johnson, director of the

> **HEALTH NOTE**
>
> Even if you do burn fewer calories as you get older, there's another way to **STAY SLIM**: Eat several small meals a day, instead of two or three big ones. Older women tend to store fat calories after eating big meals, according to a Tufts University study; mini-meals, in contrast, don't produce the same response.

ARE YOU Overweight?

Last year, the National Institutes of Health released the first federal standards regarding who should be considered overweight. Under these guidelines, a person with a body mass index of 25 or more is overweight; someone with a BMI of 30 or higher is considered obese. Overnight, 29 million Americans became overweight. The new guidelines aren't perfect: A person who is simply very muscular may have the same BMI as someone who is truly fat.

HEIGHT / WEIGHT	5'0"	5'1"	5'2"	5'3"	5'4"	5'5"	5'6"	5'7"	5'8"	5'9"	5'10"	5'11"	6'0"	6'1"	6'2"	6'3"	6'4"
100	20	19	18	18	17	17	16	16	15	15	14	14	14	13	13	12	12
105	21	20	19	19	18	17	17	16	16	16	15	15	14	14	13	13	13
110	21	21	20	19	19	18	18	17	17	16	16	15	15	15	14	14	13
115	22	22	21	20	20	19	19	18	17	17	17	16	16	15	15	14	14
120	23	23	22	21	21	20	19	19	18	18	17	17	16	16	15	15	15
125	24	24	23	22	21	21	20	20	19	18	18	17	17	16	16	16	15
130	25	25	24	23	22	22	21	20	20	19	19	18	18	17	17	16	16
135	26	26	25	24	23	22	22	21	21	20	19	19	18	18	17	17	16
140	27	26	26	25	24	23	23	22	21	21	20	20	19	18	18	17	17
145	28	27	27	26	25	24	23	23	22	21	21	20	20	19	19	18	18
150	29	28	27	27	26	25	24	23	23	22	22	21	20	20	19	19	18
155	30	29	28	27	27	26	25	24	24	23	22	22	21	20	20	19	19
160	31	30	29	28	27	27	26	25	24	24	23	22	22	21	21	20	19
165	32	31	30	29	28	27	27	26	25	24	24	23	22	22	21	21	20
170	33	32	31	30	29	28	27	27	26	25	24	24	23	22	22	21	21
175	34	33	32	31	30	29	28	27	27	26	25	24	24	23	22	22	21
180	35	34	33	32	31	30	29	28	27	27	26	25	24	24	23	22	22
185	36	35	34	33	32	31	30	29	28	27	27	26	25	24	24	23	23
190	37	36	35	34	33	32	31	30	29	28	27	26	26	25	24	24	23
195	38	37	36	35	33	32	31	31	30	29	28	27	26	26	25	24	24
200	39	38	37	35	34	33	32	31	30	30	29	28	27	26	26	25	24
205	40	39	37	36	35	34	33	32	31	30	29	29	28	27	26	26	25
210	41	40	38	37	36	35	34	33	32	31	30	29	28	28	27	26	26

Body mass index can be found using this three-step formula: 1) Multiply your weight by 704.5. 2) Determine your height in inches and square it. 3) Divide your first answer by your second. Take, say, a woman who is 5 foot 6 and weighs 140 pounds. Her weight multiplied by 704.5 is 98,630. Her height—66 inches—squared is 4,356. Dividing 98,630 by 4,356 gives a BMI of 22.6.

25 — OVERWEIGHT LIMIT

▢ OVERWEIGHT

division of continuing education at the Cooper Institute for Aerobics Research in Dallas. What sort of loss might that translate into? One pound of body fat equals approximately 3,500 calories. In theory, that means most people could lose a pound every 11 to 13 days.

But getting caught up in weight-loss formulas may be a recipe for frustration. That's because the speed at which you lose depends on your age, your starting weight, and your metabolism. Rutenberg took months to lose the first five pounds but then dropped 20 pounds in six months once she got in the groove. Pisciotta lost two pounds a month from the start. People without much to lose won't lose much at all.

Also, it's important to remember that exercise isn't the speediest way to lose weight. A study at the Baylor College of Medicine of average-size men and women found that those put on a strict diet lost 15 pounds the first year, while those told to exercise lost only six. But after the second year, most dieters had fallen off the eating plan and had regained nearly all their lost weight. The exercisers, however, were still going strong— and had maintained a five-pound weight loss.

The scale isn't the best place to look for results, anyway. Within weeks you should see what most people are really after: a stronger, leaner, more balanced body. "Some people lose fat but gain muscle," Johnson says. "That won't necessarily show up on the scale as losing weight, but the positive changes can be dramatic."

There are other ways to measure success. Richard Cotton, an exercise physiologist and a spokesperson for the American Council on Exercise, suggests one option: "Take a piece of clothing you've had for a while, and see how it fits. That's the way to see your progress."

How fast is brisk

For most people, Rippe says, a brisk pace is equivalent to "walking as if you have someplace to go: a level that's not just strolling but not all out of breath, either." Try working up to at least four miles per hour, a 15-minute-mile pace. Your version of brisk may be slower or faster, however. Pisciotta's long stride takes her a mile every 11 minutes.

How to keep it interesting

Head for the hills; hikes break the boredom of the same old spin around the neighborhood. Sign up for walkathons. Go with a buddy, your spouse, or a group.

Five years ago Dick Trautmann and his wife, Jo, got involved in the Dallas chapter of the American Volkssport Association, a national distance-walking club that stages regular walks open to anyone.

Each week the couple, both in their sixties, participate in two ten-kilometer events. "The walks are interesting in themselves because we go through different parts of the community," Trautmann says. He has lost ten pounds and kept them off; his blood pressure has come down ten points. But he especially relishes the time spent with his wife. "We talk about things and enjoy each other," he says. "When one of us doesn't feel particularly upbeat about the walk, we still go because we made a commitment to walk with each other as scheduled. And we're always glad we did."

Why you'll stick with it

Walkers might start out just wanting to lose weight, but there's something else that keeps them going day after day: the emotional payoff they

ARE Extra Pounds DANGEROUS?

Only in certain cases—though newspaper headlines would lead you to believe they always are. Last year, 29 million Americans got a rude surprise when the federal government changed its weight guidelines, thereby classifying them as overweight, and warned of dire health consequences. But there's more to the story.

Let's say you're a woman who stands 5 foot 5 and weighs 150 pounds. Under previous guidelines, your weight could go as high as 162 without your being considered overweight or unhealthy. But a panel of experts from the National Institutes of Health now says that you're both. After reviewing hundreds of studies, the panel concluded that in this weight range you're likely to be at increased risk of diabetes, stroke, heart disease, and several other health problems.

The key phrase is "likely to be." Lost in the hoopla was the importance of family history in determining your ideal weight. Does diabetes or heart disease run in your family? What about high blood pressure or high cholesterol? If you answer no to these questions, the panel says, you're healthy as long as you avoid the pound-a-year weight gain that typically begins in the thirties.

However, if any of your answers are yes, the panel would place you in the "lose weight now" category (the same goes if your waist measures more than 35 inches around for a woman, 40 inches for a man). That's because your family's health is so strongly linked to your own. Researchers at the Johns Hopkins School of Medicine, for example, found that a man in his forties whose brother or sister has a heart attack before the age of 60 is at least three times more likely to develop heart trouble than someone whose siblings are free of heart disease. For a woman with the same family history, the risk is up to two and a half times as great.

Some experts criticized the panel for not considering physical fitness. If you exercise regularly, they say, chances are you'll enjoy good health for years to come, even if you're heavy. Just 30 minutes of activity every day can ward off many of the diseases that plague the overweight. A 1995 study at the Cooper Institute for Aerobics Research in Dallas found that thin but unfit people were at greater risk of early death than plump people who exercised often.

The bottom line: Talk to your doctor. Do a careful assessment of your risk factors. Then decide if you need to shed pounds or just not gain any more. And keep in mind, a combination of eating well and exercising regularly makes sense whether or not you're officially overweight.

---

reap. "In our studies, walking has yielded enormous psychological benefits," Rippe says. In one study that he conducted, for example, a single 40-minute walk significantly lowered the subjects' levels of anxiety and tension.

At the University of Illinois in Urbana-Champaign two years ago, researchers had a group of 83 inactive men and women walk three times a week; key aspects of self-esteem steadily improved over a 20-week period. "People began to feel much more positive about their physical competence, body image, strength, and overall physical self-worth," says exercise psychologist Edward McAuley, who led the study.

Such changes, he speculates, may help counteract depression and anxiety.

That's certainly been the case for Diana Pisciotta. The walk she usually chooses takes her past blocks of stately houses before it loops around a reservoir. "When I come back, I have so much energy—and much less nervous energy," she says.

Walking made a world of difference during a trip she took to London. "People kept telling me about the subways, the tube—where to get it, how long it would take," she says. "But I looked at the distances and said, 'Why don't I just walk?' And I did. You know, you see a whole lot more of life when you're walking."

—*Nancy Bilyeau*

What About Fats?

A Food Lover's Guide to Fats

There's surprising news about the most feared ingredient in our meals. And the best part is that you can probably put back on your plate some of the foods you've pushed away.

In the German household where I grew up, the food looked so robust I assumed it was good for me. Plump potatoes, sturdy sausages, cheerful bowls of creamy peas. People had been gobbling hearty foods like these since the Neolithic, it seemed, and civilization was none the worse for it.

Then came the affliction. Beginning in the late 1970s, my mother's cooking grew strangely emaciated. Dishes that had once been buttery lost their sheen. Beef and pork became scarce and then extinct at our table. Milk grew paler by the year, until only a bluish gray substance remained, so weak it was almost transparent. In the final, most lurid stages of this culinary disease, odd growths began to appear in our kitchen: gel capsules full of fish oil and vitamin E, distended bags of unpalatable grains, loaves of unsavory soy protein. My mom's hearty German cooking had expired at last, replaced by a sickly doppelgänger called healthy cuisine.

The carrier of the disease, of course, was a campaign to improve the American diet. Fat isn't just fat, we were told. Butter, bacon, cheese, eggs, and red meat—all stalwarts of the German kitchen—are rich in saturated fat. These fats tend to congeal at room temperature, keep well, and make baked goods crispy and moist. But they also raise blood cholesterol and contribute to heart disease. The unsaturated fats in vegetable oil and fish oil, on the other hand, turn liquid at room temperature, spoil a little faster, and lower the risk of heart disease.

But now the world has changed again. Despite the grim pronouncements—saturated fats will clog your arteries, unsaturated fats will widen your waistline—nutrition researchers are discovering that the moral's not so cut and dried. Some saturated fats won't harm your heart, while some unsaturated fats are looking dangerous. Amid all the gnashing of teeth, how do you decide what to eat? On the following pages are the answers to six tricky questions food lovers have been left to ponder.

Should I go back to using butter?

Thirty years ago, when the dramatic drawbacks of saturated fats went public, millions of Americans switched from butter to margarine. More recently, though, news reports about the saturated fat in margarine have made many people wonder whether it wouldn't be wise to switch back again.

Saturated fat in margarine? Aren't most margarines made of pure vegetable oil? Yes, but there's a catch: Chemists have to tinker with that oil to keep it solid at room temperature. They do this by pumping hydrogen into it at high pressures and temperatures. In the process, about 25 percent of the unsaturated fat is turned into

Not all fats are bad:
Those in fish and olive oil
can actually lower your
risk of heart disease.

a partly saturated, hydrogenated fat.

What's more, hydrogenation turns an additional 25 percent of the fat into another form called trans fatty acids. In recent years studies have verified that trans fats are worse for your health than unsaturated ones.

Just how much worse is a matter of hot debate. Seven years ago a Dutch study found that high doses of trans fats were actually worse than saturated fat, more significantly raising low-density lipoprotein (or LDL, the bad cholesterol) and lowering high-density lipoprotein (or HDL, the good). Though follow-up studies have shown mixed results, most nutritionists now think that trans fats fall somewhere between saturated and unsaturated fats.

Not surprisingly, the hoopla has left many people with the impression that margarine is as bad for the heart as butter. "That is absolutely untrue," says Penny Kris-Etherton, a professor of nutrition at Pennsylvania State University. "Only about 20 to 26 percent of the fat in margarine is trans, but butterfat is 53 percent saturated." True, margarine contains an additional 19 percent saturated fat, but a third of it is a kind that doesn't raise cholesterol. Tally all the numbers and you'll see that margarine has significantly less unhealthy fat than you'll find in butter. In a study published in 1996, patients with high cholesterol were put on either butter- or margarine-rich diets. Those eating margarine had 10 percent lower levels of LDL at the end of the study.

Still worried? Shop for margarines that announce they're free of trans fats, or buy the softer kind that comes in a bottle or a tub. As the American Heart Association now says: The softer the margarine, the safer it is.

Can I believe all the promises about fish?

The news about fish seems to have done more flip-flops than the creatures themselves. However, nutritionists are now convinced that eating fish does the heart some real good.

The excitement began in the late 1970s, when researchers noticed that heart disease is rare among Greenland Eskimos, who eat a diet extremely rich in fish oil. Subsequent studies found that people who ate fish were blessed with markedly lower levels of LDL.

Chocolate is loaded with fat, but America's favorite sweet is healthier than you think.

But a second look at the data revealed that the subjects had eaten fish instead of meat. It was the consumption of less saturated fat, not the dose of fish oil, that was the actual source of the LDL drop. In fact, fish oil has hardly any effect on cholesterol, although it does lower the total amount of fat in the blood. Its benefits to the heart appear to lie elsewhere.

The active ingredients in fish oil are EPA (eicosapentaenoic acid) and DHA (docosahexaenoic acid). Both belong to a family of fatty acids known as omega-3s, and both help prevent blood clotting and hence heart attacks. In two separate studies people who ate fish regularly were less than half as likely to die of heart disease as people who said they ate no fish at all. But because these studies were based on the subjects' recollections, their results are still open to debate.

Other evidence suggests that in high doses EPA and DHA can prevent heart arrhythmias and even relieve arthritis. Still, the fish oil findings aren't done flip-flopping. The same Greenland Eskimos who had so few heart attacks also bled easily and suffered many more strokes than average—though in a later study fish actually seemed to reduce stroke risk. Until those issues get sorted out, health experts are unlikely to recommend daily doses of fish oil.

In the meantime, nutritionists suggest that people try to eat fish—especially fatty fish like salmon—once or twice a week. Fish oil supplements are potent; no one says they aren't. But the pills may do less good simply because they don't replace meals rich in saturated fats.

Is it true chocolate is good for me?

The term saturated fat has become a skull and crossbones of sorts in people's minds. However, not every kind of saturated fat is a killer. A chocolate truffle may epitomize devil-may-care indulgence, yet half the saturated fat in its cocoa butter is a type called stearic acid that acts more like an unsaturated fat. "Stearic acid is unique in that it doesn't raise cholesterol levels at all," says nutritionist Kris-Etherton. "It has a truly neutral effect."

Four years ago Kris-Etherton put a group of young men on a low-fat diet, then added either a high-carbohydrate snack or a chocolate bar for a few weeks. Neither the chocolate nor the snack increased the men's LDL. So chocolate might not be exactly good for you, but it isn't so bad after all.

Still, not everything containing chocolate deserves to wear a white hat. Many sweets labeled chocolate contain little cocoa butter and hence no bounty of stearic acid. Most of the bars that fill grocery store checkout racks contain less than 20 percent cocoa butter. Chocolate ice cream is

> **KITCHEN TIP**
>
> Instead of thickening soups with cream, which is rich in butterfat, add a pureed potato to the mixture. Use nonfat yogurt or buttermilk in place of sour cream in salad dressings and baked goods. For sauces, try skim or low-fat milk.

THE Disease-Fighting Fats IN A PILL

First came studies showing that fish-loving Eskimos hardly ever get heart disease; then came capsules filled with fish oil. Recent research has suggested benefits from exotic oils refined from other foods, and—no surprise—they're now available in pills. Here's what you need to know about three fatty acid supplements currently in vogue. If you decide to take any of them, tell your doctor.

FISH OIL
Omega-3s: EPA and DHA
Proven benefits Reduces heart attack risk by warding off blood clots, lowering blood pressure, and bringing down triglycerides (blood fats); crucial to brain development in fetuses and infants. At higher-than-usual doses (advisable only under a doctor's orders), fish oil relieves arthritis pain and prevents arrhythmias, a leading cause of death in heart patients.
Possible benefits May prevent certain cancers.
Known risks Because it slows clotting and prolongs bleeding, taking fish oil can slightly raise your risk of hemorrhagic stroke.
Usual dose A single one-gram capsule a day.
Bottom line Fish oil is economical insurance for people at high risk for heart disease, but eating fish a few times a week is even smarter.

FLAXSEED OIL
Linolenic Acid
Proven benefits The body converts some of this seed oil into the fatty acids in fish oil, so the benefits are the same, though much larger doses are needed.
Possible benefits May lower cholesterol.
Known risks None, though linolenic acid hasn't been studied thoroughly.

Usual dose One to three tablespoons a day.
Bottom line Fish oil is cheaper and probably more effective.

CLA
Conjugated Linoleic Acid
Proven benefits At the moment, none. Recent studies on this fatty acid, which occurs naturally in meat and dairy products, have tantalized researchers. No tests, however, have been done on people.
Possible benefits In lab animals high doses prevent some cancers, stave off heart disease, boost the immune system, and diminish body fat.
Known risks No side effects have been seen in animals given large amounts.
Usual dose Three to six one-gram capsules a day.
Bottom line Promising but unproven.

almost all butterfat. The healthiest form of chocolate is probably the purest and darkest form: bittersweet or milk chocolate bars made mostly of cocoa butter.

Are eggs getting better?

Some of them are. Several years ago egg producers made a surprise announcement: Eggs actually have a quarter less cholesterol than everyone thought, as shown by updated lab tests. Think again, they pleaded. Give eggs a break. But egg sales continued to fall.

Since then food scientists have been casting about for ways to lure back health-conscious Americans. One approach has been to rebuild eggs from the chicken feed up. At Texas A&M University, poultry scientist Mary Van Elswyk has discovered that she can successfully rework the fatty acids in eggs by feeding the chickens flax seeds.

More than half the oil in flax (also known as linseed) is the omega-3 fatty acid called linolenic acid. Some of this is changed in your body to EPA and DHA, the fish oils that help prevent heart disease. You can buy flaxseed oil in health food stores, but you'll get more DHA—and a far tastier meal—by letting chickens eat your flax for you.

Pilgrim's Pride, a Texas-based egg producer, now sells a line of eggs called EggsPlus in several states, including California and Texas. Under Van Elswyk's guidance, the company has cooked up a feed fortified with flax and vitamin E for its hens. Their eggs have about as much saturated and monounsaturated fat as regular eggs. But they also deliver six international units of vitamin E (ten times the amount in regular eggs), 100 milligrams of linolenic acid, and 100 mg of DHA. That's less than a third of the omega-3s in a salmon dinner but more than most of us get in a day's meals. EggsPlus taste, look, and cook just like normal eggs. The only evident difference is price: EggsPlus cost about $1 more per dozen than regular eggs.

Two eggs of any kind deliver a third more than the recommended daily dose of cholesterol. Still, the American Dietetic Association says that most people can eat up to four eggs a week without worrying about the cholesterol in the yolks (you can whip up as many cholesterol-free whites as you like). In moderation, then, the humble egg is still an option—economical, low in calories, and bursting with protein, vitamins, and minerals.

Which is healthier, olive or canola oil?

As almost everyone has heard by now, unsaturated fats come in two versions. The monounsaturated fats in olive and canola oils have earned a glowing reputation. Most nutritionists recommend them because they slightly lower LDL (the bad cholesterol) and slightly raise HDL (the good). The much-vaunted Mediterranean diet, for instance, is rich in olive oil.

The polyunsaturated fats in sunflower, safflower, and several other oils lower LDL, which is good, but slightly lower HDL as well, which is bad. Because polys also have a bewildering range of effects—they can bring down blood pressure or raise it, prevent cancer or promote it—their reputation is mixed. That makes it smart to choose a mono.

The wrinkle is that olive and canola oils aren't identical. Canola is primarily monounsaturated fats (62 percent), but the rest is polyunsaturated with a smidgen of saturated. Olive oil is somewhat higher in mono (72 percent) but has a good dose of saturated (17 percent)—

possibly enough to cancel out some of the mono benefits.

So which is best? If you don't find olive oil's strong flavor a big selling point, you probably ought to favor canola oil. About 10 percent of it is the flaxseed fat linolenic acid. When you eat foods with linolenic acid, your liver converts a little of it into EPA and DHA, the fatty acids in fish oil that help prevent blood clotting and cut the risk of heart attacks. Cooking with canola oil gives you two benefits for the price of one.

Can I eat all the nuts I want?

The high fat and calorie content of nuts has historically forced many people to go to extreme lengths to avoid them—or to eat their Snickers on the sly. So nut-lovers will be thrilled to hear that almonds, pea-nuts, pistachios, and many other nuts are proving to be strong defenders against heart disease. Why? Close to 60 percent of their fat is monounsat-urated, the healthy kind found in olive and canola oils.

The Adventist Health Study, pub-lished in 1992, was one of the first investigations to uncover the nut's salutary effects. Analyzing the diets of more than 31,000 Seventh-Day Adventists in California, researchers found that people who helped them-selves to nuts more than five times a week had a risk of heart disease more than 50 percent lower than subjects who rarely ate nuts. Similar results were reported recently from the Harvard Nurses' Health Study.

The clincher came last year, giv-ing the peanut—and many of its nutty cousins—a place right beside olive oil as a heart protector. Penny Kris-Etherton put 22 adults with normal or slightly elevated choles-terol levels on the typical American diet (35 percent of daily calories from fat) for almost a month. Then she had them follow a series of four other diets: a low-fat plan (25 per-cent of calories from fat), plus three that were high in total fat but rich in monounsaturates; the mono sources were olive oil, peanuts and peanut butter, and peanut oil.

The results were enough to send Kris-Etherton sprinting to the snack machine for a pack of dry-roasteds. Compared with the typical U.S. diet, the olive oil and the various peanut diets lowered subjects' total choles-terol by 11 percent and cut their LDL level by 14 percent. Even better: The low-fat diet raised levels of triglyc-erides (fatty particles that can dam-age blood vessels) by 11 percent, while the olive oil, peanut, and pea-

Peanuts as a pick-me-up? Seems so. New research shows that active women may have more stamina when they don't skimp on fat.

nut oil diets lowered them by nearly the same amount. Which means that a nutty high-fat diet is probably bet-ter for your heart than a nut-free reduced-fat one.

Of course, having a strong heart is wonderful, but won't nibbling nuts every day add inches to your waistline? Not according to several studies that show that munching nuts helps people feel satisfied—and less inclined to overeat later.

—*Burkhard Bilger &*
Alice Lesch Kelly

How Low-Fat Do You Need to Go?

For some people there's no question: A diet low in fat is a lifesaver. For others it can be risky. Figuring out what's best for you could be one of the most important things you do.

What's the key to a better diet? Ask most Americans and you'll get the same simple answer: Eat less fat. According to the Food Marketing Institute, we worry more about fat in the foods we buy than about any other ingredient, including salt, cholesterol, sugar, and calories.

Small wonder. Too much fat, we've been told time and again, is gumming up our arteries and threatening our hearts—and making us fat. Aided and abetted by food makers, who've turned the war on fat into a booming business, we serve up "lite" salad dressings, nonfat cookies, skim milk, and low-fat cheeses.

And we're making progress. Americans have cut back on fat, from 40 percent of one day's calories in 1968 to 33 percent today. That's an astonishing change in a single generation. We've eased up on saturated fat, too, that infamous clogger of arteries, from 18 percent down to 11 percent of daily calories—nearly the goal of the American Heart Association, which recommends a maximum of 30 percent total fat and 10 percent saturated. Along the way, it appears, we've trimmed our risk of heart disease significantly.

But hold on a second. Last year a group of leading nutrition scientists heated up the pages of the *New England Journal of Medicine* with some startling statements: The healthiest menu may in fact be quite high in fat, they said, as long as it's mainly unsaturated. By contrast, an extremely low-fat, high-carbohydrate diet might actually boost the danger of heart disease.

What? Now fat's good for us? Can't these scientists make up their minds and give us some advice that sticks? There's no reason to get hot and bothered. It turns out that the findings are great news for people who love to eat yet want to stay healthy.

Why some say fat is fine

The new movement takes its inspiration from the sun-drenched shores of the Mediterranean, where the traditional cuisines are hardly lean—and where heart disease has been as rare as hens' teeth. The Mediterranean diet isn't loaded with just any fat, of course. It's low in saturated fat and high in unsaturated fat, specifically the monounsaturated kind in olive oil. All told, the age-old diets of Crete and southern Italy top out at nearly 40 percent of calories from fat.

Of course, there's nothing magical about Mediterranean-style meals. Their main virtue is that they're light on meat, butter, and cheese, and rich in beans, grains, greens, and olive oil. Eating this way has been proved to lower LDL, the artery-choking kind of cholesterol, without putting a dent in HDL, the good cholesterol that carries LDL out of the bloodstream. What's more,

At 120 calories per tablespoon, olive oil isn't light. But experts say if you're not overweight there's no reason to shun it.

THE 40 percent PLAN

Loosen up, many researchers say. If you're trim and healthy it's okay to get up to 40 percent of your calories from fat. But they warn that saturated fat from butter, cheese, and fatty meat is still a villain. They likewise suggest avoiding artery-clogging hydrogenated oils, common in hard margarines, crackers, and cookies. And they cite studies hinting that polyunsaturates in corn, safflower, and generic vegetable oils may promote breast cancer.

What can you eat? Monounsaturated fats, found in olive and canola oils, and omega-3 fatty acids in fish are clearly safe bets. The big caveat: You'll have to watch your weight on this plan because fat delivers so many more calories than do carbohydrates and protein.

Feel free to buy breakfast cereals with almonds or walnuts, which are rich in monounsaturates and fiber. Pour on 1 percent or nonfat milk, however, to trim saturated fat.

For lunch try Middle Eastern sandwiches: tabbouleh or hummus on pita bread. These high-fiber fillings are meatless but flavored with olive oil or tahini (sesame paste).

Dress salads with olive oil vinaigrettes, not mayonnaise-based dressings such as thousand island. For hearty extras think chicken breast or avocado, not cheese.

Snack on peanuts and almonds instead of crackers and chips, which tend to be laced with hydrogenated or polyunsaturated fats. For extra fiber and a bit of sweetness, add some dried fruit.

If you hanker for meat, sauté, grill, or stir-fry turkey and chicken breast, pork tenderloin, beef sirloin, and other lean cuts using modest amounts of canola or olive oil.

Help yourself to fatty fish like salmon, tuna, trout, and mackerel.

Choose pasta sauces such as primavera, made with vegetables and oil, instead of alfredo, which is loaded with butter, cheese, and cream.

Mediterranean meals hold down the bloodstream level of fat particles called triglycerides. That's key because triglycerides appear to increase heart disease risk by damaging blood vessels. When triglyceride levels climb, HDL cholesterol also tends to fall, further adding to the danger. Making a bad situation worse, high triglycerides and insulin resistance seem to be linked. In overweight people, that combination raises the threat of adult-onset diabetes.

A diet high in unsaturated fat appears to sidestep all these hazards. Indeed, when Harvard researchers looked at the mealtime habits of more than 80,000 women between the ages of 34 and 59, they found that the total amount of fat the women ate had no impact on their risk of developing coronary artery disease—only the amount of saturated fat did. Replacing saturated fat with unsaturated cut their risk by 42 percent.

One study suggests that even people who already have heart disease can benefit. In the Lyon Diet Heart Study in France, researcher Serge Renaud divided 605 heart patients into two groups. One took up a lower-fat diet along the lines of the American Heart Association's recommendations; the other ate from a Mediterranean menu that replaced saturated with unsaturated fat, mostly monounsaturated. After 27 months heart attacks and deaths were 70 percent less common in the Mediterranean group than in the low-fat group.

There is one downside: Fat is fattening. Gram for gram, fat delivers more than twice the calories that carbohydrates do. "Maintaining a healthy weight means consuming only as many calories as you burn," says William Connor, a nutrition professor at Oregon Health Sciences University in Portland. "Given how little physical activity most Americans get, that's a very limited number of calories. If we spend 40 percent of those on fats, we've got that much less to spend on far more important sources of nutrients, such as fruits and vegetables."

Still, if you aren't striving to cut calories (and you don't need to lose weight), the Mediterranean plan may be your best bet for lowering heart disease risk. That's especially true if your HDL level is low or your triglycerides are high. Replacing saturated fat with unsaturated fat should improve both numbers. This relatively high-fat diet might reduce your risk of developing insulin resistance (and possibly diabetes) as

Do You Know What "Light" Means?

It's a rare food product that can't find something reassuring to say about itself: No Salt Added. 100% Natural. 14 Essential Vitamins and Minerals. Contains Fiber-Rich Oat Bran. No Tropical Oils. 97% Fat-Free. These statements are influential, if frequently misunderstood, nutritional claims. Following are six wordings often prominently displayed on food items. Take this true-or-false quiz to see if you know the meaning behind the message.

1 Cholesterol-Free
This means the cholesterol has been removed by the manufacturer.

TRUE OR FALSE

2 Light
The product delivers either half the fat, half the sodium, or two-thirds the calories of the regular version.

TRUE OR FALSE

3 Good Source of Calcium
This means the product has at least 20 percent of the calcium you need to get each day.

TRUE OR FALSE

4 Low-Fat
The product gets no more than 30 percent of its calories from fat.

TRUE OR FALSE

5 Reduced-Fat
The fat in this product has been cut by a minimum of 50 percent.

TRUE OR FALSE

6 See Back Panel for More
Information About Saturated Fat
and Other Nutrients
This wording is required on every food label.

TRUE OR FALSE

ANSWERS

1. **True** This label is reserved for special versions of cholesterol-heavy foods like cheesecake. But people on heart-healthy diets should check the ingredients list for partially hydrogenated oils, which can also raise your body's cholesterol levels. A label that reads "Cholesterol-Free Food" is making much ado about nothing: The food had no cholesterol in the first place.

2. **True** If you want to know which improvement was made, keep reading; the manufacturer has to state the change in percentage terms somewhere on the package.

3. **False** To qualify as a "good source," a food has to supply only 10 percent of the "daily value," which is the government-recommended amount of a vitamin, mineral, or fiber. The words "high in . . . ," on the other hand, do guarantee 20 percent of the daily value in each serving.

4. **True** "Low-fat" on the label nearly always means a food hits the 30 percent goal. But there are some exceptions. A few products, because of their small serving size—sandwich cookies, for instance—can be labeled "low-fat" with almost 40 percent of their calories coming from fat. Also: "Low-fat" 2 percent milk has five grams of fat per serving and gets about 35 percent of its calories from fat.

5. **False** To make this claim, the maker has to cut the fat per serving by a quarter compared with its regular product. Many products have cut fat by 50 percent, however; the actual percentage will be listed somewhere on the item.

6. **False** This notice is required if a product makes a nutrition claim yet delivers a lot of cholesterol, sodium, fat, or saturated fat—more than 20 percent of the daily value in one serving. Watch for these words on "high-fiber" foods like granola, which often are fatty, too.

For more information on food labels, write to FDA, Office of Public Affairs, 5600 Fishers Lane, Rockville, MD 20857. Ask for publications 94-2276 and 98-2273.

long as you also eat plenty of foods from the produce aisle and keep your weight in check.

The case for light and lean

Look to the Far East, say advocates of low-fat eating, where traditional diets are rich in rice and greens, with little meat and no dairy products. In parts of rural China where typical meals get about 15 percent of their calories from fat, heart disease is virtually unheard of. Here at home the trend toward lighter cuisine appears to have helped lower heart attack rates. So why turn back now? Connor believes a reasonable goal is between 20 and 25 percent of calories from fat. University of California researcher Dean Ornish, a leading advocate of very low fat diets, maintains the ideal is 10 to 15 percent.

In Ornish's landmark Lifestyle Heart Trial, a diet with no more than 10 percent of calories from fat—all but eliminating oil, red meat, chick-

HEALTH NOTE

Because the **FAT CONTENT OF TUNA** can vary by 500 percent depending on where the fish was caught, some tuna packed in oil may be lighter than the water-packed kind sitting next to it. Nutrition labels will clue you in; compare before you buy.

en, fish, and dairy—not only lowered cholesterol but actually helped open clogged arteries as well. "If there's anything wrong with the American diet," Ornish insists, "it's that we haven't cut back far enough on fat." He argues that high triglycerides and low HDL are risky only for people on high-fat diets. If there's little fat, there's little need for HDL's protection.

Ornish is concerned that many devotees of French and Italian cuisines have taken to using generous amounts of olive oil, drizzling it onto their green salads and pasta or sopping it up with fresh-baked bread in restaurants—without easing up elsewhere.

"Olive oil is still 100 percent fat," Ornish says. "If you add two tablespoons of olive oil to your pasta, that's the equivalent of 28 grams of fat, which is almost as much as you'd get in two scoops of Ben & Jerry's ice cream." No one should do that, he says, and expect to lose weight.

Some health experts, though, question whether

THE 20 percent PLAN

If you're hoping to lose weight, many experts suggest getting less than 30 percent of your daily calories from fat. The same researchers say that this strategy can also help reverse heart disease, while others raise concerns about potential dangers. Because fiber diminishes the possible risks from a low-fat, high-carb diet, beans and lentils are recommended instead of white rice and pasta. Only the leanest cuts of meat, poultry, and fish can take center stage on this plan. One plus, though: Because you'll be taking in so little fat, you get to serve yourself bigger portions than people on the high-fat plan.

Try to keep breakfast fat-free. That rules out eggs, muffins, and most granolas. Instead, think fresh fruit and juice, whole grain breads, and high-fiber cereals. Stick to nonfat milk and yogurt.

At lunch pledge allegiance to turkey and chicken breast, and forsake cheese on salads and sandwiches. Spread your bread with mustard alone or fat-free mayonnaise. Choose fat-free salad dressings. Order veggie pizzas, hold the cheese.

Snack on pears, berries, bananas, apples, dried fruit, and other treats that have at least 3 grams of fiber per serving.

Make your dinners meatless most of the time. Even lean red meats deliver significant amounts of fat.

Use meat as a flavoring rather than a main ingredient in soup, stew, chili, and pasta.

Measure vegetable oils by the teaspoon. Use smidgens of sesame oil to accent Asian dishes, walnut oil or extra virgin olive oil to dress salads. Sauté and stir-fry using defatted broth.

Choose low-fat fish—cod, flounder, halibut, snapper, sole.

For dessert, reach most often for fresh fruit, sorbet, or other fat-free sweets. But treat yourself regularly to small servings of milk chocolate or ultrarich ice cream, experts like Dean Ornish suggest, so you don't feel deprived.

EASY EXCHANGES: Trusty Low-Fat Substitutes

Cutting back on fat doesn't mean going hungry; it just means making wise choices. The swap chart below offers some low-fat alternatives to common foods. (Portions are average serving sizes.)

INSTEAD OF	FAT GRAMS	GO FOR	FAT GRAMS
Corn muffin	5	English muffin and jam	1
Granola	12	Nonfat yogurt sprinkled with granola	2
Bacon and eggs	37	Pancakes with syrup	6
Tuna salad sandwich	16	Turkey breast sandwich with mustard	7
Cheeseburger	30	Bagel with lox and low-fat cream cheese	10
French fries	20	Oven-fried potatoes	8
Cream of chicken soup	18	Chicken noodle soup	6
Potato chips	18	Pretzels	2
Bean dip	4	Salsa	0
Alfredo sauce	10	Tomato sauce	1
Sautéed vegetables	14	Steamed vegetables	0
Ranch-style dressing	18	Vinaigrette	8
Ice cream	18	Sorbet	0
Apple pie	16	Fig bars (4)	4

low-fat diets are really the best way to shed pounds. "All you have to do is look at the past 20 years to see that cutting fat hasn't kept Americans from getting fatter than ever," says Frank Sacks, an epidemiologist at the Harvard School of Public Health. "The typical situation is that people go on a low-fat, high-carbohydrate diet, they don't exercise, they don't lose weight, triglycerides go up, HDL goes down, and they end up worse off than when they began."

However, if you're serious about losing weight, or if you already have heart disease and hope to reverse it, cutting way back on fat is a fine strategy. "The fewer calories you get from fat, the more calories you can spend on high-fiber and nutrient-rich foods like beans, fruits and vegetables, and whole grains," says Connor. That may be especially important in view of the anticancer chemicals in the plants we eat.

"We're coming to realize that for most people, several things appear to matter more than whether they're getting 20 or 30 or 40 percent of their calories from fat," says Tim Byers, a public health expert at the University of Colorado School of Medicine in Denver. "One is reducing saturated fat. Another is eating plenty of fruits and vegetables. The third is getting regular exercise and making sure you expend as many calories as you consume." Byers' words are good news for anyone who's ever opened a menu to find the only entrée marked heart-healthy is steamed broccoli on rice.

"No single dietary recommendation is right for everyone," says Ronald Krauss, a cholesterol researcher at Lawrence Berkeley National Laboratory in California. The growing consensus seems to be that it all depends on who you are and what you're after. A low-fat diet may be best. Or—miracle of miracles—a high-fat diet might be just what the doctor ordered. The trick is to gauge the pros and cons, then choose the path that's best for you.

— *Peter Jaret*

KITCHEN TIP

To defat stocks made at home: Open a one-gallon zip-top plastic bag. Pour in the cooled, strained broth. Seal, then lift the bag and invert it over a large bowl. After a few seconds (the fat will rise), open the zipper an inch. As the fat layer nears the bottom, reseal and toss the bag.

The Lighter Side of Meat

Sure, the saturated fat in beef, pork, and lamb is nobody's friend. But you don't need to bypass the butcher if you know which cuts to buy and how to cook them.

When the nation's trend watchers checked up on eating habits recently they saw an amazing thing: Americans have started eating beef again. Up until a few years ago, the demand for red meat had been falling as consumers took their concerns about fat and cholesterol into the supermarket and purchased chicken and turkey instead of red meat. Cynics see the return to red meat as a backlash against prudent eating—even the dawning of a new era of indulgence.

But who said meat can't fit into a smart diet? If you pick the leanest cuts, trim visible fat, and cook using the right techniques and seasonings, red meat can be as light as skinless chicken—and certainly better for your heart than a vegetarian entrée dripping with butter and cheese. As the figures for saturated fat in the chart on page 84 show, you can find cuts of meat that aren't likely to harm your arteries. (A reasonable total for a day's saturated fat is about 18 grams.)

In many ways, you can't do better than meat if you're serious about getting the nutrients you need; some either can't be found or aren't available in the right amounts from the grains, dairy products, fruits, and vegetables that make up the bulk of a healthy diet. For example, most meats—including the lean cuts of poultry, pork, beef, and lamb—are rich in iron, zinc, and vitamins B-6 and B-12, all of which aid in the production of red and white blood cells. The iron in red meat and poultry is particularly valuable. Known as heme iron, it comes in a form more readily absorbed by the body than the iron found in grains and vegetables. And, of course, meat is an abundant source of protein.

In fact, ounce for ounce, red meat can be a remarkably efficient way of putting nutrients on your plate, outshining even chicken and fish. A three-ounce serving of beef, for instance, provides as much iron as three cups of raw spinach and as much zinc as three four-ounce cans of tuna. Beef also provides more than eight times the vitamin B-12 and twice the riboflavin of the typical chicken breast.

So how can you make meat part of a healthy diet? First, don't make it the star at dinner every night. You'll reap most of meat's benefits if you eat it only occasionally. Then, follow these suggestions for buying, preparing, and serving it.

Choose the best cuts

Every meat has its lean side. Ranchers and food scientists have been working for years to breed slimmer cattle, for example, and they've been remarkably successful.

When buying beef, choose top round, eye of round, and sirloin; if you're on a budget, consider round tip brisket. Stay away from fattier

For a dinner that's lean but not mean, try Lamb Chops With Black Bean–Orange Relish (see page 148 for recipe).

THE Leanest Meats IN TOWN

No butcher around? Use this chart to help you identify healthy cuts. "Prime" meats usually have the most fat, "select" the least.

	TOTAL FAT (GRAMS)	SATURATED FAT (GRAMS)	CALORIES
BEEF (select grade, trimmed of fat, 3 ounces, uncooked)			
Top round	2.1	0.7	102
Tip round	2.7	0.9	101
Eye of round	3.0	1.0	106
Sirloin	3.1	1.1	105
Top loin	3.8	1.4	113
Tenderloin	6.0	2.2	130
CHICKEN (fryer, 3 ounces, uncooked)			
Breast, without skin	1.0	0.3	94
Drumstick, without skin	3.0	0.7	102
Thigh, without skin	3.3	0.8	102
Breast, with skin	8.0	2.3	150
PORK (trimmed of fat, 3 ounces, uncooked)			
Tenderloin	3.0	1.0	102
Chop, top loin	4.5	1.6	121
Ham	4.6	1.6	116
TURKEY (young tom, 3 ounces, uncooked)			
Light meat, without skin	1.3	0.4	98
Dark meat, without skin	3.5	1.2	105
Light meat, with skin	6.0	1.6	134
Dark meat, with skin	6.8	2.0	130
LAMB (choice grade, trimmed of fat, 3 ounces, uncooked)			
Leg	3.8	1.4	109
Loin chop	5.0	1.8	122

cuts such as flank steak and ribs. When buying beef for hamburgers or meat loaf, be careful: Federal meat standards allow ground beef to be nearly one-third fat by weight. Even a quarter-pound patty made from extralean ground beef will give you 14 grams of fat. If you've got your mind set on a burger, the best option is to ask for a ground version of a leaner cut.

For healthy cuts of other meats, check the chart at left.

Trim the fat

For many of us, a meaty meal means a roast smothered in gravy, pork chops bubbling in creamy scalloped potatoes, or chicken-fried steak. But you can cook meats lightly, too.

First, use a sharp knife to cut all visible fat and the white connective tissue from meat before cooking. Avoid frying meat in fat or coating it in an eggy batter; broiling, grilling, and roasting yield flavor without lots of added fat or oil. For a quick and tasty dish using steak, cut the meat across the grain into 1/2- to 3/4-inch-thick slices. Rub with herbs, brush with soy-based teriyaki or tomato-based barbecue sauce, and pop under the broiler or on the grill.

Sautés and stir-fries are fine, but lighten them up by heating your pan before you add the oil; extra-lean cuts are less likely to stick. And let the oil get hot before you add the meat: Food absorbs cold oil more readily than hot.

Handle with care

Contaminated meat has been blamed for some of the more serious outbreaks of food poisoning this decade. Fortunately, cooking meat thoroughly kills the bacteria that can cause problems. The risk in your kitchen arises when those bugs make the leap from the raw meat to other foods or utensils. That's where you have control. Here are a few guidelines for protecting yourself and your family from food-related illness.

■ Wash your hands with soap and warm water before and after handling raw meat.

■ Defrost frozen meat in the microwave or the refrigerator.

■ Use separate plates for raw and cooked meat; wash knives and chopping boards after use.

■ Use tongs—not a fork—to turn meat. Piercing the surface can force dangerous bacteria into the meat's cooler interior, where the germs can survive cooking.

■ Test for doneness with a clean meat thermometer. Ground red meat products should be cooked to 160°; ground poultry to 165°. Unground cuts of red meat should reach 145° for medium-rare, 160° for medium, and 170° for well-done. Poultry should be cooked to at least 180°.

■ Reheat meaty carryout meals and leftovers to a minimum internal temperature of 165°.

Think small

When meat's on the menu, make the most of it. The typical adult serving should weigh in at no more than three ounces and be about the size of a deck of cards. (Restaurants often give you twice that much, although some places will serve you an artery-boggling 22 ounces.) A child's portion should be one to three ounces; teenagers can have up to six ounces.

— *Yvette Robert*

IS IT Risky to Eat WELL-DONE MEAT?

Cooking a burger is getting ever more complicated. On the one hand, we're told to make sure it's well-done to kill off possible contaminants like E. coli. Then late last year a study hinted that a diet of deeply browned meat could hike the risk of breast cancer.

This most recent wrinkle comes from research comparing the meat-eating habits of 273 women recently diagnosed with breast cancer with those of 675 healthy women. Survey respondents who preferred their burgers, steak, or bacon very well-done (heavily browned to blackened) had a risk of breast cancer 4.6 times higher than those who liked their meat rare or medium. (Those who ate at least an eighth of a pound of meat a day also had a somewhat higher risk than the less-carnivorous cohort.)

Wei Zheng, the epidemiologist at the University of South Carolina in Columbia who directed the study, believes the danger lies in compounds formed when beef, pork, fish, or chicken is heated to a high temperature. One class of such chemicals, called heterocyclic amines (HCAS), has been shown to cause mammary gland tumors in lab rats.

That certainly sounds bad, but other researchers have cited weaknesses in the survey. For example, the study was based on recollections of past eating patterns and didn't establish whether the women actually ate well-done meat, or how often.

What about that burger? Go ahead and cook it well. Most health officials argue that the big E (as in E. coli) is a much more pressing threat than the big C.

Still, to play it safe, when eating meat that has been grilled or fried, scrape off the crispy surface, which contains known carcinogens. Also, Zheng says, keeping meat moist during cooking may limit the types and amount of heterocyclic amines that develop.

Along those lines, another study, from the Lawrence Livermore National Laboratory in California, found that marinating chicken before cooking virtually eliminates HCAS. The researchers used a marinade of brown sugar, olive oil, cider vinegar, garlic, mustard, lemon juice, and salt. Results were similar whether the chicken was merely dipped in the marinade or soaked for 48 hours.

Vitamins & Minerals

Why a Good Diet Isn't Enough

If you munch carrots for snacks and steam broccoli for dinner, you may think you're getting all the vitamins you need. But you could in fact be running short on a few crucial nutrients.

Experts have long seemed unable to talk about vitamin pills without scoffing. All you get from the supplements, they'd say, is expensive pee. Just eat a balanced diet; that's enough. Well, say good-bye to the era of the scientific sneer.

Last year a panel enlisted by the venerable National Academy of Sciences announced that a good diet just isn't good enough: Even people who eat lots of fruits and vegetables seldom get all the B vitamins they need. The panel, which is responsible for setting recommended dietary allowances, approximately doubled the RDA of the B vitamin known as folic acid, or folate, to 400 micrograms for adults. The scientists pointed out that Americans get only about 200 mcg a day on average and suggested that for many people supplements are the way to go.

In explaining their embrace of vitamin pills, researchers tend to emphasize folic acid's role in preventing birth defects. But for many advocates, there's more than one motive at work. Evidence is mounting that the vitamin, along with B-6 and B-12, has the power to protect against heart attacks, and possibly strokes and colon cancer, too.

And the Bs aren't the only vitamins making supplements respectable. Often forgotten, vitamin D is calcium's silent partner in building strong bones; adequate levels are crucial to staving off osteoporosis as well as for everyday well-being.

Yet there's an unrecognized epidemic of vitamin D deficiency, says Michael Holick, an endocrinologist and vitamin D specialist at Boston University Medical Center. Up to 40 percent of Americans over the age of 50 fall short of the amount they need, he says.

Vitamin E is another nutrient that many researchers wish we would pop. Studies show this antioxidant probably protects against heart disease and might deter Alzheimer's, Parkinson's, and other diseases of age. But the benefits accrue only if you regularly get amounts well above those provided by a sensible diet.

All these tidings might tempt you to cruise your neighborhood market's supplement aisle, stocking up on the entire alphabet. Rein in your cart. There's no evidence that the average American diet leaves people deficient in the other vitamins—A, C, and K.

These nutrients are necessary, no question. Vitamin K helps blood to clot, promotes the healing of wounds, and is critical for strong bones. And your very ability to read these words comes courtesy of your stores of vitamin A, which is essential to making the pigments that enable you to see.

But it's easy to get plenty of A and K from your diet. And that's fortunate because, in the case of A at least, supplements are hazardous. Too much A can be hard on your liver, and if you're pregnant, it can cause serious birth defects. You might

A once-a-day multivitamin contains
400 micrograms of folic acid.
That's enough to reduce your risk of heart
disease and perhaps some cancers.

Buying INSURANCE

Stand in the supplement aisle of your market or pharmacy and scan the shelves. What do you see? Bottle after bottle filled with capsules, tablets, and little Elmos, Freds, and Barneys. The choices can seem daunting. When shopping, bear in mind the following:

Vitamin and mineral supplements that contain no more than 100 to 150 percent of the U.S. recommended dietary allowance (RDA) for each vitamin are fine. After all, there's a reason these are called supplements: You're getting at least some nutrients from your diet, right?

Synthetic forms are just as good as "natural"; your body treats them identically. Vitamin E is an exception: The natural form is more potent and is absorbed about twice as efficiently.

Added ingredients such as choline, inositol, and PABA serve no dietary purpose for most people.

Excess amounts of vitamins can interfere with lab test results and interact with medications.

Vitamin supplements complement your daily diet— they can't make up for poor eating habits.

suppose you could avoid danger by taking supplements of beta-carotene—a building block of vitamin A that your body uses only as needed. Yet even beta-carotene isn't risk-free. A few years ago scientists were shocked to discover that smokers who took high doses raised their chances of developing lung cancer.

Perhaps no vitamin illustrates the need for caution better than that celebrity of supplements, vitamin C. Without enough C your muscles and ligaments would lose their stretch, like old rubber bands. You'd be plagued by bleeding gums, fatigue, and wounds that wouldn't heal. Some researchers believe C's benefits extend to warding off heart attacks and strokes, and to bolstering the immune system against colds, flu, and even cancer.

No wonder many people take huge doses. Yet a study last year suggested the vitamin may have a Jekyll-and-Hyde character: At 500 milligrams daily—a dose higher than the RDA but lower than the amount frequently taken to beat back colds—it may cause the kind of genetic damage that can lead to cancer. Until all the facts are in, says Chris Rosenbloom, a spokeswoman for the American Dietetic Association, it's wise to rely on your diet for C; if you want to supplement, do so with caution.

So it's a trio of vitamins—the Bs, D, and E— that's bringing us into this new era. The view from here: You may scorn junk food and swill milk by the quart, but you still ought to think about whether you're falling short on these crucial nutrients. Here's how to know whether you need extra—and how much.

The B vitamins

When the government's advisory panel raised the RDA for folic acid last year, the scientists were primarily concerned with women of child-bearing age. The panel said these women should take 400 mcg of folic acid daily to prevent birth defects such as anencephaly, in which the fetal brain fails to develop fully, and spina bifida, an incomplete closing of the fetus's spinal column. The advice is intended for *all* premenopausal women, not just pregnant ones, because damage to a fetus can occur before a woman knows she has conceived.

But even if there's no bassinet in your future, it's wise to heed the Bs. "It looks like getting B vitamins—from foods or supplements—is nearly as important as stopping smoking, lowering high cholesterol, and controlling blood pressure in preventing a heart attack," says epidemiologist Eric Rimm of Harvard University.

In February 1998, Rimm and his colleagues reported that women who got ample folic acid and B-6 suffered heart attacks only about half as often as women who took in meager amounts. The finding may help explain a long-standing puzzle in heart disease: Half of all heart attack victims have cholesterol levels that are in the safe range. Increasingly, scientists are looking into a substance called homocysteine as a likely culprit in some of these cases. Homocysteine is thought to scar blood vessel walls, setting the stage for artery-narrowing deposits. Unfortunately, your body busily produces this chemical whenever it digests animal protein.

Experts think that folic acid, B-6, and B-12 help dispose of homocysteine before it can wreak havoc on arteries. The Harvard study—which followed 80,000 women for 14 years—is the first to show a direct link between these vitamins and a reduction in the risk of heart disease.

It remains possible, of course, that something else was protecting the women who had high levels of B vitamins; indeed, it's likely that these fruit-and-vegetable lovers or vitamin takers exercised more and smoked less. "The jury is still out," says endocrinologist JoAnn Manson of Harvard Medical School, "but the evidence is strong, very promising."

Let's assume you're sold on the Bs. Do you really need a supplement? For one thing, the Food and Drug Administration requires enriched grains to be fortified with folic acid. The rule covers rice or flour that's had the germ and bran removed and nutrients added back. It doesn't make white bread preferable to whole wheat, but it does mean that almost every serving of bread or cereal moves you toward your goal.

So you could get the folic acid you need (400 mcg) from a daily bowl of fully fortified cereal. But would you really stick to the breakfast habit? You could vow to eat more lentils and spinach and to drink more orange juice, and more power to you. But keep in mind that the folic acid in food is fickle—it's unstable and also more difficult for your body to use than the synthetic variety used in vitamin pills or sprayed onto cereal. Levels in food vary according to growing conditions and may easily be halved by exposure to heat, air, or light.

Vitamin B-6 is found in a wide variety of foods including chicken, turkey, bananas, watermelon, and potatoes. Nevertheless, many people don't get enough: 15 percent of young women and up to half of women over 50 fall short, according to the government panel.

And B-12? Besides this vitamin's role in sweeping your body clean of homocysteine, researchers long ago established that it's crucial in the formation of red blood cells as well as in the functioning of the nervous system. A severe deficiency can produce symptoms that range from irritating to horrifying—from tingling or loss of feeling in the hands and feet to irreversible dementia.

The vitamin is plentiful in milk, meats, and other animal products. However, because people tend to produce less stomach acid with age, up to a third of those over 50 have trouble absorbing the nutrient from food.

To B or not to B? To serve you well, these vitamins must be in the proper balance. An overload of folic acid can disguise symptoms of a B-12 deficiency, for example. Besides, excessive doses of some Bs can be dangerous in their own right. High doses of niacin—sometimes used to control cholesterol—can harm the liver and shouldn't be taken except under a doctor's supervision.

The bottom line: Take a once-a-day multivitamin. Most contain 400 mcg of folic acid, 2 mg of B-6, and 6 mcg of B-12. And make sure your diet is rich in fruits and vegetables.

Vitamin D

Ironically, Americans' desire to do the right thing for their health may be leading to rampant vitamin D deficiency. "Anyone who doesn't drink much milk and doesn't get out in bright sun very often is a candidate for supplements," says Suzanne Murphy, a nutrition scientist at the University of Hawaii.

The vitamin is vital to the health of your bones, not to mention the quality of your days. Although calcium gets all the attention in osteoporosis prevention campaigns, it's D that shepherds calcium to your bones. If you lack vitamin D, an abundance of calcium won't keep your skeleton strong. What's more, a shortage of D can bring on muscle aches, weakness, and symptoms resembling those of arthritis.

"We see many people with deep bone pain who doctors thought had arthritis but who turn out to be deficient in vitamin D," says endocrinologist Holick. "Their lives improve tremendously when they receive supplements."

It might seem easy to get enough vitamin D, considering that every carton of pasteurized milk is fortified with it. Not only that, your body is a vitamin D factory fueled by sunlight. With 15 minutes of sun exposure three times a week, most people can make all the D they need.

But studies show that fortified milk doesn't always deliver as

> **KITCHEN TIP**
>
> To preserve water-soluble vitamins, rinse rather than soak fresh vegetables when cleaning. And don't cut them up until you're ready to pop them into your mouth or into the pan.

promised. "Three-quarters of all milk sold contains less D than the label states, and 15 percent of skim milk contains no vitamin D at all," Holick says. And D-rich foods like liver and fatty fish probably don't make a daily appearance on your table. Meanwhile, rising rates of skin cancer have put a chill on many a summer afternoon. Sunscreen with a sun protection factor (SPF) of more than 8 can reduce vitamin D synthesis by 80 percent. "Sunscreen doesn't create problems for most people because they don't put it on properly," Holick says. "But older adults apply it correctly and faithfully." Yet these are just the people who could use a boost in production, not a barrier to it, since the body's efficiency at manufacturing D drops with age.

HEALTH NOTE

There's now evidence that folic acid and vitamin B-12 may **PROTECT YOUR EARS.** Researchers have found that women with impaired hearing had up to 38 percent lower levels of these nutrients in their blood than their sharp-eared counterparts .

Even if your sunscreen use is spotty, catching some rays can be more complicated than it sounds. From November to February in the northern hemisphere, the ozone layer absorbs a good deal of sunlight before it can hit the earth. Consequently, in much of the United States during winter months you simply can't get the kind of sunlight you need for adequate D production. Some people face a year-round hurdle to getting their daily D. "Melanin acts like sunscreen," Holick says, "so many African Americans have insufficient levels."

The D decision: Depending on your skin color and on where you spend your winters, you may do just fine with a faceful of sun for 15 minutes three times a week (before applying sunscreen) if you are under age 50. After that, you could likely use a supplement.

But D is not a more-the-merrier kind of vitamin. Overdoses—more than about 2,000 international units daily—can cause headaches and fatigue. If you really go overboard with supplements, you might wind up with kidney stones and calcified heart valves. Reckless megadosing can even be fatal.

The bottom line: For those 50 to 70 years old, young African Americans, or young people of any race who spend the winter in northern regions (think of a line running from Boston to the California-Oregon border), a multivitamin will do the trick; most contain 400 IU of vitamin D. If you're older than 70 and avoiding the sun, add a separate calcium-plus-D supplement, to total 600 to 800 IU. Don't take two multivitamins, or you may end up with an overdose of vitamin A.

Vitamin E

In the past decade scientists have made a strong case for vitamin E's power to guard the heart. In one of the most persuasive studies, people with heart disease were given 400 or 800 IU of the vitamin or a dummy pill; those taking either dose of E turned out to be only half as likely to suffer a heart attack as the placebo group. Such research has prompted many investigators to recommend vitamin E to heart patients or people at risk—and to take it themselves.

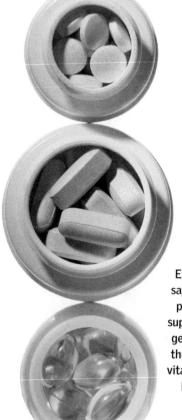

Experts now say that many people need supplements to get enough of three types of vitamins: D, the Bs, and E.

Evidence for other benefits is in the promising-but-preliminary category. In 1997, says Tufts nutrition scientist Jeffrey Blumberg, one study showed that patients in the early stages of Alzheimer's disease who took high doses of the vitamin deteriorated more slowly than similar patients given a placebo.

On the other hand, the support for cancer prevention is weak, says Harvard epidemiologist Rimm, who's been investigating vitamin E for years. A well-publicized study last year showed fewer deaths from prostate cancer among Finnish men who took supplements. But a number of other sizable studies have failed to register the benefit.

Taken as a whole, though, the findings have convinced Blumberg and many other researchers that the RDA should get an upward shove this year from the current setting of 15 IU. More than a minimal boost in the RDA would constitute an implicit endorsement of supplements. The fact is, for a do-gooder vitamin, E keeps company with some oily characters: nuts, margarine, and mayonnaise. Sunflower seeds are a good source, but you'd need to eat a few cups of them to get a decent dose.

Capsule advice on E: A supplement provides cheap, low-risk health insurance, especially for anyone with heart disease or risk factors such as a family history of the condition.

The pills come in natural and synthetic versions. Check the label: The prefix *d-* identifies natural, *dl-* synthetic. Natural vitamin E is more potent and is absorbed twice as efficiently as the man-made variety. You'll notice that it's also twice as expensive.

In any case, resist the temptation to load up. Vitamin E is generally safe, but it does inhibit blood clotting, so it should be treated with respect. More than 1,000 IU daily may cause bleeding. If you regularly take aspirin, warfarin, or another blood-thinning medication, ask your doctor how much vitamin E is safe for you.

The bottom line: To reduce the risk of cardiovascular disease, researchers suggest 100 to 400 IU daily. For people who have heart disease or are at particularly high risk, the suggested dose climbs to between 400 and 800 IU. That's also the amount advised for those hoping to keep Alzheimer's at bay. Most multivitamins contain only 30 IU, so you'll need to purchase a separate E supplement. — *Harriet A. Washington*

Go to the SOURCE

Here's a handy list of foods that are rich in vitamins C, A, and E and folic acid. The RDA (recommended dietary allowance) figures show you the minimum to aim for daily.

VITAMIN C
RDA: *60 milligrams*

	mg
Red bell peppers, 1 cup, raw, chopped	283.0
Green bell peppers, 1 cup, raw, chopped	133.0
Brussels sprouts, 6, raw	96.0
Strawberries, 1 cup, halves	86.2
Broccoli, 1 cup, raw, chopped	82.0
Kiwifruit, 1 medium, no skin	74.5
Orange, 1 medium	64.7

VITAMIN A
RDA: *4,000–5,000 international units*

	IU
Carrots, 1 cup, raw, chopped	28,129
Pumpkin, canned, 1 cup, without salt	22,056
Sweet potatoes, 1 cup, strained	20,063
Red chile pepper, 1, raw	10,750
Apricots, dried, 1 cup, stewed halves	7,240
Spinach, 1 cup, raw	6,715
Red bell peppers, 1 cup, raw, chopped	5,700

VITAMIN E
RDA: *15 international units*

	IU
Wheat germ oil, 1 tablespoon	39.0
Sunflower seeds, 1 ounce, dry-roasted, without salt	21.0
Wheat germ, 1 cup	20.0
Peanut butter, 2 tablespoons	4.8
Almonds, 10	4.3
Butter, 1 pat, with salt	1.2
Peanuts, dry-roasted, 10, without salt	1.0

FOLIC ACID
RDA: *400 micrograms**

	mcg
Lentils, cooked, 1 cup	358.0
Pinto beans, cooked, 1 cup	294.0
Wheat germ, toasted, 1/4 cup	99.5
Green peas, 1 cup, raw	94.3
Spinach, 1 cup, raw	58.3
Fortified breakfast cereal, 1 cup	44.0
Romaine lettuce, 1/2 cup, shredded	38.0

600 mcg for pregnant women

From Iron to Zinc: Mind Your Minerals

Is your blood pressure edging up? Are you alarmed about cancer in your family? Have you been warned about diabetes? You may benefit from one or another of a few key minerals.

Michael LeVesque stocks his health food store in San Francisco with a dizzying array of dietary supplements, but it's the minerals that are dearest to his heart. His own mineral regimen includes calcium, potassium, and magnesium for, he says, "good energy." A dash of chromium to "level out my blood sugar." And zinc. "Because when I'm getting sufficient zinc, food tastes better." LaVesque gazes fondly at the shelves crammed with bottles. "Minerals are really incredible," he says softly.

LaVesque has a lot of company. In 1997 Americans swallowed 750 million dollars' worth of mineral pills, powders, and potions, 27 percent more than in 1990. Health food stores and pharmacies draw customers who want minerals with established benefits—calcium and iron, for example—as well as exotics like bottled silver, "the only known substance that will kill all types of viruses and bacteria," or Amazing Organic Germanium, which earns high praise from a handout: "She regained the ability to write after five months of germanium treatment, and in ten months, she was walking again."

As was the case with vitamins, long-standing wisdom held that anyone with a balanced diet would not be mineral deprived. (See the chart on page 98 for four of the many minerals crucial to your well-being.) But given the less-than-ideal state of the typical American diet, researchers now acknowledge that a pill may be just what many people need to avoid shortage-related ailments. What's more, recent studies have raised the possibility that large doses of some minerals may have medicinal power over problems that aren't linked to nutritional deficiencies, including cancer.

Such research has propelled the current rush of products, many of which, unfortunately, promise far more than science has shown they deliver. Take zinc, a best-seller.

The recommended daily dose of zinc is 12 milligrams for women and 15 for men, yet you can buy tablets that pack six to eight times that amount. Such megadoses are promoted as bolstering the immune system—a perfect example of how research gets twisted, says Bonnie Liebman, nutrition director of the Center for Science in the Public Interest (CSPI) in Washington, D.C. "Supplement makers take studies that describe what happens when you're deficient in a mineral and turn it around to imply that if you take more of the mineral, you'll get the benefit."

True, zinc occupies an important position in the immune system, and studies have shown that high doses can improve immune response in people who are zinc deficient. But because few Americans are short on zinc, amounts above the recommended dietary allowance (RDA) are of little use. And as with many minerals, big doses can be hazardous. Consuming 50 mg of zinc a day for several weeks

Will iron pills give you more energy? Possibly, if tests show you're anemic.

can drive down the body's supply of copper, heightening the risk of high cholesterol and heart disease.

Still, a few mineral supplements may be valuable for people who fit certain profiles. If you're nagged by any of the following worries, consider buying some mineral insurance. (For the complete story on calcium, see "Making the Most of Calcium," page 100.)

Think your diet could be better?

A multivitamin with minerals can cover your nutritional bases. Taking one a day might be especially advisable if certain foods never make it onto your plate. Vegetarians, for instance, may be short on zinc and iron, since lean red meat is the richest source of both.

But choose carefully. While most brands offer essentially the same laundry list of vitamins, they can vary wildly when it comes to minerals. Look for a formula with as many mineral ingredients as possible in amounts approaching 100 percent for minerals with RDAs. (You won't find the recommended amount of calcium, because it can't fit into a little pill.)

Don't bother paying extra for high-octane compounds with names like Ultra Mega Minerals. Despite the imposing label, that kind of formula actually does most of its dose-boosting among the vitamin, not the mineral, ingredients.

Feel like you might be anemic?

Iron supplements usually solve that problem. But first you need to make sure you really have "tired blood," as Geritol's famous slogan put it. Lately, concerns that women get too little iron have been eclipsed by worries that some take in too much.

That's because an estimated 12 percent of Americans carry a gene causing them to absorb 50 percent more iron from their food than is normal, explains Victor Herbert, a professor of medicine at Mt. Sinai and Bronx Veteran's Affairs Medical Centers in New York City. Because only menstruation or having blood drawn rids the body of excess iron, carriers of this gene are at risk for iron overload. In extreme cases iron overload damages tissues and organs and raises the risk of heart attack. A blood test analyzing transferrin, a protein that transports iron, can tell you whether you have iron overload, which can be treated by having blood drawn.

Researchers debate whether the iron-absorption problem is as dangerous or as prevalent as Herbert maintains. But most agree that people need a supplement only if they're low in iron or anemic; the exception is during pregnancy, when women's iron needs double. A standard blood test will tell you if you have low iron stores or anemia.

Blood pressure edging up?

Potassium may help reverse the trend. According to a 1997 analysis of 33 clinical trials, people with high blood pressure saw their numbers drop by four to five points when they took potassium supplements, while people with normal blood pressure who took the pills had a drop of one to two points. Such results mean that potassium supplements could keep some people off hypertension medication and reduce their risk of stroke as well.

Potassium doesn't work equally well for everyone. But if you're worried about your blood pressure (and if you have healthy kidneys) there's no harm in taking a supplement. "People with high blood pressure

HEALTH NOTE

If your breakfast includes cereal, don't be shy about slurping down the last drops of **MILK** in your bowl. That's where many of the cereal's vitamins and minerals end up.

THE ESSENTIAL Vitamin & Mineral Guide

VITAMINS	POSSIBLE BENEFITS	BEST SOURCES	HIGH-DOSE RISKS
Vitamin A (BETA-CAROTENE) RDA Women: 4,000 IU Men: 5,000 IU	**BETA-CAROTENE** is converted to vitamin A, which helps cells develop, promotes bone and tooth growth, and boosts the immune system. You also need vitamin A to help you see at night.	You're well on your way to getting enough if you regularly eat dairy products and eggs or baked goods made with eggs. Leafy green vegetables, carrots, broccoli, cantaloupe, peaches, and squash are also great sources.	Vitamin A is generally safe up to 10,000 IU daily, but toxic above 50,000 IU. During pregnancy, doses of 20,000 IU or more can cause birth defects. Beta-carotene is believed safe up to 83,000 IU per day, but supplements may raise a smoker's risk of lung cancer.
Vitamin B-6 RDA Adults to age 50: 1.3 mg Pregnant women: 1.9 mg Women over 50: 1.5 mg Men over 50: 1.7 mg	**B-6** helps the body process proteins, fats, and carbohydrates, helps supply energy to muscles, and aids in the production of blood cells. Important to the immune system.	Chicken, fish, pork, liver, eggs, spinach, bananas, whole wheat bread, peanut butter—the list is so long and varied that most people don't have to worry about getting enough.	Safe up to 100 mg per day. Higher levels may be risky; taking 2,000 mg daily can cause nerve damage within two months.
Vitamin B-12 RDA Adults: 2.4 mcg Pregnant women: 2.6 mcg	**B-12** helps the body use fats and carbohydrates. Vital to cell development, especially blood cells. Also helps the nervous system work properly.	Meats, chicken, fish, and dairy products are great sources. B-12 is added to some breakfast cereals.	Believed safe up to 100 mcg daily. No known risks.
Vitamin C RDA Adults: 60 mg	**VITAMIN C** is needed to produce collagen, which makes up connective tissue. The vitamin acts as an antioxidant, protecting cells from natural deterioration that occurs with aging.	If you eat fruits or vegetables every day—especially citrus fruits, broccoli, leafy greens, and bell peppers—you're probably over the RDA.	Generally safe up to 500 mg daily. Doses above that can cause diarrhea and may act to promote, not prevent, cell damage of the kind that leads to cancer.
Vitamin D RDA Adults to age 50: 200 IU Adults 51–70: 400 IU Adults over 70: 600 IU	**VITAMIN D** regulates the formation and repair of bone and cartilage. It also controls the amount of calcium and phosphorus your body absorbs from foods.	If you drink milk regularly, you're probably getting plenty. Your body also forms vitamin D when your skin is exposed to the sun. Older men and women should consider daily supplements to protect their bones.	Safe up to 2,000 IU daily. Supplements may be risky if you drink more than a quart of milk a day. Doses of 5,000 IU or more per day can cause irreversible kidney damage.
Vitamin E RDA Adults: 15 IU	**VITAMIN E** appears effective in preventing heart disease. It is an antioxidant that helps shield cells from wear and tear. Helps prevent blood clots. Involved in making red blood cells.	Plentiful in vegetable oil, margarine, meats, nuts, and leafy greens. To protect the heart, a daily supplement of 400 IU is considered best.	Safe up to 800 IU daily, though the body doesn't readily absorb more than 400 IU per day.

VITAMINS	POSSIBLE BENEFITS	BEST SOURCES	HIGH-DOSE RISKS
Folic Acid RDA Adults: 400 mcg Pregnant women: 600 mcg	**FOLIC ACID** helps reduce the risk of heart disease. Insufficient levels increase a woman's chance of having a baby with neurological defects. Needed for red blood cell production.	If you eat lots of leafy greens, peas and beans, citrus fruits, fortified cereals, and whole grains, you're probably getting enough. Women trying to become pregnant should eat plenty of these foods or take a supplement.	Safe up to 1,000 mcg per day. Doses above this may promote zinc loss and can mask vitamin B-12 deficiency, opening the door to irreversible nerve damage.
Niacin RDA Women: 14 mg Pregnant women: 18 mg Men: 16 mg	**NIACIN** aids in processing fat and producing blood sugar. It helps tissues get rid of waste materials. It also lowers cholesterol levels in the blood, reducing the risk of heart disease.	Plentiful in meats, niacin is also formed in the body from protein in eggs and milk. It's added to the flour in breads, pasta, and other products, so most people get plenty.	Safe up to 35 mg per day. Niacin capsules can cause itching, tingling, and rashes. Supplements can also cause liver damage.

MINERALS

Calcium
 	
RDA
Adults to age 50: 1,000 mg
Adults over 50: 1,200 mg
Postmenopausal women
  not taking estrogen:
  1,500 mg
	CALCIUM works to keep bones strong and healthy, helping prevent osteoporosis. It does the same for teeth. It's also essential in muscle relaxation and contraction.	Milk, yogurt, and cheese are the richest sources. Leafy greens, corn tortillas, and tofu will provide some. Women who don't eat much dairy should consider taking a supplement.	Safe up to 2,500 mg daily. More can keep you from absorbing iron and zinc. Excessive doses can cause nausea and other symptoms and may lead to kidney stones and calcium deposits in soft tissues.

Chromium RDA Adults: 50 to 200 mcg	**CHROMIUM** helps convert blood sugar into energy. You need it so insulin can work effectively, which helps prevent diabetes.	Peanuts and beer both offer healthful amounts, as do cheese, whole grains, broccoli, wheat germ, and liver.	Safe at 50 to 200 mcg daily.
Iron RDA Women: 15 mg Men: 10 mg	**IRON** is essential to making red blood cells and hemoglobin.	Plentiful in meats, eggs, lentils, nuts, cheddar cheese, mussels, whole grains, and pumpkin seeds.	Believed safe up to 75 mg daily. More than 100 mg can interfere with zinc and calcium absorption; more than 10,000 mg per day can be lethal.
Zinc RDA Women: 12 mg Men: 15 mg	**ZINC** helps red blood cells carry carbon dioxide to the lungs for disposal. It aids in keeping senses alert and healing wounds. It may also help ease cold symptoms.	Plentiful in red meats, bread and other grain products, eggs, seafood (especially oysters), milk, sunflower seeds, soybeans, and chicken.	Safe up to 15 mg daily. 50 mg per day may increase the risk of heart disease. 2,000 mg or more per day can cause vomiting.

RDA=recommended dietary allowance   **IU**=international units   **MG**=milligrams   **MCG**=micrograms

should take supplements, especially if they're not interested in following a diet that's rich in potassium—a diet of fruits, vegetables, and fruit juices," says Frank Sacks, a professor of nutrition at the Harvard School of Public Health.

You don't need a big dose. So many foods contain potassium that even a junk-food diet will deliver about two of the three and a half to four grams you need a day. Take one 500 mg pill in the morning and another 500 mg at night.

Been warned about diabetes?

Chromium shows promise in thwarting the condition. You may remember chromium from a few years back when it was pitched as a "miracle mineral" that would pare those thunder thighs down into lean, mean muscle. Those claims have largely been discredited. But Richard Anderson, a biochemist with the USDA's Human Nutrition Research Center in Beltsville, Maryland, says 20 years of studies have convinced him that most people with diabetes should take chromium.

"The results with Type 2 diabetes are nothing short of phenomenal," he says. "In a study we conducted in China, we were taking people from diabetic to normal simply by giving them chromium."

Anderson believes some cases of diabetes are linked to a chromium deficiency. Though that point is debated, researchers agree the mineral is necessary to the work of the hormone insulin, which regulates blood sugar levels. "It makes insulin more efficient," says Anderson.

Plenty of experts are skeptical about Anderson's work. It's not clear, they say, how many Americans are in the same boat as the Chinese subjects, who were probably short on chromium. (There's no way to test

for this deficiency.) Without more evidence, the American Diabetes Association isn't recommending chromium supplements.

Still, chromium is the safest of all the trace elements, so taking a supplement won't hurt you. Anderson advises healthy people who want to try chromium to take 200 micrograms a day. People with diabetes, he says, should take 200 to 300 mcg twice a day—more than the recommended dietary allowance but less than the 1,000 mcg a day given to the people in the China study.

Alarmed by cancer in your family?

Selenium offers hope. A University of Arizona study published in 1996 showed that men and women who swallowed 200 mcg a day developed dramatically fewer cases of prostate, lung, and colon cancer (though not breast cancer) than did those who took placebos.

"If I were at high risk for one of those cancers, I'd consider taking it," says CSPI's Liebman, who is no pushover for pills. Unless you are inordinately fond of brazil nuts, a supplement is the only way to get a large enough dose.

Exciting as the prospect of a cancer prevention pill is, most experts, including the authors of the selenium study, agree that the results need to be duplicated before they know the mineral is effective. In the meantime, talk to your doctor about whether your family history or habits put you at special risk of cancer and whether taking a daily selenium pill is worth the expense.

You can safely take a 200 mcg pill. But don't take too much. More than 1 mg a day can cause hair loss, fatigue, nausea, and vomiting. With selenium, as with so many minerals, a little goes a long way.

—Susan Freinkel

Making the Most of Calcium

The great bone builder may not be doing its job even if you're drinking milk and taking supplements. Follow these steps to make sure this essential mineral works.

Make no bones about it: Calcium is one temperamental mineral. Unlike other highly important nutrients, calcium pretty much keeps to the dairy case, with a few oddball exceptions. When it does venture forth into foods like spinach and rhubarb, it does so with heavy irony—accompanied by a naturally occurring chemical that prevents the body from absorbing it. It clings so tightly to the wheat bran found in many high-fiber cereals that your digestive system can't pry the two apart, so some of the calcium in your breakfast milk goes unused. What's more, all the calcium in the world won't do you a bit of good if you don't commit to some sort of bone-building exercise like jumping rope or strength training.

It's hard enough for most Americans to meet the daily requirement for calcium without worrying about these complicating factors. In 1996 only 27 percent of women got the entire 800-milligram daily minimum. And now that the government has raised that number to 1,000 mg for people ages 31 to 50 and 1,200 mg for anyone 51 or older (the National Osteoporosis Foundation recommends 1,500 mg for postmenopausal women not taking estrogen), reaching the goal will be even tougher.

The body does have a resourceful, albeit self-destructive, means of making up for a chronic shortfall: It steals calcium from the bones.

Hardly the inanimate objects we imagine them to be, bones are actually in a constant state of flux—taking in calcium, losing it, taking it in again. Imagine scavenging the timbers of your house to provide wood for your stove. As long as you keep replacing the wood that's been removed, you can pry away the pieces of your shelter indefinitely. But if you dismantle too much without replenishing the source, you make the structure so unstable it'll crack with the first strong wind.

That's essentially how you get osteoporosis. Over time your bones grow thinner and weaker, setting you up for crippling fractures and spinal deformities later in life. Left unchecked, osteoporosis could easily leave you with 30 percent less bone than you had in your prime, which can translate into 50 percent less bone strength.

If you use it correctly, though, calcium can help prevent skeletal weakening. To get the most out of this bone-building mineral, all you have to do is aim your shopping cart—and your exercise habits—in a slightly different direction. Check out these suggestions on how to do just that.

Drink your milk

Brimming with 316 mg of calcium in each eight-ounce glass, milk can keep your body from nibbling away at its own framework. And unlike calcium supplements, milk is an important source

An eight-ounce glass of milk delivers almost a third of the calcium you need in a day. Cheeses are good sources, too.

of other nutrients that work in concert with the mineral to promote strong bones—nutrients such as potassium, magnesium, and vitamin D. Which milk is best? Hands down, it's nonfat, which contains far fewer calories than 2 percent or whole.

There are even varieties of milk designed for people with lactose intolerance, a condition in which dairy products cause gas, bloating, or constipation. Moreover, lactose intolerance varies greatly in severity, so while you may have trouble digesting a glass of milk by itself, that same milk might go down smoothly when taken with food. You can also try retraining your intestines by gradually introducing milk into your diet: Drink a third to a half cup with each meal for one week, then bump it up to one cup the next.

The fact is, if you're a dedicated milk drinker it's pretty easy to get 1,000 mg of calcium per day. But if you're like the average American, who drinks milk with just three meals a week, you'll probably need to rely on other calcium sources.

Don't overlook yogurt and cheese

A slice of reduced-fat swiss cheese layered inside a sandwich ratchets up the calcium by 272 mg. A cup of nonfat cottage cheese with your salad boosts the plate's content by 150 mg. Two tablespoons of parmesan cheese dusted onto your pasta bring 138 mg. If you really want to go for the gusto, head for the nonfat yogurt: One cup packs about 500 mg.

Seek out other calcium-rich foods

Turn to nondairy foods for some of your daily calcium. Fortified orange, grapefruit, or apple juice is your best bet; these have about the same amount of calcium as milk. At 211 mg, a small can of salmon is also a reasonable choice, as is firm tofu, with 204 mg per half-cup serving. After that, however, the purveyors of calcium either don't deliver very much—corn tortillas have only 46 mg apiece—or are foods that people don't

---

HEALTH NOTE

Women on hormone replacement therapy shouldn't skimp on calcium. Researchers analyzed 31 studies and found that **ESTROGEN** takers who got about 1,200 mg of calcium each day increased their bone mass at least one and a half times more than did those who got only 560 mg— a typical intake for women in middle age.

---

regularly heap on their plates: things like sardines (184 mg per four-ounce serving, if you eat them bones and all) or collard greens (226 mg per cup, cooked). Still, if you pick and choose from each of these groups, nondairy foods can contribute about 300 mg of calcium per day.

Beware of foods that inhibit absorption

Meals rich in animal protein, wheat bran, or oxalic acid—a substance found in many foods, including green beans, spinach, peanuts, and summer squash—are the main culprits here. A plate of spinach, for instance, contains 240 mg of calcium, but once the oxalic acid does its dirty work, your body will hang on to a scant 3 percent of that amount. The 1,000 mg minimum for calcium presumes that you'll be eating four ounces of animal protein a day, but for every ounce you take in above that, you need an extra 100 mg of calcium to stay even. And in one study, a regular 1.5-ounce serving of wheat bran cereal reduced absorption of the calcium in the milk by one-third.

No one's suggesting you steer clear of these foods. It's just that you may need to boost your calcium intake to compensate for these absorption inhibitors.

Make up for your shortfall with supplements

If you just don't have time to work calcium into every meal, or if you're lactose intolerant, it's fine to use supplements as a backup. But they shouldn't be your only source.

"Some pills can be hard to swallow and can have a constipating effect," says Connie Bales, an associate research professor of medicine at Duke University and the editor of *Eating Well, Living Well With Osteoporosis.* "So I start by asking a woman if she'd be willing to have, say, one more serving of milk a day. Then I'll prescribe a supplement amount that would make up the difference."

Not all pills contain the same amount of calcium. Those made from calcium carbonate have

Are You Hip to Healthy Bones?

More than 28 million Americans either have or are at risk for osteoporosis, a disease in which bones become fragile and are more likely to break. Indeed, it's responsible for 1.5 million fractures every year, primarily of the hip and vertebrae. But dowager's hump is not inevitable—there's plenty you can do to lower your odds. Are you doing all you should to stand tall?

1 Women begin losing bone density around the time they reach menopause.

TRUE OR FALSE

2 Who is *not* at risk for osteoporosis?

A) AFRICAN AMERICAN WOMEN
B) MEN
C) YOUNG PEOPLE
D) NONE OF THE ABOVE

3 In the United States, the incidence of hip fracture among women equals that of

A) BREAST CANCER
B) UTERINE CANCER
C) OVARIAN CANCER
D) THE TOTAL OF THESE THREE

4 Exercise of any type strengthens bones.

TRUE OR FALSE

5 Bone density tests use X-rays, so you should wait until you're at high risk to get an exam.

TRUE OR FALSE

6 Once you've found out you have low bone density, there's nothing you can do to treat it.

TRUE OR FALSE

ANSWERS

1 **False.** The skeleton is 98 percent complete by age 20. After 40 it's all downhill; by menopause bone loss may be as high as 4 percent a year.

2 **D.** Osteoporosis usually strikes older Caucasian and Asian women, but people of all ages and races are vulnerable (2 million American men have the disease). Other risk factors include smoking, excessive use of alcohol, early menopause, a family history of osteoporosis, an inactive lifestyle, and a diet low in calcium.

3 **D.** And a hip fracture can lead to a fatal decline. Nearly 25 percent of women over 50 die within a year of suffering one.

4 **False.** While all exercise brings benefits to the body, bone-building cells go to work only when the skeleton is stressed. Weight lifting, hill hiking, and step aerobics fit the bill.

5 **False.** Don't let fear of radiation stop you. New tests use ultrasound, which is safe and cheap.

6 **False.** Although there is no cure for osteoporosis, you and your doctor can devise a treatment plan that may help slow bone loss. It will most likely ensure that you get enough calcium and weight-bearing exercise, and may include medication. Several drugs have been approved to treat osteoporosis, among them Raloxifene and Fosamax. Estrogen supplements may help, too.

FOODS HIGH IN Calcium

How much do you need? The National Academy of Sciences recommends 800 milligrams a day for children four through eight years old. Adolescents (up to age 18) should get at least 1,300 mg. Adults need 1,000 mg; that number rises to 1,200 for anyone older than 50. To ward off thinning bones, the National Osteoporosis Foundation recommends 1,000 mg a day after age 25 and 1,500 mg a day for post-menopausal women (1,000 mg if they're on hormone replacement therapy). Along with plenty of calcium-rich foods, make sure you're getting enough vitamin D, which is vital for calcium absorption. Salmon, shrimp, and other kinds of seafood are good sources of D.

MILLIGRAMS PER SERVING

Ricotta cheese, part-skim, ½ cup	337
Milk, nonfat, 1 cup	316
Calcium-fortified orange juice, 1 cup	300
Swiss cheese, 1 ounce	272
Yogurt, nonfat, ½ cup	244
Salmon, canned, 3.5 ounces	211
Cheddar cheese, 1 ounce	204
Tofu, firm, ½ cup	204
Almonds, ¼ cup	160
Dried figs, 5	135
Soybeans, ½ cup, cooked	130
Turnip greens, ½ cup, cooked	99
Corn tortillas, 2	92
Baked beans, ½ cup, cooked	77
Navy beans, ½ cup, cooked	64
Pinto beans, ½ cup, cooked	60
Orange, 1 medium	52
Kale, ½ cup, cooked	47
Broccoli, ½ cup, cooked	36

the most; 40 percent of the tablet is the mineral itself. But that figure drops to 38 percent for pills made with calcium phosphate and 21 percent for calcium citrate. Any type will do the job, provided you take more pills—or bigger pills—of the latter varieties to equal the amount of calcium in calcium carbonate. A simple solution to the whole mess: Keep on hand some extra-strength Tums (made of calcium carbonate), each of which contains almost as much calcium as a glass of milk.

If you decide to go with supplements, don't take your pills all at once. Any system, whether it's a lawn mower confronting tall grass or your digestive tract facing a megadose of calcium, tends to balk at being overloaded. Indeed, your body's efficiency at absorbing calcium drops off when you take the mineral in one big lump rather than in smaller amounts throughout the day. You'll also wring an additional 10 percent from your supplements if you take them when you're finished eating rather than on an empty stomach, assuming that your meal isn't loaded with calcium-inhibiting foods.

And don't fret about lead. A recent study showed that some calcium supplements contain surprisingly high levels of this potentially dangerous metal. But experts say the amount in most pills is generally so minute—less than what's naturally present in milk, canned peaches, or wine—that it's not a concern. Still, it's wise to avoid supplements made from unrefined bone-meal, dolomite, and oyster shell, which have the highest amounts of lead.

Remember vitamin D

If calcium is the wayward traveler making its way through your digestive tract, vitamin D is the traffic cop that flags down the mineral and channels it into the bloodstream and bones.

Fortunately, with 15 minutes of sun exposure three times a week, most people can make all the D they need. To maintain stockpiles during the colder months, try eating fish, eggs, liver, and meat, which naturally contain vitamin D. While milk is artificially fortified with D, studies show that most samples fall short of the amount listed on the label. One foolproof strategy is to take a multivitamin that contains D. For more on how to get all the D you need, see "Why a Good Diet Isn't Enough," page 88.

A Grown-up's GUIDE TO JUMPING ROPE

Jump rope fans tout it as one of the most effective whole-body workouts around. It's not only a quick calorie consumer (five minutes of jumping rope burns as many calories as 15 minutes of brisk walking), it's a weight-bearing exercise—important for warding off osteoporosis. If you limit your workout to bicycling, swimming, or walking, you're missing the impact crucial for building new bone. Cover your bets by bouncing for a few minutes several times a week. Though jumping rope may seem intimidating, getting started couldn't be easier.

WHAT YOU NEED

The rope You can get a decent one for $5 at a sporting goods store. Choose a lightweight rope with wood or foam-covered handles. As for length, doubled up it should reach from the floor to your armpits.

The clothes Wear athletic shoes with good arches and ankle support. Any comfortable outfit that you don't mind sweating in and that won't interfere with the rope will do.

The place Find a forgiving surface—a wood floor, a rubber mat, or a cinder track. Avoid concrete if you can.

HOW TO PROCEED

Be patient Chances are, you'll spend your first sessions trying to stay tangle-free; also, expect one to two minutes of uninterrupted jumping to leave you panting.

Start slowly Try hopping twice for every revolution. Work up to single jumps as your endurance increases.

Conserve energy Increase your speed and endurance by jumping just high enough to clear the rope. Keep your hands at waist level and turn the rope with your wrists to prevent your arms from tiring.

Jump to music As with other aerobic exercises, an up-tempo beat can help you maintain a rhythm.

Set a realistic goal As your stamina and coordination improve, you'll be able to extend your workout. Your goal should be five to ten minutes of jumping three or four times a week.

Stretch after each session Shin muscles tend to tighten up from the repeated bouncing. After your workout, sit on the floor with your legs straight in front of you, then point your toes out and down.

For more information For *The Basic Single Rope Instructional Video*, send $26.95 to the U.S.A. Jump Rope Federation, Box 569, Huntsville, TX 77342. —*Willow Older*

Make an impact

None of this finagling over when and how to take your calcium is worth a damn if you don't also do some sort of regular bone-building exercise. In 1996 epidemiologist Bonny Specker of South Dakota State University reviewed 17 studies that looked at the effects of exercise on bone density, all of which included information about the volunteers' calcium intake. She came to some startling conclusions: Exercise made bones stronger only in subjects who took in more than 1,000 mg a day, and the mineral didn't do any good unless the person was moderately active.

The ideal bone-building regimen combines strength training with a weight-bearing activity such as step aerobics, climbing stairs (the real kind, not the impact-absorbing stair steppers at gyms), jumping rope, or racket sports. This combination stresses the bones so that they retain calcium. It also targets the hip bones and vertebrae, which are most prone to fractures as the body ages. While walking won't build bone, evidence suggests that it will slow bone loss.

There's one more paradoxical point, just to complete the loop. Yes, you need to exercise to make your calcium do its job. But if you exercise hard, your calcium may call it quits in another way—by hightailing it out of your body in a heavy sweat. Not to worry: If your bone-saving workout leaves you drenched, just drink an extra glass of milk that day or reach for one more supplement.

—*David Sharp*

> **HEALTH NOTE**
>
> New research shows that bone-building calcium may also ward off **COLON CANCER**, a leading killer of women. When women with a history of colorectal polyps took in 1,200 mg of calcium daily for one year, the number of abnormal cells in their colons fell considerably.

Recipes

Salads & Starters
Main Dishes
Desserts & Sweets

Sensational Dishes From Super Foods

All those powerful cancer fighters, bone builders, and heart defenders can't work if they don't make it into your meals. For optimum nutrition, dig in to these 140 light and easy recipes.

Add up all the latest nutrition news, and you get this kindly message: To stay healthy as the years tick by, stop focusing on the supposedly bad old foods and reach instead for the great new ones. Cantaloupe, strawberries, garlic, green beans— the list of super foods is long and getting longer.

But nobody eats only ingredients. People eat dinners, lunches, desserts, snacks. And that's where reliable recipes come in. Ripe tomatoes may be scrumptious simply sliced and salted, but what else can you do with them? Try Panzanella With Chicken (page 137), Orange Roughy With Parmesan Tomatoes (page 175), or Tomato and Potato Herb Frittata (page 157).

Want to work some soy into your diet? Try a Double Strawberry Shake (page 188), a Tangy Tropical Smoothie (page 189), or some Classic Stir-Fried Tofu and Vegetables (page 157).

All of these dishes are light and supremely healthful. Just as important, they make eating— and cooking—a pleasure. To make putting them together even simpler, consider equipping your kitchen with some first-rate tools.

A **nonstick skillet** is just the thing for low-fat sautéing, and you can count on the latest versions to hold up to metal spoons and spatulas. Look for a pan with a heavy bottom and sides, and handles that are riveted or welded, not screwed, to the skillet body. All-Clad Nonstick, Anolon, Berndes, and Calphalon Nonstick have all gotten good reviews.

The knife you grab can make chopping vegetables a joy—or a brutal chore. No wonder chefs say a wide, sharp blade is absolutely essential. Buy a top-quality one, and keep it keen with an **electric knife sharpener** such as the Chef's Choice Diamond Hone Sharpener.

Have you ever hoisted a scalding pot of soup off the burner and over to the blender or food processor? Give yourself a break. Make quick purees right on the stovetop with a **handheld blender.** Highly rated brands include Braun and Cuisinart.

Steaming vegetables preserves precious vitamins, and for that task your best bet is a stainless steel **stockpot and steamer.** It comes with a pair of perforated inserts: a shallow one for steaming vegetables and fish, a deep one for boiling and then draining pasta and corn on the cob.

A **fat separator** greatly simplifies defatting homemade chicken stock. It looks like a watering can. You pour in your stock, then pour it out, leaving the grease behind. Shop for a version made of polycarbonate, a plastic that withstands high temperatures.

Of course, you don't need to purchase any of these products to enjoy the many recipes on the following 80 pages. That's the great part about enlightened cooking: Not only is it good for you, it's easy, too.

White Bean, Tuna, and Tomato Salad, page 116

Thai-Style Shrimp and Eggplant Wraps, page 172

Lamb and Veggie Burger With Feta Spread, page 149

Creamy Vanilla Cheesecake With Fresh Strawberries, page 176

Caramelized Onion and Fennel Pie

SERVES 6

CRUST

3 cups shredded peeled baking potato

⅓ cup chopped onion

⅛ teaspoon salt

1 large egg, lightly beaten

cooking spray

Preheat oven to 400°. Combine first 4 ingredients in a medium-size bowl. Press mixture into bottom and up sides of a 10-inch deep-dish pie plate coated with cooking spray. Mist potato mixture with cooking spray. Bake 40 minutes. Remove from oven. Reduce oven temperature to 350°.

FILLING

1 teaspoon olive oil

2 cups vertically halved and slivered onion

1⅓ cups thinly sliced fennel bulb
   (about 1 medium bulb)

½ cup nonfat milk

½ cup (2 ounces) grated fresh parmesan cheese

2 tablespoons nonfat sour cream

¼ teaspoon salt

¼ teaspoon pepper

4 large eggs

Heat oil in a large nonstick skillet coated with cooking spray over medium-high heat. Add onion and fennel; cook 20 minutes or until golden, stirring frequently. Remove from heat; cool slightly.

Combine milk and remaining ingredients in a large bowl, whisking until well blended. Stir in fennel mixture. Pour into prepared potato crust. Bake 45 minutes or until set. Let stand 10 minutes.

Per serving: Calories 203 (35% from fat), Fat 8 g (3 g saturated), Protein 13 g, Carbohydrate 21 g, Fiber 2 g, Cholesterol 191 mg, Iron 2 mg, Sodium 374 mg, Calcium 193 mg

Corn and Onion Focaccia

SERVES 12

1 package active dry yeast

1 cup warm (100°) water

½ teaspoon salt

2 tablespoons olive or salad oil, divided

¾ cup cornmeal

about 2¼ cups all-purpose flour, divided

1 cup corn kernels, fresh or frozen

2 tablespoons minced fresh sage leaves

1 small red onion (about 3 ounces), thinly sliced

1 tablespoon lemon juice

½ cup shredded jack cheese

Preheat oven to 400°. In a large bowl, sprinkle yeast over water; let stand about 5 minutes. Stir in salt, 1 tablespoon oil, cornmeal, and 1 cup flour. Beat with a mixer until dough is stretchy, 3 to 5 minutes. Stir in 1 more cup flour.

Coat a board with remaining ¼ cup flour and scrape dough onto it. Knead dough until smooth and elastic, 7 to 10 minutes. Add a little more flour if dough sticks.

Place dough in a bowl, cover with plastic wrap, and let rise in a warm spot until doubled, about 45 minutes. Punch dough down in bowl to expel air bubbles. Pour remaining 1 tablespoon oil into a 10" × 15" baking pan. Turn dough in oil to coat, then press and pat dough to evenly fill pan. Sprinkle with corn kernels and sage; press firmly into dough, using your palm. Separate onion slices into rings and mix with lemon juice. Scatter onion rings over dough and press down gently with your palm. Cover pan lightly with plastic wrap, and let dough rise in a warm place until puffy, about 30 minutes.

Bake, uncovered, on the lowest rack until dough is well browned on edges and bottom, about 35 minutes; sprinkle with cheese and bake just until cheese begins to melt, about 2 minutes. Serve hot, warm, or at room temperature, cut into squares.

Per serving: Calories 168 (21% from fat), Fat 4 g (1 g saturated), Protein 5 g, Carbohydrate 27 g, Fiber 2 g, Cholesterol 4 mg, Iron 1 mg, Sodium 133 mg, Calcium 44 mg

Caramelized Onion
and Fennel Pie

Individual Corn-Chile Soufflés

SERVES 6

2 medium-size ears corn (about 10 inches
    long and about 1½ pounds total) or
    2 cups frozen corn kernels

1 cup nonfat milk

2 tablespoons cornstarch

1 teaspoon ground cumin

¼ cup canned diced green chiles

¼ pound light jarlsberg cheese, shredded

2 large eggs, separated

4 large egg whites (discard yolks or reserve
    for another use)

½ teaspoon cream of tartar

salt to taste

Preheat oven to 375°. Remove husks and silks from corn, reserving 12 of the longest and widest pieces of husk. Immerse reserved husks in cool water.

Rinse ears. With a sharp knife, cut corn kernels off cobs.

In a 1½- to 2-quart pan, mix milk with cornstarch and cumin; add corn and chiles. Stir over high heat until boiling. Add cheese and stir until melted. Remove from heat and stir in egg yolks.

Drain husks and divide into pairs; make a cross with each pair. Nest a pair in each of 6 lightly oiled soufflé baking dishes, 1¼- to 1½-cup size. (If using frozen corn, omit husks and do not oil dishes.)

Put 6 egg whites in a deep bowl; add cream of tartar and whip with mixer on high speed until whites hold soft peaks. Stir about ⅓ of whites into corn mixture, then gently fold corn mixture into remaining whites; mixture can be streaked. Divide mixture equally among soufflé dishes.

Bake until well browned; allow 20 minutes for creamy soufflé centers, 25 minutes for firmer centers. Serve immediately with salt to taste.

Per serving: Calories 235 (31% from fat), Fat 8 g (3 g saturated), Protein 14 g, Carbohydrate 32 g, Fiber 3 g, Cholesterol 82 mg, Iron 1 mg, Sodium 199 mg, Calcium 236 mg

Salade Niçoise With Aioli

SERVES 8

AIOLI

½ cup low-fat buttermilk

½ cup egg substitute

2 tablespoons water

4 teaspoons lemon juice

2 teaspoons dijon mustard

¼ teaspoon salt

¼ teaspoon ground red pepper

6 cloves garlic, halved

2 tablespoons olive oil

½ cup fresh bread crumbs

Prepare the aioli before starting the salad. Place first 8 ingredients (through garlic) in a food processor; process until smooth, scraping sides of bowl occasionally.

With food processor on, slowly pour oil through chute; process until well blended. Add bread crumbs; process until smooth. Cover and chill. Makes 1 cup.

Per serving: Calories 58 (59% from fat), Fat 4 g (1 g saturated), Protein 3 g, Carbohydrate 4 g, Fiber 0 g, Cholesterol 0 mg, Iron 0 mg, Sodium 155 mg, Calcium 30 mg

SALADE NIÇOISE

¼ cup red wine vinegar

½ teaspoon dried oregano

½ teaspoon dried basil

3 cloves garlic, minced

4 6-ounce tuna steaks

8 red potatoes (about 1½ pounds)

½ pound green beans, trimmed

cooking spray

1 large tomato, cut into ¼-inch-thick wedges

1 can (14 ounces) artichoke hearts,
    drained and halved

8 cups chopped romaine lettuce

1 cup thinly sliced red onion, separated into rings

1 can (2¼ ounces) sliced black olives, drained

Combine vinegar, oregano, basil, and garlic in a large zip-top plastic bag. Add tuna to bag; seal. Marinate in refrigerator 30 minutes, turning bag occasionally.

Place potatoes in a saucepan; cover with water. Bring to a boil. Reduce heat and simmer 20 minutes or until tender; drain. Cover and chill. Cut potatoes into thin slices; set aside. Steam beans, covered, 5 minutes or until tender. Rinse in cold water; drain and chill.

Remove tuna from bag; discard marinade. Place tuna on a broiler pan coated with cooking spray; broil 7 minutes on each side or to desired degree of doneness. Arrange tuna, potatoes, beans, tomato, and artichokes on a large lettuce-lined serving platter; top with onion, olives, and a generous spoonful of aioli.

Note: Aioli, green beans, potatoes, and tuna can be prepared ahead of time; cover and chill.

Per serving: Calories 300 (28% from fat), Fat 9 g (2 g saturated), Protein 27 g, Carbohydrate 28 g, Fiber 4 g, Cholesterol 32 mg, Iron 4 mg, Sodium 302 mg, Calcium 101 mg

Tabbouleh With Orange-Marinated Shrimp

SERVES 8

⅔ cup fresh orange juice (about 2 oranges)

2 tablespoons olive oil

1 tablespoon honey

½ teaspoon salt

¼ teaspoon cracked black peppercorns

1 pound peeled cooked medium shrimp

4 cups water

1 cup uncooked bulgur or cracked wheat

2 cups thinly sliced spinach

1 cup diced seeded, peeled cucumber

1 cup orange sections (about 3 oranges)

⅔ cup chopped fresh mint

½ cup thinly sliced red onion

⅓ cup chopped fresh parsley

Combine first 5 ingredients (through peppercorns) in a large bowl; whisk well. Add shrimp; cover and marinate in refrigerator 1 hour.

Combine water and bulgur in a large bowl. Cover and let stand 30 minutes; drain well. Add bulgur, spinach, and remaining ingredients to shrimp mixture; cover and marinate in refrigerator at least 1 hour, stirring occasionally.

Per serving: Calories 183 (22% from fat), Fat 4 g (1 g saturated), Protein 15 g, Carbohydrate 22 g, Fiber 5 g, Cholesterol 111 mg, Iron 3 mg, Sodium 290 mg, Calcium 62 mg

IN SEASON

Superjuicy valencia oranges are at their freshest in early spring, including a late-ripening navel that typically appears in March.

BEST BUYS
Shop for fruit that's firm, heavy for its size, and free of soft spots. Don't pass up oranges with brown patches or green highlights; they're just as sweet and tasty.

COOKING TIPS
A splash of valencia juice revitalizes fruit salads and perks up cakes and muffins. For a festive light salad, slice peeled oranges and jicama, then arrange on a bed of watercress; dress with a vinaigrette of equal parts extra virgin olive oil, wine vinegar, and fresh orange juice. For a side dish with roast pork or chicken, slice sweet potatoes, oranges, and red onions into a casserole. Sprinkle with raisins and olive oil. Cover and bake at 350°, stirring a few times, until potatoes soften, about 30 minutes.

HEALTH BONUS
Loaded with vitamin C, oranges are also rich in limonene, a compound that may strengthen the body's defenses against cancer.

Grilled Southwestern Chicken Salad

SERVES 4

2 teaspoons chili powder, divided

2 teaspoons ground coriander, divided

½ teaspoon garlic salt

4 4-ounce skinned, boned chicken breast halves

cooking spray

½ cup reduced-calorie ranch dressing

10 cups gourmet salad greens (lettuces, spinach,
*   arugula, radicchio, mizuna)*

1 cup cherry tomatoes, halved

Prepare grill or preheat broiler. Combine 1½ teaspoons chili powder, 1½ teaspoons coriander, and garlic salt; sprinkle over chicken. Place chicken on grill rack or broiler pan coated with cooking spray; cook 5 minutes on each side or until done.

Combine ½ teaspoon chili powder, ½ teaspoon coriander, and ranch dressing. In a large bowl, combine salad greens, tomatoes, and dressing mixture; toss gently to coat. Divide salad evenly among 4 plates. Cut chicken into thin slices and arrange on salad.

Per serving: Calories 218 (29% from fat), Fat 7 g (1 g saturated), Protein 29 g, Carbohydrate 9 g, Fiber 4 g, Cholesterol 66 mg, Iron 3 mg, Sodium 543 mg, Calcium 76 mg

Quinoa Salad With Peanut Dressing

SERVES 4

1 cup quinoa

2 cups reduced-sodium nonfat chicken broth

1 small (about 2 ounces) carrot, cut into long thin
*   strands or shredded*

½ cup finely shredded red cabbage

¼ cup green onions, ends trimmed, thinly sliced

2 tablespoons chopped fresh cilantro, plus fresh
*   cilantro sprigs for garnish*

Peanut Dressing (recipe follows)

Rinse quinoa in a fine-mesh strainer; drain. Pour quinoa into a 1½- to 2-quart pan. Stir over medium heat until lightly browned, 8 to 10 minutes. Add broth, then bring to a boil over high heat. Reduce heat, cover, and simmer until most of liquid is absorbed and quinoa is just tender, 10 to 15 minutes. Drain and discard remaining liquid; let quinoa cool completely.

In a large bowl, combine quinoa, carrot, cabbage, green onions, and chopped cilantro. Pour peanut dressing over the mixture and stir gently. Serve, or cover and chill up to 2 hours. Garnish with cilantro sprigs.

PEANUT DRESSING
In a bowl, whisk together 2 tablespoons chunky peanut butter, 3 tablespoons rice or cider vinegar, 2 teaspoons reduced-sodium soy sauce, 1 tablespoon lemon juice, 1 clove minced garlic, 2 teaspoons minced fresh ginger, and ⅛ to ¼ teaspoon dried hot red chile flakes.

Per serving: Calories 221 (24% from fat), Fat 6 g (1 g saturated), Protein 9 g, Carbohydrate 34 g, Fiber 4 g, Cholesterol 0 mg, Iron 4 mg, Sodium 135 mg, Calcium 48 mg

Jicama and Orange Salad

SERVES 6

1 medium-size jicama, peeled and diced

¼ cup fresh lime juice

salt to taste

2 navel oranges, sectioned and diced

pure powdered chiles to taste

2 tablespoons chopped fresh cilantro

1 head leaf lettuce or 2 cups baby salad greens

Toss together jicama, lime juice, and salt. Let sit at room temperature 1 hour, tossing occasionally. Add remaining ingredients except lettuce and toss. Let mixture sit at least 15 minutes, preferably 2 hours.

Line a large bowl or platter with lettuce, top with jicama mixture and serve.

Per serving: Calories 45 (0% from fat), Fat 0 g (0 g saturated), Protein 2 g, Carbohydrate 10 g, Fiber 4 g, Cholesterol 0 mg, Iron 1 mg, Sodium 13 mg, Calcium 16 mg

TECHNIQUES

How to Chop an Onion

Cut an onion quickly and cleanly, and you'll shed fewer tears. The first step is to make sure that your knife is very sharp—a dull one can slip and hurt your fingers. Then, with the onion's peel still on, trim both ends, leaving intact as much of the woody root end as possible.

1 Slicing straight down through the trimmed ends, cut the onion in half. Peel away and discard the papery skin. Lay both halves cut side down on a cutting board. Hold one half lightly with your fingertips.

2 Position the knife against the stem end, parallel to the cutting board, 1/2 inch from the bottom. Slice nearly to—but not through—the root end. Make one or two more parallel cuts 1/2 inch apart.

3 Place the knife tip near the root end, and cut straight down to the cutting board, making several parallel cuts 1/2 inch apart. Leave the sections attached at the far end.

4 Holding the half with your fingertips curled under, slice the onion crosswise in parallel cuts 1/2 inch apart. Discard the last 1/2 inch. Repeat steps for second half.

Italian Tuna, Red Pepper, and Rice Salad

SERVES **4**

2 cups water

1 cup uncooked long-grain rice

¼ cup fresh lemon juice

2 tablespoons olive oil

1 tablespoon chopped green onions

1 teaspoon grated lemon zest

¼ teaspoon salt

1 cup diced red bell pepper

2 6-ounce cans albacore tuna, drained

*1 cantaloupe, peeled, seeded, and cut
    lengthwise into 16 slices*

Bring water to a boil in a medium-size saucepan; add rice. Cover, reduce heat, and simmer 15 minutes or until liquid is absorbed. Remove from heat; let stand 5 minutes. Fluff with a fork; cool.

Combine lemon juice, oil, onions, zest, and salt in a large bowl; stir well. Stir in rice, bell peppers, and tuna. Cover and chill. Serve with cantaloupe.

Per serving: Calories 399 (21% from fat), Fat 9 g (2 g saturated), Protein 21 g, Carbohydrate 59 g, Fiber 4 g, Cholesterol 24 mg, Iron 3 mg, Sodium 393 mg, Calcium 43 mg

White Bean, Tuna, and Tomato Salad

White Bean, Tuna, and Tomato Salad

SERVES **4**

⅓ cup chopped green onions

1 teaspoon grated lemon rind

2 tablespoons fresh lemon juice

1 tablespoon white wine vinegar

1 tablespoon olive oil

2 cups halved cherry tomatoes

*1 can (16 ounces) cannellini beans
    or other white beans, rinsed
    and drained*

1 can (6 ounces) albacore tuna

in water, drained and flaked

3 tablespoons minced fresh basil

4 large leaves red leaf lettuce

Combine first 5 ingredients in a large bowl. Add tomatoes, beans, and tuna; toss gently to coat. Stir in basil; cover and chill. Serve on lettuce-lined plates.

Per serving: Calories 244 (25% from fat), Fat 7 g (1g saturated), Protein 17 g, Carbohydrate 32 g, Fiber 7 g, Cholesterol 12 mg, Iron 5 mg, Sodium 290 mg, Calcium 148 mg

Shrimp With Lime-Mustard Marinade

SERVES **6**

½ cup thinly sliced sweet onion, separated into rings

¼ cup fresh lime juice

2 tablespoons capers

2 teaspoons dijon mustard

¼ teaspoon hot sauce

1 cup water

¼ cup white wine vinegar

3 whole cloves

1 bay leaf

1 pound medium shrimp, peeled and deveined

Combine onion, lime juice, capers, mustard, and hot sauce in a large shallow dish; set mixture aside.

Combine water, vinegar, cloves, and bay leaf in a large saucepan; bring to a boil. Add shrimp and cook 1 minute or until done, stirring constantly. Add shrimp mixture to onion mixture; stir well. Cover and marinate in refrigerator up to 2 hours, stirring occasionally.

Discard cloves and bay leaf. Serve with crackers.

Per serving: Calories 67 (11% from fat), Fat 1 g (0 g saturated), Protein 12 g, Carbohydrate 2 g, Fiber 0 g, Cholesterol 111 mg, Iron 2 mg, Sodium 403 mg, Calcium 25 mg

Tabbouleh With Snow Peas and Red Peppers

SERVES 8

1½ cups bulgur, rinsed

1½ cups boiling water

1 cup chopped seeded, peeled cucumber

½ cup diagonally sliced snow peas

½ cup chopped red bell pepper

⅓ cup lemon juice

¼ cup chopped fresh parsley

¼ cup chopped red onion

2 tablespoons minced fresh mint

2 tablespoons olive oil

½ teaspoon salt

⅛ teaspoon pepper

Combine bulgur and boiling water in a large bowl; stir well. Let stand 40 minutes or until water is absorbed. Add remaining ingredients; toss well. Cover and chill.

Per serving: Calories 134 (26% from fat), Fat 4 g (1 g saturated), Protein 4 g, Carbohydrate 23 g, Fiber 6 g, Cholesterol 0 mg, Iron 1 mg, Sodium 154 mg, Calcium 21 mg

Red Cabbage Coleslaw With Apples and Blue Cheese

SERVES 6

¼ cup raspberry-flavored vinegar

¼ cup water

1 tablespoon honey

2 teaspoons vegetable oil

1 teaspoon dijon mustard

⅛ teaspoon salt

⅛ teaspoon pepper

4 cups sliced peeled red delicious
  or granny smith apples

3 cups thinly sliced red cabbage

¼ cup (1 ounce) crumbled blue cheese

Combine first 7 ingredients (through pepper) in a bowl; stir well. Add remaining ingredients; toss well.

Cover and chill 1 hour. Toss immediately before serving.

Per serving: Calories 96 (31% from fat), Fat 3 g (1 g saturated), Protein 2 g, Carbohydrate 17 g, Fiber 3 g, Cholesterol 4 mg, Iron 0 mg, Sodium 142 mg, Calcium 48 mg

Roasted Asparagus With Orange-Scented Onions

SERVES 4

2 cups slivered onions

1 tablespoon water

1 teaspoon chopped fresh thyme

1 teaspoon olive oil

2 2" × ½" pieces orange rind, cut into thin strips

dash of freshly ground black pepper

1½ pounds fresh asparagus

1 teaspoon olive oil

Preheat oven to 400°. Combine onions, water, thyme, olive oil, and orange rind in a 13" × 9" × 2" baking dish; stir well. Cover and bake 45 minutes or until onions are golden and tender. Remove from oven. Stir in pepper; push onion mixture to side of dish. Reduce heat to 350°.

Snap off tough ends of asparagus; remove scales with a knife or vegetable peeler, if desired. Add asparagus to dish; drizzle with 1 teaspoon oil, tossing gently. Spoon onion mixture over asparagus. Cover and bake 15 minutes or until asparagus is crisp-tender.

Per serving: Calories 64 (37% from fat), Fat 3 g (0 g saturated), Protein 3 g, Carbohydrate 9 g, Fiber 2 g, Cholesterol 0 mg, Iron 1 mg, Sodium 12 mg, Calcium 31 mg

IN SEASON

Spring is the time for asparagus, the young shoots of a fernlike plant in the lily family. Tender and sweet when steamed, the spears make an appealing side dish or warm salad.

BEST BUYS
Fresh asparagus is bright green with purplish tips. Shop for firm spears of medium thickness whose tips are tightly closed and not bruised or mushy.

COOKING TIPS
To remove the woody ends, take each stalk in both hands, set about 3 inches apart. Bend until the stalk snaps. If the spears are especially tough or fat, peel the lower portions with a potato peeler. Rinse thoroughly, then place spears in a large steamer set in a wide pan over simmering water. Cover, and cook 8 to 10 minutes. Dress with extra virgin olive oil, lemon juice, salt, and pepper.

HEALTH BONUS
With just 4 calories a spear, asparagus ties cooked spinach as the lean, green vegetable with the most heart-protecting folic acid.

Pear and Pasta Spinach Salad

SERVES 6

2 cups corkscrew macaroni

3 tablespoons cider vinegar

2 tablespoons packed brown sugar

1½ tablespoons olive oil

1 tablespoon water

1 teaspoon brown mustard

¼ teaspoon dried hot red pepper flakes

3 cups tightly packed torn fresh spinach

1 cup (1 medium) sliced pear

1 cup (1 small) sliced yellow summer squash

¼ cup sliced red onion

3 tablespoons crumbled feta or farmer cheese

Cook pasta as directed on package; drain. Rinse under cold water; drain again. Transfer to a large bowl.

In a container with a tight-fitting lid, combine vinegar, brown sugar, olive oil, water, mustard, and red pepper flakes. Cover and shake well. Add to pasta; toss gently. Cover and refrigerate at least 2 hours, up to 24 hours.

Add spinach, pear, squash, and red onion just before serving; toss gently. Sprinkle individual servings with crumbled feta cheese.

Per serving: Calories 221 (20% from fat), Fat 5 g (1 g saturated), Protein 6 g, Carbohydrate 38 g, Fiber 3 g, Cholesterol 3 mg, Iron 2 mg, Sodium 78 mg, Calcium 70 mg

Asian Pasta-Vegetable Salad

SERVES 5

3 ounces linguine or fettuccine, broken
    in 3-inch lengths

2 large carrots, cut in julienne strips

2 tablespoons rice vinegar or wine vinegar

1 tablespoon low-sodium soy sauce

1 tablespoon honey

1 tablespoon vegetable oil

¼ teaspoon dry mustard

¼ teaspoon toasted sesame oil

dash hot pepper sauce

3 cups shredded chinese cabbage or spinach

2 teaspoons toasted sesame seeds

Cook pasta and carrots together as directed on the pasta package; drain. Rinse under cold water; drain again. Transfer to a medium-size bowl.

Combine vinegar, soy sauce, honey, vegetable oil, mustard, sesame oil, and hot pepper sauce in a small bowl. Add to pasta mixture; toss gently. Cover and chill at least 2 hours or up to 24 hours.

Add cabbage before serving; toss gently. Sprinkle with sesame seeds.

Per serving: Calories 112 (32% from fat), Fat 4 g (0 g saturated), Protein 3 g, Carbohydrate 17 g, Fiber 2 g, Cholesterol 0 mg, Iron 1 mg, Sodium 154 mg, Calcium 50 mg

Warm Wild-Mushroom Salad

SERVES **4**

2 teaspoons olive oil, divided

1 cup sliced fresh oyster mushrooms

1 cup sliced fresh shiitake mushroom caps

2 tablespoons minced shallots

¼ teaspoon dried marjoram

2 cloves garlic, minced

1 tablespoon balsamic vinegar

1 tablespoon water

⅛ teaspoon salt

1 cup diced seeded tomato

6 cups gourmet salad greens

Heat 1 teaspoon oil in a medium-size nonstick skillet over medium heat. Add mushrooms, shallots, marjoram, and garlic; sauté 5 minutes. Add remaining oil, vinegar, water, and salt; cook over low heat 1 minute. Remove from heat; stir in tomato.

Combine warm mushroom mixture and greens in a large bowl and toss gently. Serve immediately.

Per serving: Calories 55 (44% from fat), Fat 3 g (0 g saturated), Protein 2 g, Carbohydrate 7 g, Fiber 2 g, Cholesterol 0 mg, Iron 1 mg, Sodium 84 mg, Calcium 9 mg

Poached Leeks With Tomato Salsa

SERVES **4**

1 cup diced seeded tomato

2 tablespoons coarsely chopped fresh basil

1 tablespoon thinly sliced green onions

1 teaspoon finely chopped fresh mint

⅛ teaspoon salt

2 teaspoons fresh lime juice

2 teaspoons olive oil

12 small leeks (about 3½ pounds)

½ cup low-sodium chicken broth

1 sprig fresh basil

freshly ground black pepper to taste

For the salsa, combine first 7 ingredients (through oil) in a bowl; toss gently and set aside.

Remove roots, outer leaves, and tops from leeks, leaving 5 inches of each leek. Cut diagonally into thirds, then diagonally in half. Rinse leeks and drain.

Combine leeks, chicken broth, and basil sprig in a large skillet; bring to a boil. Cover, reduce heat, and simmer 20 minutes or until tender. Place leeks on a platter; discard poaching liquid. Top leeks with salsa, and serve with freshly ground pepper.

Per serving: Calories 109 (23% from fat), Fat 3 g (0 saturated), Protein 2 g, Carbohydrate 21 g, Fiber 2 g, Cholesterol 0 mg, Iron 3 mg, Sodium 100 mg, Calcium 80 mg

> ### KITCHEN **TIP**
> Tomatoes can brighten almost any dish, but tomato seeds can be bitter. Luckily, seeding a tomato is easy: Cut it as you would a grapefruit, along the equator. Separate the halves. Grasp one half in your hand and squeeze gently to release the seeds; using a spoon, scoop out any that remain. Repeat with the other half.

The Best Way To Store Leftovers

As long as you're cooking, it's smart to fix more than you need today and keep the rest for a quick meal tomorrow. But how to keep those heat-and-eat meals fresh? These simple storing techniques can help.

Transfer hot leftovers to the refrigerator as soon as possible. Tiny amounts of bacteria that might not be enough to make you sick are apt to multiply at room temperature. Poultry is particularly risky; in two hours an innocuous salmonella colony can grow into a population large enough to do serious damage.

Store hot food in small containers. Whether it's soup or pasta, it won't cool fast enough in large quantities to stop harmful bacteria from multiplying. For faster cooling, select containers that are no deeper than 4 inches, and place them side by side in the refrigerator instead of stacking them.

Fill containers to the top, and seal them tightly. Oxygen is what makes food turn sour and smelly, so try to minimize how much air touches the food. Plastic, glass, and stainless steel containers with snap-down lids are equally effective. Plastic bags with zipper seals or twist ties also are fine, though because they're thinner, oxygen has a better chance of getting through.

Make sure that your leftovers don't come into contact with dirty utensils, hands, or cutting boards en route to the fridge. Any of these little lapses can introduce bacteria into your food—some that can make you ill and some that can make your food spoil sooner.

Lentil and Spinach Soup

SERVES 6

1 tablespoon olive oil

1 medium onion, chopped

3 or 4 cloves garlic, minced or pressed, divided

2 cups lentils, washed and sorted for stones

2 quarts water

1 bay leaf

1 parmesan cheese rind (optional)

salt to taste

freshly ground black pepper to taste

1 pound spinach or chard, stemmed and coarsely chopped

¼ cup chopped fresh parsley

plain nonfat yogurt for garnish

Heat oil over medium-low heat in a heavy-bottomed soup pot; add onion. Cook, stirring, until onion is tender, 3 to 5 minutes. Add half of the garlic and stir about 30 seconds, until garlic smells fragrant. Stir in lentils, water, bay leaf, and parmesan rind. Bring to a boil; reduce heat, cover, and simmer 40 minutes or until lentils are tender. Stir in remaining garlic, and add salt and freshly ground pepper to taste.

Discard bay leaf and parmesan rind. Puree a cup of the lentils in a blender or food processor, and stir mixture back into soup. Add spinach, cover, and simmer 5 to 10 minutes, stirring occasionally. Stir in parsley and serve. Top each bowl with a dollop of yogurt.

Per serving: Calories 264 (10% from fat), Fat 3 g (0 g saturated), Protein 21 g, Carbohydrate 42 g, Fiber 22 g, Cholesterol 0 mg, Iron 8 mg, Sodium 68 mg, Calcium 118 mg

How to Make Vegetable Stock

Preparing broth for your soups is a mess of trouble, right? Not if you follow these steps. Your work in the kitchen takes just minutes, and the stock cooks in the span of a "Seinfeld" rerun. Ingredient amounts are flexible, and you can toss in that leftover onion from the veggie drawer.

1 With a chef's knife, chop the white part of 2 leeks (or 1 bunch green onions), 1 yellow onion, 2 large carrots, and 2 celery ribs (including some tops). With the side of the knife, crush 4 or 5 peeled garlic cloves.

2 Heat 1 tablespoon olive oil in a soup pot over medium-high heat. Add chopped leeks, onion, carrots, and celery. Cook, stirring until vegetables are lightly browned and fragrant, 5 to 10 minutes.

3 Add 2 quarts water, garlic, 1 or 2 bay leaves, 1/2 teaspoon dried thyme, 1 teaspoon whole black peppercorns, and several parsley sprigs. Bring to a boil; lower heat and simmer, uncovered, for 30 minutes.

4 Add 1 teaspoon salt or more to taste. Strain broth into a second pot if using right away; otherwise, strain into containers that can be chilled or frozen. Discard vegetables and use stock for soups or sauces.

Shrimp and
Papaya Kabobs

Roasted Tofu With Sweet-and-Sour Plum Sauce

SERVES **8**

ROASTED TOFU

2 tablespoons low-sodium soy sauce

1 tablespoon dry sherry

1½ teaspoons dark sesame oil

1½ teaspoons vegetable oil

⅛ teaspoon crushed red pepper

*1 package (about 12 ounces) reduced-fat extrafirm
   tofu, drained*

Preheat oven to 450°. Combine first 5 ingredients
(through red pepper) in a shallow dish; stir with
a whisk. Cut tofu crosswise into 8 slices; cut each
slice into 3 triangles. Add tofu to mixture in dish,
turning to coat. Let stand 30 minutes, stirring
occasionally. Bake 20 minutes or until browned,
stirring after 10 minutes.

SWEET-AND-SOUR PLUM SAUCE

⅓ cup sugar

3 tablespoons white vinegar

1 tablespoon water

⅛ teaspoon crushed red pepper

2 teaspoons bottled plum sauce

Combine first 4 ingredients (through red pepper)
in a small saucepan; bring to a boil, stirring frequently. Reduce heat to medium-low, and simmer
5 minutes. Remove from heat; add plum sauce,
stirring with a whisk. Pour sweet-and-sour sauce
into a small bowl and serve alongside roasted tofu.

Per serving: Calories 70 (26% from fat), Fat 2 g (0 g saturated),
Protein 3 g, Carbohydrate 10 g, Fiber 0 g, Cholesterol 0 mg, Iron
1 mg, Sodium 162 mg, Calcium 21 mg

Teriyaki Chicken Kabobs

SERVES 4

8 green onions

½ cup low-sodium teriyaki sauce

1 teaspoon grated peeled fresh ginger

1 teaspoon dark sesame oil

2 cloves garlic, minced

1 pound skinned, boned chicken breast, cut
   lengthwise into 16 strips

cooking spray

Prepare grill. Remove green tops from onions and reserve for another use. Cut white portion of each onion into 1-inch pieces.

Combine onions and next 5 ingredients (through chicken) in a large zip-top plastic bag. Seal and marinate in refrigerator 30 minutes. Remove chicken and onions from bag, reserving marinade.

Thread chicken and onions alternately onto 8 10-inch skewers. Place on rack coated with cooking spray; grill 3 minutes on each side or until done, basting often with marinade.

Per serving: Calories 170 (15% from fat), Fat 3 g (1 g saturated), Protein 28 g, Carbohydrate 8 g, Fiber 1 g, Cholesterol 66 mg, Iron 1 mg, Sodium 589 mg, Calcium 37 mg

Shrimp and Papaya Kabobs

SERVES 4

1 pound large shrimp, peeled and deveined

16 1-inch chunks peeled papaya

16 1-inch pieces green bell pepper

16 1-inch chunks onion

⅓ cup water

2 tablespoons thawed orange juice concentrate

½ teaspoon ground coriander

¼ teaspoon salt

cooking spray

Prepare grill. Thread first 4 ingredients alternately onto 8 10-inch skewers. Combine ⅓ cup water, juice concentrate, coriander, and salt in a small bowl; brush over kabobs. Place kabobs on grill rack coated with cooking spray; grill 7 minutes on each side or until shrimp are done.

Per serving: Calories 157 (11% from fat), Fat 2 g (0 g saturated), Protein 19 g, Carbohydrate 16 g, Fiber 3 g, Cholesterol 129 mg, Iron 3 mg, Sodium 277 mg, Calcium 75 mg

Mexican Pork Kabobs With Salsa

SERVES 6

2 ears corn, shucked

cooking spray

1 cup sliced red onion, cut ½ inch thick

1½ cups chopped tomato

2 tablespoons red wine vinegar

1 tablespoon minced fresh cilantro

½ teaspoon salt, divided

1 clove garlic, minced

2 teaspoons ground cumin

2 teaspoons chili powder

⅛ teaspoon pepper

1½ pounds pork tenderloin, cut into 24 1-inch cubes

Prepare grill. To make salsa, place corn on grill rack coated with cooking spray; grill 15 minutes or until corn is lightly browned, turning every 5 minutes. Allow to cool. Cut kernels from ears of corn to measure 1¼ cups. Grill onion slices 2 minutes on each side. Chop onion. Combine corn, onion, tomato, vinegar, cilantro, ¼ teaspoon salt, and garlic in a small bowl. Set salsa aside.

To prepare pork, combine ⅛ teaspoon salt, cumin, chili powder, and pepper in a large zip-top bag. Add pork. Seal and shake well to coat.

Thread 4 pork cubes onto each of 6 10-inch skewers. Place on rack coated with cooking spray; grill 4 minutes per side or until done. Serve with salsa.

Per serving: Calories 168 (19% from fat), Fat 4 g (1 g saturated), Protein 25 g, Carbohydrate 9 g, Fiber 2 g, Cholesterol 74 mg, Iron 2 mg, Sodium 268 mg, Calcium 25 mg

Gyro-Style Kabobs

SERVES **4**

1 teaspoon dried oregano

1 teaspoon ground cumin

¼ teaspoon each salt and pepper

2 cloves garlic, minced

8 ounces plain nonfat yogurt

1 pound boned leg of lamb, cut into 16 1-inch cubes

1 onion, cut into 16 1-inch chunks

16 large cherry tomatoes

cooking spray

Prepare grill. Combine first 5 ingredients (through yogurt) in a large zip-top plastic bag; add lamb. Seal and marinate in refrigerator 8 hours, turning bag occasionally. Remove lamb from bag; discard marinade. Thread lamb, onion, and tomatoes onto 8 10-inch skewers.

Place kabobs on rack coated with cooking spray; grill 5 minutes per side or to desired doneness.

Per serving: Calories 243 (27% from fat), Fat 7 g (3 g saturated), Protein 28 g, Carbohydrate 16 g, Fiber 3 g, Cholesterol 76 mg, Iron 3 mg, Sodium 236 mg, Calcium 104 mg

Caribbean Pork and Pineapple Kabobs

SERVES **4**

⅔ cup water

½ cup packed brown sugar

2 tablespoons fresh lime juice

2 tablespoons white rum

2 teaspoons vanilla extract

1 large sweet potato (about 1 pound),
    peeled and cut into 40 ½-inch chunks

1 pound pork tenderloin, cut into
    16 1½-inch cubes

1 teaspoon vegetable oil

1 teaspoon garlic powder

½ teaspoon ground allspice

¼ teaspoon salt

⅛ teaspoon ground red pepper

16 1-inch cubes fresh pineapple

cooking spray

Prepare grill. Combine first 5 ingredients (through vanilla) in a small saucepan; cook over medium heat 10 minutes. Increase heat to medium-high; cook 7 minutes or until syrup is thin. Reserve ⅓ cup syrup for basting kabobs; pour remaining syrup into a small bowl.

Place sweet potato in a small microwave-safe bowl; cook on high 4 minutes, until slightly soft.

Combine pork and oil in a bowl. Combine garlic powder, allspice, salt, and pepper; sprinkle over pork, tossing to coat.

Thread 5 sweet potato pieces, 2 pork cubes, and 2 pineapple cubes alternately onto each of 8 10-inch skewers. Place kabobs on grill rack coated with cooking spray; grill 9 minutes or until pork is done and sweet potato is tender, turning and basting frequently with ⅓ cup reserved syrup. Serve remaining syrup with kabobs.

Per serving: Calories 392 (14% from fat), Fat 6 g (2 g saturated), Protein 26 g, Carbohydrate 58 g, Fiber 4 g, Cholesterol 79 mg, Iron 3 mg, Sodium 226 mg, Calcium 58 mg

Butternut Squash Soup With Ginger Cream

SERVES **6**

⅓ cup plain nonfat yogurt

1 tablespoon chopped crystallized ginger

1 3-pound butternut squash

2 cups defatted chicken broth (page 126)

> **KITCHEN TIP**
>
> Bamboo kabob skewers
> are cheap and convenient, but
> they're also combustible.
> To prevent them from igniting on
> your grill, soak them in
> water, up to several hours, while
> you marinate your beef,
> pork or chicken.

¼ teaspoon salt

⅛ teaspoon pepper

1 can (12 ounces) evaporated nonfat milk

To make the ginger cream, combine yogurt and ginger; stir well. Set aside.

To make the soup, preheat oven to 400°. Place squash on a baking sheet and bake 1 hour or until tender, turning once. Let cool 10 minutes. Peel squash and cut in half lengthwise; remove and discard seeds and membranes. Mash pulp.

Combine squash, chicken broth, salt, and pepper in a food processor or blender; process until smooth.

Place squash mixture in a medium saucepan. Gradually add milk, whisking until blended. Place over medium heat and cook 3 minutes or until hot, stirring constantly.

Ladle soup into individual bowls. Top each with 1 tablespoon ginger-yogurt cream.

Per serving: Calories 126 (0% from fat), Fat 0 g (0 g saturated), Protein 7 g, Carbohydrate 26 g, Fiber 2 g, Cholesterol 3 mg, Iron 2 mg, Sodium 180 mg, Calcium 261 mg

Vegetable Bisque

SERVES 5

2 cups water

*3 cups small fresh broccoli florets
(about 1 large head), divided*

1 cup diced carrot, divided

½ cup chopped onion

1 cup coarsely chopped fresh cauliflower

¼ teaspoon salt

¼ teaspoon dry mustard

¼ teaspoon dried whole dill weed

⅛ teaspoon pepper

1 cup nonfat milk

*¾ cup (3 ounces) shredded reduced-fat sharp
cheddar cheese*

½ cup diced yellow squash

IN SEASON

The new crop of butternut squash, the tastiest of the winter squashes, arrives in October.

BEST BUYS

Shop for heavy midsize squashes with smooth unblemished rinds. The flesh should be firm and deep orange.

COOKING TIPS

For an easy soup to serve 4, remove the rind from a 2-pound squash using a sharp potato peeler. Trim ends, scoop out seeds, then cut flesh into chunks. Boil in 4 cups fat-free chicken broth 20 minutes. Puree squash and broth in a blender with 1 cup cold water, 1 cup canned tomatoes, plus 1 large clove garlic and 1 onion, chopped and sautéed. Simmer soup in saucepan 5 to 10 minutes. Add salt and pepper to taste. Garnish with nonfat sour cream.

HEALTH BONUS

Butternut squash is loaded with beta-carotene, a strong antioxidant that appears to impair the growth of cancer cells.

Bring water to a boil in a large saucepan; add 2 cups broccoli, ½ cup carrot, and onion. Cover, reduce heat, and simmer 15 minutes or until vegetables are tender.

Place broccoli mixture in a blender or food processor. Cover and process until smooth. Return broccoli puree to saucepan.

Add remaining 1 cup broccoli, remaining ½ cup carrot, cauliflower, salt, mustard, dill weed, pepper, and milk; bring to a boil. Reduce heat and simmer, uncovered, 10 minutes or until vegetables are tender.

Add cheese and squash; cook an additional 5 minutes, stirring, until cheese melts.

Per serving: Calories 108 (31% from fat), Fat 4 g (2 g saturated), Protein 9 g, Carbohydrate 11 g, Fiber 3 g, Cholesterol 12 mg, Iron 1 mg, Sodium 292 mg, Calcium 256 mg

Defatted Chicken Broth

MAKES 2 QUARTS

10 cups cold water

1 teaspoon salt

6 black peppercorns

4 sprigs parsley

3 sprigs thyme

2 medium-size onions, peeled and halved

2 medium-size carrots, cut into pieces

2 celery stalks, cut into pieces

2 medium-size parsnips, cut into pieces

1 4-pound broiler-fryer chicken, cut into
    standard pieces

Combine all ingredients in an 8-quart stockpot; simmer 1 hour. Skim foam from top. Increase heat to medium and simmer 30 minutes.

Remove chicken from broth; let cool. Remove skin and bones from chicken; reserve chicken for another use. Return skin and bones to broth; simmer an additional 30 minutes.

Strain broth through a sieve into a large bowl; discard solids. Cover broth and chill 8 hours. Skim fat and discard. Refrigerate 1 to 2 days, or freeze up to 6 months.

Per cup: Calories 22 (0% from fat), Fat 0 g (0 g saturated), Protein 1 g, Carbohydrate 2 g, Fiber 0 g, Cholesterol 0 mg, Iron 0 mg, Sodium 5 mg, Calcium 0 mg

Ribollita

SERVES 6

12 ¼-inch-thick slices french bread,
    diagonally cut

olive oil–flavored cooking spray

1 clove garlic, halved

1 tablespoon olive oil

1 cup chopped onion

1 cup chopped carrot

1 cup chopped celery

1 cup diced baking potato

3 cloves garlic, minced

3 cups defatted chicken broth

2 cups shredded green cabbage

2 cups shredded kale

½ teaspoon dried oregano

1 can (14½ ounces) tomatoes, chopped

1 cup zucchini, halved lengthwise and thinly sliced

1 cup yellow squash, halved lengthwise
    and thinly sliced

1 can (15 ounces) cannellini or other
    white beans, drained

3 tablespoons grated fresh parmesan cheese

Preheat oven to 350°. Place bread slices in a single layer on a baking sheet coated with cooking spray. Bake 7 minutes or until bread is toasted; rub with garlic halves. Set bread slices aside.

Heat oil in a stockpot or dutch oven over medium-high heat. Add onion, carrot, celery, potato, and minced garlic; sauté 5 minutes. Stir in chicken broth, cabbage, kale, oregano, and tomatoes (with liquid); bring to a boil. Reduce heat and simmer, covered, 10 minutes. Stir in zucchini, yellow squash, and beans; simmer 15 minutes or until zucchini and squash are tender.

Arrange 2 toast slices in each of 6 individual bowls. Ladle 1½ cups stew into each bowl, and sprinkle each with 1½ teaspoons cheese.

Per serving: Calories 347 (13% from fat), Fat 5 g (1 g saturated), Protein 13 g, Carbohydrate 61 g, Fiber 7 g, Cholesterol 4 mg, Iron 4 mg, Sodium 631 mg, Calcium 178 mg

French Onion Soup
With Garlic-Cheese Croutons

SERVES 8

GARLIC-CHEESE CROUTONS

8 ½-inch-thick slices french bread (about 4 ounces)

butter-flavored cooking spray

1 clove garlic, halved

½ cup (2 ounces) shredded reduced-fat swiss cheese

2 tablespoons grated parmesan cheese

Prepare the croutons first. Preheat oven to 400°. Coat both sides of french bread with cooking spray and arrange on a baking sheet. Bake 5 minutes or until golden. Rub cut sides of bread with garlic; return to baking sheet. Sprinkle cheeses evenly over tops; bake 5 minutes more or until cheese melts. Makes 8 croutons.

Per serving: Calories 68 (20% from fat), Fat 2 g (1 g saturated), Protein 4 g, Carbohydrate 8 g, Fiber 0 g, Cholesterol 4 mg, Iron 0 mg, Sodium 114 mg, Calcium 99 mg

FRENCH ONION SOUP

butter-flavored cooking spray

4 cups thinly sliced onion

3½ cups defatted chicken broth, divided

1½ cups thinly sliced leek

¼ cup thinly sliced garlic (about 20 cloves)

1 tablespoon sugar

2 tablespoons all-purpose flour

½ cup dry white wine

½ teaspoon dried thyme

⅛ teaspoon ground allspice

¼ teaspoon salt

¼ teaspoon pepper

2 cans (29 ounces) fat-free beef broth

Garlic-Cheese Croutons

Place a large saucepan coated with cooking spray over medium heat until hot. Add onion, ¼ cup chicken broth, leek, and garlic. Cover and cook 20 minutes or until vegetables are tender, stirring occasionally.

Add sugar; cook, uncovered, 30 minutes over medium-high heat or until golden. Add flour; cook 2 minutes. Add remaining 3¼ cups chicken broth, wine, and next 5 ingredients (through beef broth); bring to a boil. Reduce heat; simmer, uncovered, 5 minutes.

Place a crouton in each bowl; top each with 1 cup soup.

Per serving: Calories 153 (11% from fat), Fat 2 g (1 g saturated), Protein 12 g, Carbohydrate 22 g, Fiber 2 g, Cholesterol 4 mg, Iron 1 mg, Sodium 316 mg, Calcium 139 mg

Essential ingredients: Garlic, onions, and olive oil add soul to Mediterranean dishes made with mild-flavored eggplant and squash.

Black Bean Soup

SERVES 4

1 cup dried black beans, washed, sorted,
  and soaked overnight

6 cups water

1 medium-size onion, chopped

4 large cloves garlic

salt to taste

½ pound tomatoes, peeled

1½ teaspoons ground cumin

1 tablespoon canola oil

½ cup plain nonfat yogurt for garnish

IN SEASON

Though they're often available in winter, snow peas—the original edible-pod peas—are especially tender, sweet, and crisp in spring.

BEST BUYS
Look for thin, bright green pods with tiny seeds. Pass up any that are limp, pale, or yellowed.

COOKING TIPS
Don't let snow peas linger in the fridge; their flavor and crispness fade in days. When you're ready to use them, briefly rinse and pinch the tips off both ends. For a crunchy spring salad, combine whole raw snow peas with baby spinach and grated carrot; dress with a lemony vinaigrette. Or sauté snow peas and sliced scallions in a little olive oil; add some slivered fresh basil, a pinch of crushed red pepper, and salt to taste.

HEALTH BONUS
Compared ounce for ounce with oranges, snow peas have even more vitamin C and folic acid, nutrients that might help ward off cancer and heart disease.

12 ½-inch-thick slices sourdough bread, toasted
  and rubbed with garlic

Drain beans and combine with water and half the onion in a soup pot. Bring to a boil and skim off any foam that rises, then add 2 cloves of garlic. Reduce heat, cover, and simmer 1 hour. Add salt and simmer another 30 to 60 minutes, until beans are tender.

Meanwhile, blend together tomatoes, remaining onion, remaining garlic, and cumin. Heat oil in a heavy nonstick pan over medium-high heat, and add a bit of the puree. If it sizzles, add the rest (wait a couple of minutes if it doesn't). Cook, stirring, 5 to 10 minutes, until mixture is thick and sticking to pan.

Stir in 1 cup of liquid from beans, turn heat to medium low, and simmer 15 minutes until mixture is thick and fragrant. Stir into beans.

Blend beans in batches in a blender or food processor. The texture should be somewhat coarse. Return to pot, heat through, and add more salt or cumin as desired. Top each bowl with a dollop of yogurt and 3 garlic croutons.

Per serving: Calories 452 (14% from fat), Fat 7 g (1 g saturated), Protein 20 g, Carbohydrate 79 g, Fiber 11 g, Cholesterol 1 mg, Iron 5 mg, Sodium 488 mg, Calcium 196 mg

Mulligatawny
(Curried Chicken and Apple Soup)

SERVES 7

1 tablespoon margarine

1 cup chopped onion

1 cup chopped carrot

1 cup chopped celery

1 cup chopped peeled golden delicious apple

¼ cup all-purpose flour

2 tablespoons curry powder

¾ teaspoon salt

4 cups defatted chicken broth

3 cups chopped cooked chicken

1 tablespoon fresh lemon juice

½ teaspoon grated lemon rind

3½ cups hot cooked rice

Melt margarine in a large dutch oven over medium-high heat. Add onion, carrot, and celery; sauté 5 minutes. Add apple; cover and cook 5 minutes, stirring occasionally. Add flour, curry powder, and salt; cook 1 minute, stirring constantly. Add broth and bring to a boil. Reduce heat and simmer, covered, 15 minutes. Add chicken, lemon juice, and rind; cook 2 minutes or until chicken is heated.

Spoon rice into bowls, and ladle soup over rice.

Per serving: Calories 301 (20% from fat), Fat 7 g (2 g saturated), Protein 21 g, Carbohydrate 36 g, Fiber 3 g, Cholesterol 58 mg, Iron 3 mg, Sodium 328 mg, Calcium 46 mg

Hot-and-Sour Soup

SERVES 8

¼ cup water

3 tablespoons cornstarch

3 cans (16 ounces each) fat-free, reduced-sodium chicken broth

1⅔ cups sliced shiitake mushroom caps

½ cup canned bamboo shoots, cut into strips

2 tablespoons rice vinegar

1 tablespoon low-sodium soy sauce

1 teaspoon grated peeled fresh ginger

¼ teaspoon pepper

1 package (about 12 ounces) reduced-fat extra-firm tofu, drained and julienned

¼ cup sliced green onions

½ teaspoon dark sesame oil

1 large egg, lightly beaten

Whisk together water and cornstarch in a small bowl; set aside. In a dutch oven, bring broth to a boil; add mushrooms and next 6 ingredients (through tofu). Reduce heat; simmer 4 minutes. Add cornstarch mixture; bring to a boil. Cook 1 minute, stirring constantly.

Remove from heat; gradually stir in onions, sesame oil, and egg. Serve immediately.

Per serving: Calories 64 (18% from fat), Fat 1 g (0 g saturated), Protein 7 g, Carbohydrate 6 g, Fiber 0 g, Cholesterol 28 mg, Iron 1 mg, Sodium 463 mg, Calcium 28 mg

Toasted Corn Soup With Basil Salsa

SERVES 4

4 medium-size ears corn (about 10 inches long and 3¼ pounds total) or 4 cups frozen corn kernels

4 cups low-sodium chicken broth

1 large carrot (about ¼ pound), peeled and chopped

1 medium-size onion (about 6 ounces), chopped

2 cloves garlic, pressed or minced

Basil Salsa (recipe follows)

fresh basil sprigs for garnish

salt to taste

Remove and discard corn husks and silks; rinse ears. Place a 10- to 12-inch frying pan over medium-high heat. When pan is hot, add ears of corn and sauté, turning as needed, until kernels are lightly browned, about 10 minutes. Remove corn from pan and let cool. (Follow same procedure for frozen corn kernels.)

In a 3- to 4-quart pan, combine broth, carrot, onion, and garlic. Bring to a boil over high heat, then cover and simmer over low heat until vegetables are tender, about 10 minutes.

Meanwhile, with a sharp knife, cut kernels off cobs and add kernels to broth mixture. Simmer, covered, 5 minutes. A portion at a time, puree soup in a blender until smooth. Rub pureed soup through a fine strainer set over a bowl; discard residue. Reheat soup in pan, or serve soup cool (cover and chill up to 1 day). Ladle into bowls and add to each an equal portion of basil salsa. Top with basil sprigs. Add salt to taste.

BASIL SALSA

Core and dice 1 large, firm, ripe tomato (about ½ pound). Mix tomato with ¼ cup chopped fresh basil, 2 tablespoons lime juice, and 1 tablespoon minced and seeded fresh jalapeño chile.

Per serving: Calories 425 (6% from fat), Fat 3 g (1 g saturated), Protein 16 g, Carbohydrate 100 g, Fiber 14 g, Cholesterol 0 mg, Iron 3 mg, Sodium 93 mg, Calcium 49 mg

Sautéed Chicken Breasts With Mango and Papaya Salsa

SERVES 4

1½ tablespoons fennel seeds

1 tablespoon ground cumin

1 teaspoon ground coriander

½ teaspoon paprika

⅛ teaspoon ground red pepper

1 teaspoon sugar

¼ teaspoon salt

1 cup diced plum tomato

1 cup diced peeled mango

1 cup diced peeled papaya

1 tablespoon chopped fresh cilantro

1 teaspoon lime juice

4 4-ounce skinned, boned chicken breast halves

1 tablespoon vegetable oil

Place fennel seeds in a large heavy-duty zip-top plastic bag. Seal bag; finely crush seeds using a meat mallet or rolling pin. Combine crushed fennel seeds and next 4 ingredients (through red pepper) in a large nonstick skillet. Cook over medium heat 2 minutes or until toasted, stirring frequently. Remove from heat; stir in sugar and salt.

For salsa, combine 1 teaspoon spice mixture, tomato, and next 4 ingredients (through lime juice) in a medium-size bowl. Place rest of spice mixture in a plastic bag.

Place each chicken breast half between 2 sheets of heavy-duty plastic wrap; flatten to ¼-inch thickness using a meat mallet or rolling pin. Add chicken to spice mixture in plastic bag; seal and shake to coat.

Heat oil in skillet over medium-high heat. Add chicken; cook 4 minutes on each side or until done. Top with fruit salsa.

Per serving: Calories 213 (23% from fat), Fat 5 g (1 g saturated), Protein 27 g, Carbohydrate 14 g, Fiber 2 g, Cholesterol 66 mg, Iron 2 mg, Sodium 155 mg, Calcium 43 mg

Chicken Enchiladas

SERVES 4

5 cups water

1 onion, quartered

2 cloves garlic, peeled and crushed

1 large whole chicken breast, skinned and split

½ teaspoon dried thyme or oregano

or a combination

salt to taste

Green Tomatillo Salsa (recipe follows), made with

reserved chicken stock

vegetable oil to coat baking dish

12 corn tortillas, heated

¼ cup feta or mexican queso fresco, crumbled

2 slices yellow onion, broken into rings

sliced radishes for garnish

First, cook the chicken. Combine water, quartered onion, and crushed garlic in a large saucepan or dutch oven and bring to a boil over medium heat. Add chicken. Skim off any foam that rises, then add dried herbs. Cover partially, reduce heat to low, and simmer 13 to 15 minutes, until chicken is cooked through. Add salt. Allow chicken to cool in broth if there is time. When chicken is cool enough to handle, remove from broth, bone, and shred. Strain the stock through a cheesecloth-lined sieve into a bowl. Prepare green salsa.

To assemble the enchiladas, shortly before serving, preheat the oven to 350°, lightly oil a baking dish that will hold 12 rolled enchiladas, and heat green salsa to a gentle simmer.

Toss chicken with ½ cup of the green salsa and keep warm. Pour a cup of the salsa into a wide soup bowl. Dip a tortilla into salsa, flip over to coat, and place a scant 2 tablespoons of the chicken across the center. Roll up tortilla and place in baking dish. Repeat with remaining tortillas. Pour remaining salsa over enchiladas, spread to cover ends, and wrap tightly with foil.

Sautéed Chicken Breasts With
Mango and Papaya Salsa

Warm enchiladas in oven 10 minutes (no longer, or they will fall apart). Uncover and sprinkle with cheese, onion, and radishes.

Per serving: Calories 353 (20% from fat), Fat 8 g (2 g saturated), Protein 21 g, Carbohydrate 51 g, Fiber 7 g, Cholesterol 43 mg, Iron 3 mg, Sodium 646 mg, Calcium 203 mg

GREEN TOMATILLO SALSA

1 pound (about 8 large) fresh tomatillos, husked
    and rinsed, or 26 ounces canned tomatillos
2 to 5 jalapeño or serrano chiles to taste,
    coarsely chopped
½ small white onion, coarsely chopped
1 large clove garlic, chopped coarsley
½ to 1 teaspoon salt to taste
8 or more sprigs fresh cilantro to taste
2 teaspoons canola or safflower oil
2 cups vegetable or chicken stock

If using fresh tomatillos, cover in water and simmer 10 minutes. Drain and place in a blender or food processor fitted with steel blade. If using canned tomatillos, drain and place in blender. Add chiles, onion, garlic, salt, and cilantro. Puree mixture.

Heat oil in a heavy saucepan or a nonstick skillet over medium heat. Drizzle a bit of the tomatillo mixture into the pan; if it sizzles loudly, add the rest (wait if it doesn't). Cook tomatillo puree until it thickens and begins to stick to the pan, about 5 minutes. Add stock, stir, and simmer 15 to 20 minutes, stirring occasionally, until mixture is thick enough to coat spoon. Remove from heat, taste, and adjust salt.

Per serving: Calories 77 (35% from fat), Fat 3 g (0 g saturated), Protein 1 g, Carbohydrate 12 g, Fiber 3 g, Cholesterol 0 mg, Iron 1 mg, Sodium 412 mg, Calcium 15 mg

Chicken and White Bean Cassoulet

SERVES 7

¼ teaspoon salt
¼ teaspoon pepper
¾ pound skinned, boned chicken breast
1 tablespoon olive oil
2 slices bacon
6 cups sliced cabbage
3 cups vertically sliced yellow onions
3 cloves garlic, minced
½ teaspoon dried rosemary
1 can (19 ounces) white beans, drained
olive oil–flavored cooking spray
⅓ cup dry bread crumbs

Preheat oven to 375°. Sprinkle salt and pepper over chicken. Heat oil in a large nonstick skillet over medium-high heat. Add chicken; cook 2 minutes on each side or until browned. Cut chicken into ¾-inch cubes; set aside.

In a large nonstick skillet over medium-high heat, cook bacon until crisp. Remove bacon from skillet; crumble and set aside. Add cabbage, onions, and garlic to skillet; sauté 4 minutes or until cabbage is crisp-tender.

Combine chicken, cabbage mixture, rosemary, and beans in a 3-quart casserole coated with cooking spray. Top with bread crumbs.

Bake 30 minutes or until heated through. Top with crumbled bacon.

Per serving: Calories 203 (19% from fat), Fat 4 g (1 g saturated), Protein 18 g, Carbohydrate 24 g, Fiber 5 g, Cholesterol 30 mg, Iron 2 mg, Sodium 220 mg, Calcium 95 mg

Mexican Cheese–Stuffed Chicken in Chipotle Sauce

SERVES 4

4 6-ounce skinned chicken breast halves
½ cup (2 ounces) preshredded reduced-fat mexican
    cheese blend, divided
¼ cup finely crushed baked tortilla chips
    (about 8 chips)
¼ cup chopped fresh cilantro
⅓ cup hickory-flavor barbecue sauce
4 canned chipotle chiles in adobo sauce,*
    drained and minced

Preheat oven to 375°. Cut a horizontal slit through thickest portion of each chicken breast half to form a pocket. Combine ¼ cup cheese, crushed chips, and cilantro. Stuff 3 tablespoons cheese mixture into each pocket; close each opening with a wooden toothpick. Place chicken, breast side up, in an 11" × 7" baking dish.

Combine barbecue sauce and chiles. Spread mixture over chicken. Bake 40 minutes. Sprinkle with ¼ cup cheese. Bake an additional 5 minutes or until cheese melts.

Per serving: Calories 310 (24% from fat), Fat 8 g (3 g saturated), Protein 47 g, Carbohydrate 9 g, Fiber 1 g, Cholesterol 125 mg, Iron 2 mg, Sodium 453 mg, Calcium 151 mg

*Canned chipotle chiles can be ordered from International Hot Foods. Call 800/505-9999.

Superfast Chicken Fajitas

SERVES 4

8 fat-free 6-inch flour tortillas, plain or
    jalapeño flavor
¾ pound skinned, boned chicken breasts, cut into
    ½-inch strips
1 tablespoon mild mexican seasoning blend (such
    as McCormick's)
1 tablespoon vegetable oil
1 cup red bell pepper strips
1 cup green bell pepper strips
¾ cup vertically sliced red onion
2 cloves garlic, minced
¼ cup green salsa
⅛ teaspoon salt
½ cup coarsely chopped fresh cilantro
½ cup (2 ounces) preshredded sharp cheddar cheese
½ cup low-fat sour cream

Heat tortillas according to package directions.

Combine chicken and seasoning blend. Heat oil in a large nonstick skillet over medium-high heat. Add chicken; stir-fry 3 minutes. Add bell peppers, onion, and garlic; stir-fry 3 minutes or until chicken is done. Stir in salsa and salt.

Divide mixture evenly among warm tortillas. Top each with 1 tablespoon cilantro and 1 tablespoon cheese; roll up. Serve with sour cream.

Per serving: Calories 415 (28% from fat), Fat 13 g (6 g saturated), Protein 30 g, Carbohydrate 43 g, Fiber 3 g, Cholesterol 76 mg, Iron 4 mg, Sodium 837 mg, Calcium 163 mg

Tunisian Chicken

SERVES 4

1 3½-pound chicken, cut into sections and skinned
    (or 3 pounds skinless chicken pieces with bones)
1 tablespoon olive oil
1 medium-size onion, chopped
4 cloves garlic, minced or pressed
4 tablespoons tomato paste, divided
½ teaspoon cayenne pepper
½ teaspoon ground caraway seed (optional)
½ teaspoon freshly ground black pepper
3 cups water
salt to taste
20 imported green olives (such as italian-style),
    pitted and halved lengthwise
fresh cilantro or parsley, chopped

Use fresh chiles to add tongue-tingling warmth to light southwestern dishes. From top, cayenne, jalapeño, poblano, and cascabel peppers.

Rinse chicken pieces and pat dry with paper towels. Set chicken aside.

Heat olive oil over medium heat in a large heavy-bottomed casserole or dutch oven, and add onion. Cook, stirring, until tender, about 5 minutes, and add garlic. Stir about 30 seconds, then add 3 tablespoons tomato paste, cayenne, caraway seed (if desired), and black pepper. Stir 2 minutes, until mixture is fragrant.

Add chicken pieces to pot and stir until they're coated with tomato paste and onions, about 2 minutes. Add 3 cups water, stir, and bring to a simmer. Add salt to taste, cover, reduce heat to low, and simmer 40 minutes, stirring occasionally. Add olives and simmer, covered, another 20 minutes, or until chicken begins to fall off bones.

Using tongs, remove chicken pieces and place them in a bowl. Add remaining tablespoon tomato paste to broth, and turn up heat so mixture boils briskly. Reduce by about half, until sauce is thick and fragrant. Taste, and add salt and cayenne as desired. Return chicken pieces to sauce, and heat through.

Garnish each serving with chopped cilantro or parsley, and spoon over hot couscous or rice.

Per serving: Calories 311 (35% from fat), Fat 12 g (2 g saturated), Protein 42 g, Carbohydrate 8 g, Fiber 2 g, Cholesterol 133 mg, Iron 3 mg, Sodium 661 mg, Calcium 54 mg

Chicken With Grapefruit and Olives

SERVES 4

3 large grapefruit

1 teaspoon fennel seeds

½ teaspoon cracked black peppercorns

¼ teaspoon salt

1 clove garlic, minced

4 4-ounce skinned, boned chicken breast halves

2 tablespoons all-purpose flour

1 teaspoon olive oil

1 tablespoon brown sugar

¼ teaspoon crushed red pepper

12 pitted ripe black olives, halved

Peel and section grapefruit; squeeze membranes over a bowl to extract juice. Set sections aside; reserve ½ cup juice. Discard membranes. Combine fennel, cracked peppercorns, salt, and garlic in a small bowl. Rub fennel mixture evenly over chicken; sprinkle with flour.

Heat oil in a large nonstick skillet over medium-high heat. Add chicken breast halves; cook 4 minutes on each side or until browned.

Remove chicken from pan. Add reserved grapefruit juice, sugar, and red pepper to pan, scraping pan to loosen browned bits; cook 1 minute. Return chicken to pan; cover, reduce heat, and simmer 12 minutes or until chicken is done. Stir in grapefruit sections and olives; cook 1 minute.

Per serving: Calories 233 (16% from fat), Fat 4 g (1 g saturated), Protein 28 g, Carbohydrate 21 g, Fiber 2 g, Cholesterol 66 mg, Iron 2 mg, Sodium 327 mg, Calcium 54 mg

Country Captain

SERVES 6

⅔ cup thinly sliced dried apricots

½ cup raisins

⅓ cup coarsely chopped pitted dates

½ cup dry red wine

2 tablespoons honey

cooking spray

2 teaspoons vegetable oil

3 skinned, boned chicken thighs (about ½ pound), cut into ½-inch pieces

1 cup chopped onion

1 cup chopped red bell pepper

3 cloves garlic, minced

2 cups chopped tomato

1½ cups diced granny smith apples

1½ cups uncooked long-grain rice

3½ cups water

2 teaspoons curry powder

½ teaspoon salt

¼ teaspoon ground cumin

⅛ teaspoon ground cinnamon

¼ cup sliced almonds, toasted

How to Bone a Chicken Breast

Chicken breasts are a nutritional bargain, but the boneless version can be pricey. Save money by choosing whole breasts (the halves still joined), and doing a little easy knife work. Use a stiff, sharp blade, and start by placing the whole breast, skin side down, on a cutting board.

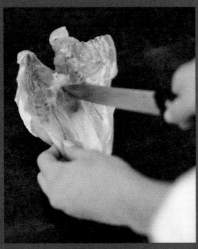

1 Locate the keel—the large dark red bone at the center. With your knife, make a short shallow slit in the whitish membrane covering the bone.

2 Pick up the breast in both hands, and with the wide end away from you, flex the halves back so that the keel pokes out. Set the breast down again.

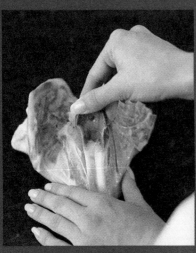

3 Grasp the keel at its widest point, and pull it away from the rib bones and flesh. Next, cut the breast halves apart, slicing forcefully down through the wishbone. (Start with step 4 if you bought bone-in breast halves.)

4 Place each half with the skin side down. From the narrow end, carefully slice off the ribs, lifting them as you cut. Then, with your fingertips, find the wishbone bits near the wide end; cut them out. Finally, trim off the skin.

Combine first 5 ingredients (through honey) in a small saucepan; bring to a boil, stirring occasionally. Remove from heat, cover, and set aside.

In a dutch oven coated with cooking spray, heat oil over medium-high heat. Add chicken, onion, bell pepper, and garlic; cook 6 minutes or until vegetables are tender, stirring frequently. Stir in apricot mixture, tomato, and next 7 ingredients (through cinnamon); bring to a boil. Cover, reduce heat, and simmer 20 minutes or until chicken is done. Sprinkle with almonds.

Per serving: Calories 318 (17% from fat), Fat 6 g (1 g saturated), Protein 12 g, Carbohydrate 59 g, Fiber 5 g, Cholesterol 31 mg, Iron 3 mg, Sodium 253 mg, Calcium 67 mg

Chili-Spiced Chicken With Black Bean and Corn Salsa

SERVES 8

1¼ cups frozen whole-kernel corn, thawed

¾ cup chopped red bell pepper

¾ cup chopped red onion

⅓ cup balsamic vinegar

¼ cup chopped fresh cilantro

1 tablespoon finely chopped seeded jalapeño pepper

2 tablespoons dijon mustard

1 can (15 ounces) black beans, rinsed and drained

2 tablespoons chili powder

2 teaspoons ground cumin

¼ teaspoon garlic salt

8 4-ounce skinned, boned chicken breast halves

2 tablespoons butter or stick margarine, divided

Thai-Style Chicken and Vegetable Stir-Fry

To make salsa, combine first 8 ingredients (through beans) in a bowl; set aside.

Combine chili powder, cumin, and garlic salt; sprinkle over chicken.

Melt 1 tablespoon butter in a large nonstick skillet over medium-high heat. Add 4 chicken breast halves; cook 6 minutes on each side or until done. Keep warm. Repeat procedure with remaining butter and chicken breasts.

Top chicken with salsa. Accompany with warm corn tortillas or rice.

Per serving: Calories 235 (21% from fat), Fat 6 g (2 g saturated), Protein 30 g, Carbohydrate 16 g, Fiber 3 g, Cholesterol 74 mg, Iron 3 mg, Sodium 384 mg, Calcium 40 mg

Panzanella With Grilled Chicken

SERVES **4**

⅓ cup extra virgin olive oil

3 tablespoons balsamic vinegar

1 teaspoon dried rosemary, crushed

1 clove garlic, minced

½ teaspoon salt

½ teaspoon freshly ground black pepper

4 skinless, boneless chicken breast halves

4 large slices italian bread or 8 slices
    french baguette

1 cup canned cannellini beans, rinsed and drained

4 cups torn romaine lettuce

2 cups chopped tomato

¼ cup chopped fresh basil

Combine oil and next 5 ingredients (through pepper). Mix well with a fork or shake in a jar with a tight-fitting lid.

Place chicken on a plate. Pour 3 tablespoons oil mixture over chicken, turning to coat. Cover and refrigerate chicken and reserved oil mixture at least 10 minutes, up to 8 hours.

Prepare grill. Place chicken on grill over medium coals or in heated ridged grill pan. Pour any remaining marinade from plate over chicken. Grill 5 minutes on each side or until no longer pink in center. Brush both sides of bread with 2 tablespoons oil mixture; grill until lightly toasted.

In a large bowl, combine beans, lettuce, tomato, and basil. Add remaining oil mixture; toss well. Cut toasted bread into cubes and add to salad. Toss again, and divide among 4 plates. Top with grilled chicken. Season with additional pepper, if desired.

Per serving: Calories 477 (40% from fat), Fat 22 g (3 g saturated), Protein 40 g, Carbohydrate 31 g, Fiber 5 g, Cholesterol 82 mg, Iron 3 mg, Sodium 627 mg, Calcium 73 mg

Thai-Style Chicken and Vegetable Stir-Fry

SERVES **4**

2 cups water

1 cup uncooked long-grain rice

¼ to ½ teaspoon salt to taste

1 bag precut vegetables (1 pound), such as
    mixed vegetable stir-fry

1 tablespoon canola oil

½ pound boneless, skinless chicken breast, cut
    into strips about ¼ inch thick and 1 inch long

¼ cup prepared spicy thai peanut sauce

Bring water to a boil in a medium saucepan; add rice and salt. Cover, reduce heat, and simmer 15 minutes or until liquid is absorbed. Remove from heat and keep warm. While rice is cooking, pierce bag containing vegetables in several places. Microwave bag on high for 3 minutes. Let stand 1 minute before carefully removing vegetables from bag.

Heat a large nonstick frying pan or wok over medium-high heat until hot enough to evaporate a drop of water on contact. Add oil and chicken. Cook, stirring constantly, 2 to 3 minutes, until meat is cooked through with no traces of pink. Add vegetables. Stir for 1 minute, remove from heat, and stir in peanut sauce.

Fluff rice with a fork; spoon onto plates. Top with chicken mixture.

Per serving: Calories 338 (16% from fat), Fat 6 g (1 g saturated), Protein 21 g, Carbohydrate 47 g, Fiber 2 g, Cholesterol 34 mg, Iron 3 mg, Sodium 927 mg, Calcium 52 mg

Chicken With Olives, Capers, and Fettuccine

SERVES **4**

4 4-ounce skinned, boned chicken breast halves

¼ cup all-purpose flour

½ teaspoon dried italian seasoning

⅛ teaspoon salt

⅛ teaspoon pepper

cooking spray

1 tablespoon olive oil

½ cup dry white wine

2 tablespoons capers

10 chopped kalamata olives

1 package (9 ounces) uncooked fresh fettuccine

2 cups small broccoli florets

6 tablespoons grated parmesan cheese

Place each chicken breast half between sheets of heavy-duty plastic wrap; flatten to ¼-inch thickness using a meat mallet or rolling pin. Combine flour, italian seasoning, salt, and pepper in a shallow dish. Dredge chicken in flour mixture.

In a large nonstick skillet coated with cooking spray, heat oil over medium-high heat. Add chicken; sauté 2 minutes on each side or until done. Remove chicken from skillet; set aside, and keep warm. Add wine, capers, and olives to skillet. Bring to a boil; cook 30 seconds (sauce will be thin). Remove from heat, and set aside.

Cook fettuccine and broccoli in boiling water 3 minutes; drain. Spoon fettuccine and broccoli onto 4 plates; top with chicken, sauce, and cheese.

Per serving: Calories 428 (21% from fat), Fat 10 g (3 g saturated), Protein 39 g, Carbohydrate 45 g, Fiber 2 g, Cholesterol 118 mg, Iron 4 mg, Sodium 740 mg, Calcium 155 mg

Spiced Chicken Breasts With Tomatillo Relish

SERVES **4**

1 teaspoon ground coriander

1 teaspoon ground cumin

½ teaspoon salt

½ teaspoon ground red pepper

4 4-ounce skinned, boned chicken breast halves

1 tablespoon vegetable oil

1 cup diced yellow bell pepper

¾ cup diced red onion

½ cup diced tomatillos (about 3 medium-size tomatillos)

2 cloves garlic, minced

1 tablespoon hot pepper jelly

2 tablespoons chopped fresh cilantro

Combine first 4 ingredients (through red pepper). Sprinkle both sides of chicken breasts with spice mixture.

Heat oil in a large nonstick skillet over medium-high heat. Add chicken and sauté 6 minutes on each side or until done. Remove chicken from pan; keep warm.

Add bell pepper, onion, tomatillos, and garlic to pan; sauté 8 minutes or until bell pepper is tender. Add jelly; stir until melted. Spread vegetable mixture over chicken and sprinkle with cilantro. Accompany with warm corn tortillas or rice.

Per serving: Calories 201 (24% from fat), Fat 5 g (1 g saturated), Protein 28 g, Carbohydrate 10 g, Fiber 2 g, Cholesterol 66 mg, Iron 2 mg, Sodium 382 mg, Calcium 39 mg

Chicken Thighs With Lemon-Caper Sauce

SERVES 4

1 pound skinned, boned chicken thighs

¼ cup all-purpose flour

1 teaspoon olive oil

½ cup fat-free less-sodium chicken broth

2 tablespoons extra-dry vermouth

1 tablespoon capers

1 tablespoon fresh lemon juice

¼ teaspoon freshly ground black pepper

chopped fresh parsley (optional)

Place each chicken thigh between 2 sheets of heavy-duty plastic wrap and flatten to ¼-inch thickness using a meat mallet or rolling pin. Place flour in a large zip-top plastic bag. Add chicken and seal; shake to coat.

Heat oil in a large nonstick skillet over medium-high heat. Add chicken and cook 2 minutes on each side or until lightly browned. Reduce heat to medium; add broth and next 4 ingredients (through pepper). Cover and cook 6 minutes or until done. Remove chicken from skillet; keep warm.

Increase heat to high; boil broth mixture 1 minute, stirring frequently. Spoon lemon-caper sauce over chicken. Garnish with chopped parsley, if desired.

Per serving: Calories 180 (28% from fat), Fat 6 g (1 g saturated), Protein 24 g, Carbohydrate 7 g, Fiber 0 g, Cholesterol 94 mg, Iron 2 mg, Sodium 326 mg, Calcium 14 mg

A cornucopia of disease-fighting compounds: carotenoids in corn and carrots, sulphoraphane in bok choy, fiber in apples, lentinan in shiitake mushrooms.

Chicken Provençale With Herbed Rice Timbales

SERVES 4

2 tablespoons grated lemon zest, divided

¼ cup fresh lemon juice

3 tablespoons chopped fresh thyme, divided

3 tablespoons minced fresh flat-leaf parsley, divided

1½ tablespoons dijon mustard

1 tablespoon chopped fresh rosemary

2 teaspoons olive oil

½ teaspoon salt, divided

4 skinned, boned chicken breast halves

1 10½-ounce can low-salt chicken broth

1 cup uncooked long-grain rice

⅓ cup golden raisins

cooking spray

Combine 1 tablespoon of the zest, juice, 2 tablespoons thyme, 2 tablespoons parsley, mustard, chopped rosemary, oil, and ¼ teaspoon salt in large zip-top plastic bag. Add chicken to bag; seal. Marinate in refrigerator 1 hour, turning occasionally.

Add water to broth to equal 2 cups. Place broth mixture in a large saucepan; bring to a boil. Add rice; cover, reduce heat, and simmer 15 minutes. Stir in 1 tablespoon zest, 1 tablespoon thyme, 1 tablespoon parsley, ¼ teaspoon salt, and raisins. Divide rice mixture evenly among 4 8-ounce custard cups coated with cooking spray; press firmly.

Preheat broiler. Place chicken on a broiler rack coated with cooking spray. Broil chicken 6 minutes on each side or until done. Invert rice onto dinner plates; place chicken alongside rice.

Per serving: Calories 381 (12% from fat), Fat 5 g (1 g saturated), Protein 31 g, Carbohydrate 51 g, Fiber 2 g, Cholesterol 67 mg, Iron 4 mg, Sodium 575 mg, Calcium 58 mg

Chicken Chilaquiles Skillet

SERVES **4**

4 6-inch corn tortillas

1½ cups egg substitute

¾ cup mild or medium-hot bottled salsa (such as Pace), divided

½ cup thinly sliced green onions

¾ pound skinned, boned chicken breasts, cut into ½-inch strips

1 tablespoon mild mexican seasoning blend (such as McCormick's)

2 teaspoons vegetable oil

Cut tortillas in half, then crosswise into ½-inch strips. Combine tortilla strips, egg substitute, ½ cup salsa, and green onions in a medium-size bowl; let stand 10 minutes.

Combine chicken and seasoning in a bowl; toss gently to coat. Heat oil in a large nonstick skillet over medium-high heat. Add chicken mixture; sauté 4 minutes or until done. Add tortilla mixture; cook 3 minutes or until set, stirring constantly.

Serve with remaining salsa.

KITCHEN TIP

Coming soon to a supermarket near you: organic chicken. Federal regulators have okayed the tag "certified organic" for meats from animals raised in a humane environment without hormones, antibiotics, or other drugs. Until now, such products usually have been labeled as "corn-fed" or "free-range."

Per serving: Calories 229 (16% from fat), Fat 4 g (1 g saturated), Protein 31 g, Carbohydrate 17 g, Fiber 3 g, Cholesterol 49 mg, Iron 3 mg, Sodium 358 mg, Calcium 114 mg

Moroccan Tagine With Dates and Lime

SERVES **6**

½ cup fresh lime juice (about 3 large limes)

3 chicken breast halves, skinned

3 chicken drumsticks, skinned

3 chicken thighs, skinned

⅓ cup minced green onions

⅓ cup minced fresh cilantro

¼ cup minced fresh parsley

¼ teaspoon each salt and pepper

1 clove garlic, minced

1 tablespoon olive oil

1½ cups fat-free less-sodium chicken broth

1 can (14.5 ounces) diced tomatoes with garlic and onion, with liquid

15 whole pitted dates, halved

1 large lime, peeled and sliced thinly

4 cups hot cooked couscous

Combine lime juice and chicken in a large zip-top plastic bag, and seal; marinate in refrigerator 1 hour, turning once. Remove chicken from bag; discard juice.

Combine onions and next 5 ingredients (through garlic) in a bowl. Dredge chicken in onion mixture. Heat oil in a large nonstick skillet over medium-high heat. Add chicken, browning on all sides. Remove from pan; keep warm. Add broth to pan, scraping pan to loosen browned bits. Bring to a boil and cook 1 minute. Return chicken to pan; stir in tomatoes. Arrange dates and lime slices on top.

Bring to a boil and cover, reduce heat, and simmer 1 hour or until chicken is done. Serve over couscous.

Per serving: Calories 436 (16% from fat), Fat 8 g (2 g saturated), Protein 43 g, Carbohydrate 50 g, Fiber 4 g, Cholesterol 114 mg, Iron 3 mg, Sodium 449 mg, Calcium 61 mg

Not merely sweet and crunchy:
Bite for bite, red bell peppers deliver more
vitamin C than any other fruit or vegetable.

Chunky Chicken and Black Bean Chili

SERVES 4

¾ pound skinned, boned chicken breasts, cut into
*   1-inch pieces*
1 tablespoon chili powder
1 teaspoon ground cumin
1 tablespoon vegetable oil
1 cup chopped onion
1 cup diced red bell pepper
3 cloves garlic, minced
½ cup bottled salsa
½ cup mexican beer (such as Aztec or Corona)
1 can (14½ ounces) mexican-style stewed tomatoes
*   with jalapeño peppers and spices, with liquid*
1 can (15 ounces) black beans, rinsed and drained
¼ cup (1 ounce) grated queso quesadilla cheese or
*   asiago cheese*
minced fresh cilantro (optional)

Combine first 3 ingredients (through cumin) in a
bowl; toss gently to coat.

Heat oil in a large nonstick skillet over medium-
high heat. Add onion; sauté 5 minutes. Add chick-
en, bell pepper, and garlic; sauté 3 minutes. Add
salsa, beer, and tomatoes; cook 5 minutes. Stir in
beans; cook 5 minutes or until chicken is done.

Ladle into 4 soup bowls; sprinkle with cheese.
Garnish with fresh cilantro, if desired.

Per serving: Calories 302 (22% from fat), Fat 7 g (2 g saturated),
Protein 29 g, Carbohydrate 31 g, Fiber 6 g, Cholesterol 52 mg,
Iron 4 mg, Sodium 760 mg, Calcium 125 mg

Chicken Cacciatore

SERVES 4

cooking spray
1 teaspoon olive oil
4 skinless chicken breast halves
2 cups sliced mushrooms
1 cup chopped onion
2 cloves garlic, minced
2 cups chopped seeded tomato
½ cup water
⅓ cup dry red wine
2 tablespoons tomato paste
1 tablespoon balsamic vinegar
1½ teaspoons chopped fresh thyme (or
*   ½ teaspoon dried)*
¼ teaspoon salt
¼ teaspoon ground allspice
3 tablespoons minced fresh parsley

In a large nonstick skillet coated with cooking
spray, heat oil over medium-high heat. Add chicken
and cook 3 minutes on each side or until browned.
Remove from skillet.

Wipe skillet clean with paper towels and recoat
with cooking spray. Add mushrooms, onion, and
garlic; sauté 5 minutes or until tender. Stir in tomato and next 7 ingredients (through allspice).

Return chicken to skillet, spooning tomato mixture over chicken; bring to a boil. Cover, reduce
heat, and simmer 30 minutes or until chicken is
done. Sprinkle with parsley.

Per serving: Calories 275 (21% from fat), Fat 6 g (2 g saturated),
Protein 42 g, Carbohydrate 12 g, Fiber 3 g, Cholesterol 107 mg,
Iron 3 mg, Sodium 259 mg, Calcium 47 mg

Sausage Polenta With Tomato-Mushroom Sauce

SERVES 4

3 ounces (1 link) italian turkey sausage

⅔ cup yellow cornmeal

¼ teaspoon pepper

1 can (10½ ounces) low-salt chicken broth

2 tablespoons chopped fresh flat-leaf
* parsley, divided*

cooking spray

1 tablespoon balsamic vinegar

1 tablespoon olive oil

¼ teaspoon salt

3 cups sliced mushrooms

6 plum tomatoes, quartered

¼ cup grated asiago or parmesan cheese

Remove casing from sausage. Cook sausage in a medium-size saucepan over medium heat until browned, stirring to crumble. Remove sausage from pan.

Add cornmeal and pepper to pan; gradually add broth, whisking constantly. Bring to a boil; reduce heat to medium, and cook 2 minutes, stirring frequently. Stir in sausage and 1 tablespoon parsley. Spoon polenta into a 9-inch pie plate coated with cooking spray, spreading evenly. Press plastic wrap onto surface of polenta. Chill 15 minutes or until firm.

Preheat broiler. Combine vinegar, oil, and salt in a medium-size bowl. Add mushrooms and tomatoes; toss well. Spread mixture on a jelly-roll pan lined with foil. Broil 6 minutes or until vegetables are soft, stirring after 3 minutes.

Cut polenta into 4 wedges. Place on a baking sheet coated with cooking spray; broil 2 minutes or until lightly browned. Use a slotted spoon to distribute sauce over polenta; sprinkle with cheese and remaining parsley.

Per serving: Calories 227 (36% from fat), Fat 9 g (3 g saturated), Protein 11 g, Carbohydrate 27 g, Fiber 4 g, Cholesterol 22 mg, Iron 3 mg, Sodium 396 mg, Calcium 97 mg

Braised Beef With Lemon and Artichokes

SERVES 5

1 2¾-pound boned chuck roast

2 tablespoons dried oregano, divided

1 teaspoon pepper

2 tablespoons all-purpose flour

2 teaspoons vegetable oil

1 cup chopped red bell pepper

½ cup chopped onion

2 cloves garlic, minced

1 cup canned beef broth

1 teaspoon grated lemon rind

⅓ cup fresh lemon juice

¼ teaspoon salt

1 package (9 ounces) frozen artichoke hearts,
* thawed and chopped*

Just steam and enjoy:
One artichoke gives you three grams
of fiber for only 25 calories.

2½ cups hot cooked orzo, or rice-shaped pasta
(about 1¼ cups uncooked)

4 lemon wedges

Preheat oven to 350°. Trim fat from roast. Rub roast with 1 tablespoon oregano and pepper; sprinkle with flour.

Heat oil in a large dutch oven over medium-high heat. Add roast, browning all sides. Remove from pan; set aside. Add bell pepper, onion, and garlic; sauté 5 minutes. Remove from pan; set aside. Add broth, lemon rind, and juice, scraping pan to loosen browned bits. Return roast and vegetable mixture to pan; add 1 tablespoon oregano and salt. Bring to a boil, then remove from heat.

Cover and bake 2 hours or until roast is tender. Remove from oven. Cool 10 minutes. Shred roast using 2 forks. Return beef to pan. Stir in artichokes. Cover and bake 20 minutes. Serve over pasta. Garnish with lemon wedges.

Per serving: Calories 464 (25% from fat), Fat 12 g (4 g saturated), Protein 42 g, Carbohydrate 45 g, Fiber 3 g, Cholesterol 97 mg, Iron 7 mg, Sodium 465 mg, Calcium 69 mg

Beefy Mushroom and Barley Stew

SERVES 6

½ pound beef stew meat, cut into ½-inch cubes

½ teaspoon salt

¼ teaspoon pepper

2 tablespoons all-purpose flour

1 tablespoon olive oil

2 tablespoons worcestershire sauce

2 tablespoons water

1 cup thinly sliced carrot

1 cup chopped shallots

1 clove garlic, minced

8 ounces mushrooms, quartered

1 cup no-salt-added beef broth

1 teaspoon dried rosemary, crushed

KITCHEN TIP

Get a jump on dinner and keep up your healthy eating habits by shopping smart: Ask the butcher to cut your lean cuts of lamb, beef or pork into cubes and wrap them in three- or four-ounce packages for your freezer. If you're buying chicken, ask to have the skin removed, too. In the time it takes to cook rice, you can defrost the meat and concoct a delicious stir-fry.

1 can (14.5 ounces) diced tomatoes, with liquid

1 bay leaf

2½ cups water

1 cup uncooked pearl barley

1 can (14 ounces) quartered artichoke hearts, drained

Sprinkle beef with salt and pepper; dredge in flour. Heat oil in a large dutch oven over medium-high heat. Add beef; cook 4 minutes, browning meat on all sides. Remove from pot.

Reduce heat under pot to medium; stir in worcestershire sauce and 2 tablespoons water. Cook 1 minute, scraping pot to loosen browned bits. Add carrot, shallots, garlic, and mushrooms; sauté 3 minutes.

Return beef to pot; stir in broth, rosemary, tomatoes, and bay leaf. Bring to a boil, then cover, reduce heat, and simmer 30 minutes or until beef is tender. Discard bay leaf.

Add 2½ cups water, barley, and artichokes. Bring to a boil, then cover, reduce heat, and simmer 50 minutes or until barley is tender.

Per serving: Calories 277 (16% from fat), Fat 5 g (1 g saturated), Protein 16 g, Carbohydrate 45 g, Fiber 7 g, Cholesterol 22 mg, Iron 4 mg, Sodium 465 mg, Calcium 73 mg

Pastrami and Grilled Vegetable Sandwiches

SERVES 6

1 yellow bell pepper, cut into 6 wedges

1 red bell pepper, cut into 6 wedges

1 green bell pepper, cut into 6 wedges

1 small onion, cut into ½-inch-thick slices

1 tablespoon balsamic vinegar

cooking spray

1 14-ounce unsliced loaf french bread

Tomato-Olive Spread (recipe follows)

¼ pound thinly sliced pastrami

Combine bell peppers and onion in a large bowl. Drizzle with vinegar; toss gently.

Prepare grill. Place vegetables on grill rack coated with cooking spray; grill 5 minutes on each side or until browned.

Slice bread in half lengthwise. Hollow out bottom half of loaf, leaving a shell 1 inch thick. Spread tomato-olive spread over cut sides of each half. Arrange vegetables on bottom half. Top with pastrami and upper half of loaf. Cut loaf crosswise into 6 equal portions.

TOMATO-OLIVE SPREAD

1½ ounces (about ¾ cup) sun-dried tomatoes, packed without oil

1½ cups boiling water

1 clove garlic, minced

¼ cup chopped green onions

2 tablespoons chopped fresh chives

1 tablespoon finely shredded fresh parmesan cheese

2 tablespoons fat-free caesar dressing

¼ cup sliced green olives

Combine tomatoes and boiling water in a bowl; let stand 30 minutes. Drain. Place tomatoes, garlic, and remaining ingredients in a food processor; process until smooth, scraping sides of bowl occasionally.

Per serving: Calories 279 (25% from fat), Fat 8 g (3 g saturated), Protein 11 g, Carbohydrate 41 g, Fiber 3 g, Cholesterol 20 mg, Iron 3 mg, Sodium 754 mg, Calcium 68 mg

Pork Chops With Honey-Glazed Figs, Oranges, and Hazelnuts

SERVES 4

8 dried figs

2 oranges

¼ teaspoon grated orange rind

⅓ cup fresh orange juice

2 tablespoons honey

¼ teaspoon salt

¼ teaspoon pepper

½ teaspoon ground cumin

¼ teaspoon curry powder

4 4-ounce boned pork loin chops

2 tablespoons all-purpose flour

2 teaspoons olive oil

2 tablespoons chopped hazelnuts

Place figs in a small saucepan and cover with water. Bring to a boil. Cover, reduce heat, and simmer 20 minutes. Remove from heat; uncover and let stand 20 minutes. Drain.

Grate and set aside ¼ teaspoon rind from an orange. Peel oranges, and cut crosswise into thin slices; cut each slice into quarters. Place in a bowl, cover, and chill.

Combine rind, juice, honey, salt, and pepper; set aside.

Combine cumin and curry powder; rub spice mixture on one side of each chop. Sprinkle both sides with flour. Heat oil in a large nonstick skillet over medium-high heat. Add chops, spice side down; cook 6 minutes, turning after 3 minutes. Remove chops; keep warm. Add orange juice mixture and figs to pan, scraping pan to loosen browned bits. Return chops to pan; cover, reduce heat, and simmer 8 minutes. Remove from heat. Stir in nuts and chilled oranges.

Per serving: Calories 405 (31% from fat), Fat 14 g (4 g saturated), Protein 27 g, Carbohydrate 46 g, Fiber 8 g, Cholesterol 68 mg, Iron 2 mg, Sodium 224 mg, Calcium 105 mg

TECHNIQUES

How to Peel and Section an Orange

Orange segments are best in prepared dishes when they're free of the thin membranes that divide them. Rather than trying to strip away these clingy partitions, use a knife to release the flesh—a process called sectioning. Before you start, grate off any rind needed for your recipe.

1 Place the orange on a cutting board. With a sharp paring knife, cut about ½ inch off one end. Turn the fruit, and cut the same amount off the other end.

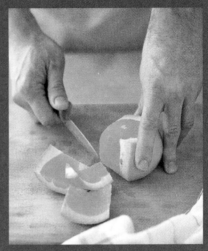

2 Stand the orange on one end, and make six to eight downward slices—following the fruit's contours—to remove the rind and slivers of the outer flesh.

3 Hold the orange over a bowl, then cut just inside one membrane to near the fruit's center. With a scooping motion, rotate the blade and slice along the facing membrane to free the section.

4 Repeat the process until you have cut away all the sections. Then, with one hand, squeeze the attached membranes so the juice from the remaining bits of flesh drips into the bowl.

Pork Medallions in Peppery Mushroom Gravy

SERVES **4**

3 cups dry medium-wide egg noodles

1 pound pork tenderloin

1 teaspoon olive oil

1 cup presliced mushrooms

½ teaspoon bottled minced garlic

1 cup beef broth

2 tablespoons sun-dried tomato sprinkles

1 tablespoon dijon mustard

1 tablespoon tomato paste

1 teaspoon dried thyme

1 teaspoon brown sugar

1 teaspoon coarsely ground black pepper

Pork Medallions in
Peppery Mushroom Gravy

Cook noodles according to package directions, omitting salt and oil. Drain.

While noodles boil, trim fat from pork; cut crosswise into 8 pieces. Place each piece between 2 sheets of heavy-duty plastic wrap; flatten to ¼-inch thickness using a meat mallet or rolling pin.

Heat oil in a large nonstick skillet over medium-high heat. Add pork; sauté 2 to 3 minutes on each side. Remove from pan; keep warm. Add mushrooms and garlic; sauté 1 minute. Add broth and remaining ingredients; bring to a boil. Cook 2 minutes, stirring frequently. Return pork to skillet, reduce heat, and simmer 2 minutes. Serve over noodles.

Per serving: Calories 389 (16% from fat), Fat 7 g (2 g saturated), Protein 35 g, Carbohydrate 45 g, Fiber 4 g, Cholesterol 138 mg, Iron 5 mg, Sodium 617 mg, Calcium 42 mg

Garlicky Pork and Vegetable Stir-Fry

SERVES **6**

1¼ pounds pork tenderloin

3 tablespoons minced jalapeño pepper

3 tablespoons low-sodium soy sauce

1½ teaspoons grated lime rind

3 tablespoons fresh lime juice

¼ teaspoon salt

9 cloves garlic, minced

¾ pound fresh green beans

1 cup julienne-cut (2-inch-long) carrot

vegetable cooking spray

2 teaspoons vegetable oil, divided

1 teaspoon cornstarch

½ cup low-sodium chicken broth

6 cups hot cooked rice (prepared without salt or fat)

Trim fat from pork, and cut pork in half lengthwise. Cut each half crosswise into ¼-inch-thick slices; set aside.

Combine jalapeño and next 5 ingredients (through garlic) in a bowl. Pour ¼ cup of sauce mixture into a large zip-top plastic bag. Add pork; seal bag, and marinate in refrigerator 30 minutes, turning occasionally.

Wash beans; trim ends and remove strings. Cut into 2-inch pieces. Place remaining sauce mixture in a large zip-top plastic bag. Add beans and carrot; seal bag and marinate in refrigerator 30 minutes, turning occasionally.

Coat a large nonstick skillet with cooking spray; add 1 teaspoon oil. Place over medium-high heat until hot. Add pork mixture; stir-fry 3 minutes. Remove pork from skillet; set aside. Add remaining teaspoon oil to skillet; place over medium-high heat until hot. Add bean mixture; stir-fry 10 minutes or until crisp-tender.

Place cornstarch in a bowl; gradually add broth, stirring until blended. Return pork to skillet; add broth mixture and stir-fry 3 minutes or until pork is tender and liquid has thickened. Serve over rice.

Per serving: Calories 386 (10% from fat), Fat 4 g (1 g saturated), Protein 26 g, Carbohydrate 59 g, Fiber 3 g, Cholesterol 61 mg, Iron 4 mg, Sodium 403 mg, Calcium 64 mg

Pork With Apples and Green Chiles

SERVES 6

1½ pounds pork tenderloin

¼ teaspoon salt

¾ teaspoon dried oregano, divided

¾ teaspoon ground cumin, divided

1 tablespoon olive oil

1 cup chopped onion

½ cup apple cider

1 tablespoon cider vinegar

2 medium-size granny smith apples, peeled, each cut into 8 wedges

1 can (4.5 ounces) green chiles

3 cups hot cooked rice

Preheat oven to 425°. Trim fat from pork. Combine ¼ teaspoon salt, ¼ teaspoon oregano, and ¼ teaspoon cumin; rub over pork.

Heat oil in a large ovenproof skillet over medium-high heat. Add pork, and brown on all sides. Remove pork from skillet. Add onion to skillet; cook over medium heat 3 minutes or until onion is lightly browned. Add cider and vinegar; simmer

2 minutes. Stir in apples, ½ teaspoon oregano, ½ teaspoon cumin, and chiles (with liquid). Return pork to skillet.

Bake, uncovered, 30 minutes. Remove pork from skillet; cut into ¼-inch slices. Serve with rice and apple-chile sauce.

Per serving: Calories 310 (16% from fat), Fat 5 g (1 g saturated), Protein 26 g, Carbohydrate 37 g, Fiber 2 g, Cholesterol 74 mg, Iron 3 mg, Sodium 177 mg, Calcium 33 mg

Sweet Potato and Pork Stew

SERVES 4

1 pound lean boneless pork loin, cut into ½-inch cubes

2 tablespoons dijon mustard

3 tablespoons all-purpose flour

vegetable cooking spray

1 teaspoon vegetable oil

2 cups cubed peeled sweet potato (about 1 pound)

¾ cup water

¾ cup unsweetened apple juice

¼ teaspoon salt

⅛ teaspoon pepper

1 cup frozen cut green beans, thawed

¼ cup sliced green onions

Combine pork and mustard in a bowl; stir well to coat. Dredge pork in flour. Coat a dutch oven with cooking spray; add oil and place over medium heat until hot. Add pork and cook 7 minutes, browning well on all sides. Add sweet potato, water, apple juice, salt, and pepper; bring to a boil. Cover, reduce heat, and simmer 15 minutes or until potato is tender.

Stir in beans and onions; cook 5 minutes or until beans are tender.

Per serving: Calories 301 (28% from fat), Fat 9 g (3 g saturated), Protein 23 g, Carbohydrate 31 g, Fiber 2 g, Cholesterol 57 mg, Iron 3 mg, Sodium 449 mg, Calcium 54 mg

Potato and Ham Provençale

SERVES 8

cooking spray

1 cup diced smoked ham

½ cup chopped green onions

2 cloves garlic, minced

8 small tomatoes (about 2½ pounds)

⅛ teaspoon salt

⅛ teaspoon black pepper

4 cups cubed yukon gold or red potatoes

¼ cup nonfat milk

¼ cup water

½ teaspoon chicken bouillon granules

½ teaspoon salt

¼ teaspoon white pepper

2 ounces (½ cup) crumbled blue cheese

Preheat oven to 375°. Heat a large saucepan coated with cooking spray over medium heat. Add ham, onions, and garlic; sauté 4 minutes. Remove mixture from saucepan and keep warm.

Cut tops off tomatoes; discard tops. Sprinkle cut sides of tomatoes with ⅛ teaspoon each salt and black pepper. Place in a 13" × 9" baking dish coated with cooking spray; bake for 15 minutes.

Place potatoes in saucepan and cover with water; bring to a boil. Reduce heat, simmer 15 minutes or until tender; drain.

Combine milk, water, and bouillon granules in a small bowl; microwave on high 1 minute or until bouillon dissolves.

Return potato to pan and mash. Stir in ham mixture, milk mixture, ½ teaspoon salt, and white pepper. Spoon potato mixture into baking dish around tomatoes. Sprinkle blue cheese evenly over top. Bake 5 minutes or until thoroughly heated.

Per serving: Calories 154 (22% from fat), Fat 4 g (2 g saturated), Protein 9 g, Carbohydrate 23 g, Fiber 3 g, Cholesterol 15 mg, Iron 1 mg, Sodium 655 mg, Calcium 65 mg

Lamb Chops With Black Bean–Orange Relish

SERVES 4

RELISH

3 oranges

½ cup chopped red onion

¼ cup chopped fresh parsley

1 tablespoon balsamic vinegar

1 tablespoon olive oil

⅛ teaspoon salt

⅛ teaspoon pepper

1 can (15 ounces) black beans, rinsed and drained

Grate 1 tablespoon rind from oranges and set aside for preparation of lamb chops.

Peel and section oranges; squeeze membranes over a bowl to extract juice (see instructions on page 145). Set sections aside; reserve ¼ cup juice. Discard membranes.

Combine 3 tablespoons reserved juice, orange sections, onion, and remaining 6 ingredients in a bowl. Cover and chill.

LAMB CHOPS

1 tablespoon grated orange rind

1 teaspoon dijon mustard

1 teaspoon dried rosemary

¼ teaspoon freshly ground black pepper

8 3-ounce lamb rib chops

Preheat broiler. Combine orange rind, 1 tablespoon reserved orange juice, mustard, rosemary, and pepper. Brush mustard mixture over both sides of lamb chops.

Place chops on a broiler pan; broil 4 minutes on each side or to desired degree of doneness. Spoon relish onto 4 dinner plates, and place 2 chops on each.

Per serving: Calories 301 (39% from fat), Fat 13 g (4 g saturated), Protein 26 g, Carbohydrate 21 g, Fiber 4 g, Cholesterol 64 mg, Iron 3 mg, Sodium 337 mg, Calcium 52 mg

Lamb and Veggie Burgers With Feta Spread

SERVES 5

½ cup uncooked bulgur

½ cup boiling water

1 cup diced baking potato

3 cups water

½ pound lean ground lamb

1 cup finely diced zucchini

½ cup chopped onion

¼ cup chopped fresh parsley

2 cloves garlic, minced

½ teaspoon salt

¼ teaspoon pepper

cooking spray

5 hamburger buns

Feta Spread (recipe follows)

5 ¼-inch-thick slices tomato

Combine bulgur and boiling water in a large bowl. Cover and let stand 30 minutes.

Meanwhile, combine potato and 3 cups water in a saucepan; bring to a boil. Reduce heat, simmer until tender, 5 to 10 minutes, and drain. Cool.

Stir together bulgur, potato, lamb, zucchini, onion, parsley, garlic, salt, and pepper in a large bowl. Divide mixture into 5 equal portions and shape into ½-inch-thick patties.

Heat a large nonstick skillet coated with cooking spray over medium-high heat. Cook patties 4 minutes on each side. Place patties on bottom halves of buns; cover each with 2 tablespoons feta spread, 1 tomato slice, and top of bun.

FETA SPREAD
Combine ½ cup nonfat sour cream, ¼ cup diced seeded peeled cucumber, ¼ teaspoon dried dill, 1 minced clove garlic, and ½ cup crumbled feta cheese.

Per serving: Calories 406 (25% from fat), Fat 11 g (4 g saturated), Protein 21 g, Carbohydrate 55 g, Fiber 4 g, Cholesterol 61 mg, Iron 3 mg, Sodium 572 mg, Calcium 113 mg

Lamb and
Veggie Burger
With
Feta Spread

Lo Mein With Eggplant and Tofu

SERVES 6

⅓ cup soy sauce

3 tablespoons mirin (japanese rice wine)
   or dry sherry

1 tablespoon plus 1 teaspoon dark roasted
   sesame oil

1 tablespoon seasoned rice vinegar

4 cloves garlic, minced

2 teaspoons minced fresh ginger root

½ teaspoon crushed red pepper flakes

1 package (10½ ounces) extrafirm or firm tofu

2 japanese or baby eggplants

3 heads baby bok choy or belgian endive

1 yellow bell pepper

1 red bell pepper

¾ pound portobello mushrooms

10 ounces udon noodles or chinese curly noodles

½ cup thinly sliced green onions or chopped cilantro

In a medium-size bowl, combine soy sauce, mirin,
sesame oil, vinegar, garlic, ginger, and pepper
flakes; mix well. Remove and reserve ¼ cup of
mixture. Cut tofu into ½-inch cubes. Add to
bowl and toss with soy sauce mixture.

Cut eggplant and bok choy in half lengthwise.
Cut bell peppers in quarters lengthwise; discard
stems and seeds. Trim ends from mushrooms.
Arrange vegetables on a platter; brush lightly with
reserved soy sauce mixture. Let vegetables and
tofu stand at room temperature while you prepare
the charcoal grill.

Cook noodles according to package directions.
Meanwhile, place vegetables on grid over medium-
hot coals. Grill 4 to 5 minutes per side or until
vegetables are crisp-tender, basting once with any
soy sauce mixture left on platter.

Transfer vegetables to cutting board; cut into 1-
inch pieces. Drain noodles; toss with vegetables.
Add tofu mixture; toss gently. Transfer to 6 warm
dinner plates; sprinkle with green onions or cilantro.

Per serving: Calories 309 (27% from fat), Fat 10 g (1 g saturated),
Protein 17 g, Carbohydrate 41 g, Fiber 5 g, Cholesterol 38 mg,
Iron 9 mg, Sodium 960 mg, Calcium 177 mg

**Lo Mein With
Eggplant and Tofu**

Pasta Fagioli

SERVES 7

1 tablespoon olive oil

2 cups water, divided

1 cup chopped onion

1 cup each thinly sliced carrot and celery

2 cups cooked farfalle (bow-tie pasta)

¼ cup chopped fresh flat-leaf (italian) parsley

1 teaspoon chopped fresh thyme

¼ teaspoon salt

⅛ teaspoon pepper

1 can (16 ounces) great northern beans

1 can (14¼ ounces) fat-free beef broth

7 tablespoons chopped tomato

7 teaspoons grated parmesan cheese

Heat oil in a large saucepan over medium-low heat;
add ½ cup water, onion, carrot, and celery. Cover
and cook 15 minutes or until tender.

Add remaining water and next 6 ingredients
(through broth); cook over medium heat 5 minutes
or until heated through. Ladle into bowls; sprinkle
with tomato and cheese.

Per serving: Calories 151 (18% from fat), Fat 3 g (1 g saturated),
Protein 7 g, Carbohydrate 25 g, Fiber 4 g, Cholesterol 1 mg, Iron
2 mg, Sodium 182 mg, Calcium 72 mg

Pad Thai With Tofu and Shrimp

SERVES 4

4 ounces dry rice-flour noodles (rice sticks)

4 cups boiling water

3 tablespoons chopped green onions

2 tablespoons chopped cilantro

2 tablespoons unsalted dry-roasted peanuts, crushed

⅓ cup water

1½ tablespoons sugar

2 tablespoons fish sauce

2 tablespoons lime juice

½ to 1 teaspoon garlic chili paste

4 teaspoons vegetable oil, divided

1 large egg, lightly beaten

1 package (about 12 ounces) reduced-fat extrafirm
    tofu, drained and diced

½ pound (about 25) medium-size shrimp, peeled
    and deveined

2 cups fresh bean sprouts

¾ cup thinly sliced leek

⅓ cup shredded carrot

Combine rice sticks and boiling water; let stand
10 minutes. Drain, chop, and set aside.

Combine onions, cilantro, and peanuts in a small
bowl; set aside.

Combine ⅓ cup water and next 4 ingredients
(through chili paste) in a bowl. Set aside.

Heat 1 teaspoon oil in a large nonstick skillet
over medium-high heat. Add egg; scramble
30 seconds. Remove egg from pan and set aside.

Add 1 teaspoon oil to pan. Add tofu; stir-fry
5 minutes or until lightly browned. Remove tofu
from pan and reserve with egg.

Add 1 teaspoon oil to pan. Add shrimp; cook
2 minutes or until done. Remove shrimp and
reserve with egg and tofu.

Add 1 teaspoon oil to pan. Add bean sprouts,
leek, and carrot; stir-fry 2 minutes. Stir in rice
sticks and fish sauce mixture; cook 2 minutes.

Return egg, tofu, and shrimp to pan; cook
30 seconds or until heated through. Spoon 1½ cups
onto each of 4 plates; top each with 2 tablespoons
peanut mixture.

Per serving: Calories 334 (26% from fat), Fat 10 g (2 g saturated),
Protein 23 g, Carbohydrate 40 g, Fiber 3 g, Cholesterol 122 mg,
Iron 4 mg, Sodium 820 mg, Calcium 103 mg

Roasted Garlic and Porcini Mushroom Risotto

SERVES 5

1 head garlic

2 cups boiling water

1 ⅞-ounce package (about ¾ cup) dried
    porcini mushrooms

1 tablespoon olive oil

2 cups finely chopped onion

1¾ cups uncooked arborio or other short-grain rice

1 teaspoon dried thyme

1 can (16 ounces) low-salt chicken broth

2 tablespoons freshly grated parmesan cheese

¼ teaspoon salt

⅛ teaspoon pepper

1 tablespoon chopped fresh parsley

Preheat oven to 400°. Remove white papery skin
from garlic head (do not peel or separate cloves).
Wrap head in aluminum foil. Bake 45 minutes;
let cool 10 minutes. Separate cloves and squeeze to
extract garlic pulp; discard skins. Set pulp aside.

Combine boiling water and mushrooms in a
bowl; cover and let stand 30 minutes. Strain mixture through a sieve into a bowl, reserving liquid.
Chop mushrooms; set aside.

Heat oil in a large nonstick skillet over medium
heat. Add onion; cover and cook 10 minutes or
until tender, stirring occasionally. Stir in rice. Add
chopped mushrooms and thyme; cook 1 minute.
Add ½ cup reserved mushroom liquid; cook until
liquid is nearly absorbed, stirring constantly.
Combine remaining mushroom liquid and chicken
broth, and add to skillet ½ cup at a time, stirring
constantly until each portion is absorbed before
adding the next (about 25 minutes total). Remove
from heat; stir in reserved garlic pulp, cheese, salt,
and pepper. Sprinkle with parsley.

Per serving: Calories 363 (12% from fat), Fat 5 g (1 g saturated),
Protein 9 g, Carbohydrate 71 g, Fiber 3 g, Cholesterol 2 mg, Iron
4 mg, Sodium 199 mg, Calcium 80 mg

Pasta Alla Puttanesca

SERVES 6

2 tablespoons olive oil

4 anchovy fillets, rinsed well and chopped

3 cloves garlic, minced or pressed

¼ teaspoon red pepper flakes

1 can (28 ounces) crushed tomatoes in puree

salt to taste

½ teaspoon dried oregano

2 tablespoons capers, drained and rinsed

8 imported black olives such as kalamata,
* pitted and halved*

1 pound hot cooked spaghetti

¼ cup chopped fresh parsley

Let a large pot of water heat for the pasta while you prepare the sauce. Heat the olive oil and anchovies in a large, heavy-bottomed, nonstick frying pan over medium-low heat until the anchovies begin to sizzle. Cook, stirring and crushing with a wooden spoon, until anchovies fall apart. Add garlic and red pepper. Cook, stirring, until garlic begins to color and smell fragrant, 30 seconds to 1 minute.

Stir in tomatoes and salt to taste, and raise the heat to medium. Cook, stirring often, about 10 minutes.

Add oregano, capers, and olives, and continue to cook, stirring often, 5 to 15 minutes, until tomatoes begin to stick to pan. Taste, and add salt or more red pepper flakes as desired. Keep warm.

Cook pasta and toss with sauce and parsley.

Per serving: Calories 379 (19% from fat), Fat 8 g (1 g saturated), Protein 12 g, Carbohydrate 64 g, Fiber 3 g, Cholesterol 1 mg, Iron 4 mg, Sodium 567 mg, Calcium 63 mg

Fried Rice With Soybeans

SERVES 6

cooking spray

2 large eggs, beaten

3 teaspoons dark sesame oil,
* divided*

1½ cups fresh bean sprouts

⅓ cup shredded carrot

¼ cup thinly sliced green onions

2 cloves garlic, minced

4 cups cold cooked rice

3 tablespoons low-sodium soy sauce

½ teaspoon salt

½ teaspoon grated peeled fresh ginger

1 can (15 ounces) soybeans, rinsed and drained

Heat large nonstick skillet coated with cooking spray over medium-high heat. Add eggs; scramble 30 seconds or until set. Remove from pan, and keep warm.

Heat 1 teaspoon sesame oil in skillet over medium-high heat. Add sprouts, carrot, onions, and

Pasta Alla Puttanesca

garlic; stir-fry 1 minute. Add 2 teaspoons sesame oil, rice, and remaining ingredients; stir-fry 5 minutes. Stir in cooked egg.

Per serving: Calories 288 (24% from fat), Fat 8 g (1 g saturated), Protein 13 g, Carbohydrate 42 g, Fiber 3 g, Cholesterol 74 mg, Iron 5 mg, Sodium 534 mg, Calcium 84 mg

Linguine Verde

SERVES 6

3 skinned, boned chicken breast halves

salt and pepper to taste

cooking spray

¾ pound dry linguine

1 tablespoon olive oil

1 cup thinly sliced leeks

1 medium-size bulb fennel, cored and thinly
    sliced lengthwise (to make 2 cups)

4 cloves garlic, thinly sliced

½ pound mushrooms, halved

½ cup dry white wine

½ cup low-sodium chicken or vegetable broth

1 large jar (15 ounces) marinated artichoke hearts,
    drained and rinsed

2 cups frozen peas

2 tablespoons chopped fresh thyme
    (or 2 teaspoons dried thyme)

¾ cup fat-free half-and-half

¼ cup grated parmesan

Preheat broiler. Place each chicken breast half between 2 sheets of heavy-duty plastic wrap; flatten to ¼-inch thickness using a meat mallet or rolling pin. Season to taste with salt and pepper. Place chicken on broiler pan coated with cooking spray; broil until golden brown, about 5 minutes each side. When cool enough to handle, slice breasts lengthwise into pieces ¼ inch wide and 1 inch long. Transfer to a bowl, cover with foil, and set aside.

Meanwhile, cook linguine according to package directions.

In a large sauté pan over medium-high heat, warm oil and sauté leeks until translucent, about 5 minutes. Add fennel and garlic, and cook another 3 to 4 minutes. Add mushrooms and wine, and simmer until liquid is reduced by half. Add broth, and simmer 1 to 2 minutes. Stir in artichoke hearts and peas. Add thyme, and season to taste with salt and pepper. Simmer until heated through, 1 to 2 minutes.

Stir in chicken and half-and-half, and cook until sauce thickens slightly. Toss immediately with linguine and sprinkle with cheese.

Per serving: Calories 475 (31% from fat), Fat 15 g (2 g saturated), Protein 27 g, Carbohydrate 55 g, Fiber 7 g, Cholesterol 39 mg, Iron 4 mg, Sodium 467 mg, Calcium 140 mg

Pasta Provençale

SERVES 6

2 tablespoons extra virgin olive oil

2 tablespoons balsamic vinegar

3 cloves garlic, minced

2 large ripe tomatoes, halved

1 large yellow squash, quartered lengthwise

1 large zucchini, quartered lengthwise

8 ounces asparagus, trimmed

½ cup canned low-salt chicken or vegetable broth

¼ cup chopped fresh basil

1 tablespoon each chopped fresh thyme and
    rosemary (or 1 teaspoon each dried)

½ teaspoon salt

½ teaspoon freshly ground black pepper

12 ounces sun-dried tomato or regular penne
    pasta, uncooked

1 baguette (about 12 ounces), cut crosswise
    into thirds and each third halved lengthwise

½ cup grated parmesan cheese or crumbled
    goat cheese

fresh thyme and rosemary sprigs for garnish (optional)

Prepare charcoal grill. Combine olive oil, vinegar, and garlic in a large bowl. Brush vegetables lightly with 2 tablespoons oil mixture. Add broth, basil, thyme, rosemary, salt, and pepper to mixture in bowl, and set aside.

Cook pasta according to package directions.

While pasta is cooking, place squash, zucchini, and asparagus on grill grid over medium-hot coals. Grill 4 minutes. Turn vegetables; add tomatoes cut side up to grill. Continue to grill 4 to 5 minutes or until vegetables are tender. Transfer to a platter and cover to keep warm.

Place bread cut side down on grid. Grill 3 to 4 minutes until lightly toasted.

Cut grilled vegetables into 1-inch chunks; add to bowl and toss with herb mixture. Drain pasta; toss gently with herb-and-vegetable mixture.

Transfer to serving plates. Top with cheese, garnish with thyme and rosemary sprigs, and serve with additional freshly ground black pepper, if desired. Serve with grilled bread.

Per serving: Calories 328 (29% from fat), Fat 11 g (3 g saturated), Protein 13 g, Carbohydrate 47 g, Fiber 6 g, Iron 3 mg, Cholesterol 10 mg, Sodium 848 mg, Calcium 221 mg

Pasta Shells With Chickpeas and Tomatoes

SERVES 6

2 cans (15 ounces each) chickpeas, drained and
   rinsed, divided

3 or 4 large cloves garlic

1 can (14½ ounces) low-sodium chicken
   broth, divided

¾ pound dry pasta shells

1 tablespoon olive oil

¼ pound prosciutto, cut into ¼-inch pieces

1 large onion, finely chopped

1 can (28 ounces) chopped tomatoes

1 tablespoon chopped fresh marjoram
   (or 1½ teaspoons dried marjoram)

salt and pepper to taste

Place half of chickpeas (amount from one whole can) with garlic and ½ cup broth in a blender or food processor fitted with a metal blade. Pulse until beans are pureed. Set aside.

In a large pan, heat oil and cook prosciutto until crisp, about 3 minutes. Add onion and continue to

cook until translucent. Stir in tomatoes, pureed and whole chickpeas, remaining broth, and marjoram.

Meanwhile, cook shells according to package directions.

Simmer sauce over low heat, 10 to 12 minutes. Season to taste with salt and pepper. Toss sauce with pasta.

Per serving: Calories 507 (14% from fat), Fat 8 g (1 g saturated), Protein 23 g, Carbohydrate 87 g, Fiber 11 g, Cholesterol 16 mg, Iron 5 mg, Sodium 989 mg, Calcium 110 mg

Pasta With Shiitakes, Sweet Potato, and Peas

SERVES 5

2 10½-ounce cans low-salt chicken broth

2 cups julienne-cut peeled sweet potato

2⅓ cups sugar snap peas (about 8 ounces), trimmed

1 ⅞-ounce package (scant 1 cup) dried
   shiitake mushrooms

1 tablespoon margarine

3 cups thinly sliced onion

4 cloves garlic, minced

½ teaspoon salt

8 ounces farfalle (bow-tie pasta), uncooked

¼ cup freshly grated parmesan cheese, divided

¼ cup chopped fresh flat-leaf (italian) parsley

¼ cup chopped fresh chives

Bring broth to a boil in a large saucepan. Add sweet potato; cover and cook 1 minute. Add peas; cover and cook 2 minutes. Add mushrooms; cover and cook 1 minute. Strain mixture through a colander into a large bowl, reserving liquid.

Remove mushrooms from vegetable mixture; discard stems and thinly slice caps. Set caps aside. Return reserved liquid to pan; bring to a boil and cook 10 minutes or until reduced to ¼ cup. Remove from heat; set aside.

Cook pasta in boiling water according to package directions, omitting fat and salt. Drain and set aside.

Melt margarine in a large nonstick skillet over medium-high heat. Add onion and garlic; sauté

Pasta With Shiitakes, Sweet Potato, and Peas

10 minutes or until tender. Add sweet potato, peas, sliced mushroom caps, ¼ cup reduced liquid, and salt; bring to a boil and cook 1 minute, stirring constantly. Combine vegetable mixture, cooked pasta, 2 tablespoons of the cheese, parsley, and chives in a large bowl; toss gently. Sprinkle remaining cheese over pasta. Serve immediately.

Per serving: Calories 383 (14% from fat), Fat 6 g (2 g saturated), Protein 14 g, Carbohydrate 68 g, Fiber 8 g, Cholesterol 4 mg, Iron 5 mg, Sodium 408 mg, Calcium 143 mg

Lamb, Tomato, and White Bean Penne

SERVES 6

1 tablespoon olive oil

1 pound lamb sirloin, trimmed of fat and
    cut into ½-inch cubes

salt and pepper to taste

1 onion, finely chopped

2 carrots, finely chopped

2 stalks celery, finely chopped

3 cloves garlic, minced

½ cup dry white wine

1 can (28 ounces) crushed tomatoes

2 cans (15 ounces each) cannellini beans,
    drained and rinsed

¼ cup chopped fresh sage leaves
    (or 4 teaspoons dried sage)

pinch red pepper flakes

¾ pound dry penne pasta

In a nonstick sauté pan over medium-high heat, heat oil and sear lamb in batches until golden brown on all sides. Season to taste with salt and pepper. Set aside on a plate lined with paper towels.

Add onion to pan and cook until translucent, about 5 minutes. Add carrots, celery, and garlic, and cook another 2 to 3 minutes. Add wine and simmer until reduced by almost half. Add tomatoes, lamb, beans, sage, and red pepper flakes. Season to taste with salt and pepper.

Meanwhile, cook penne according to package directions.

Simmer sauce 10 minutes or until beans and lamb are heated through, adding water if necessary. Spoon penne onto plates or into pasta bowls; top with sauce.

Per serving: Calories 536 (18% from fat), Fat 10 g (3 g saturated), Protein 31 g, Carbohydrate 77 g, Fiber 11 g, Cholesterol 49 mg, Iron 7 mg, Sodium 561 mg, Calcium 141 mg

Soft Tacos With Squash, Corn, Tomatoes, and Onions

SERVES **6**

1 tablespoon olive oil

1 medium-size bermuda onion or ½ torpedo onion, chopped

½ to 1 teaspoon salt

2½ cups diced yellow pattypan squash or yellow zucchini

2½ cups diced green pattypan squash or zucchini

3 large cloves garlic, minced or pressed

6 medium-size tomatoes, peeled, seeded, and chopped

1 green anaheim chile, seeded and finely chopped

1 jalapeño chile, seeded and finely chopped

kernels from 2 ears of corn, preferably white

½ cup fresh cilantro, chopped

1 cup canned pinto or black beans

12 corn tortillas, heated

½ cup nonfat cottage cheese, blended until smooth with 2 tablespoons yogurt

Classic Stir-Fried Tofu
and Vegetables

Heat oil in a large nonstick skillet over medium heat; add onion. Cook, stirring, until tender, about 5 minutes. Add a couple of pinches salt and the squash. Stir together and continue to cook about 5 minutes, until squash begins to soften. Add a few tablespoons water if vegetables stick to pan. Add garlic and stir about 1 minute, until garlic begins to smell fragrant.

Add 4 of the tomatoes and the chiles. Turn heat to medium-low and cook, stirring often, about 10 minutes, until vegetables are tender and aromatic. Add corn and cook about 3 minutes, until kernels are crisp-tender. Add all but 2 tablespoons of cilantro, the remaining tomatoes, and the beans. Stir together, taste, and adjust salt. Remove pan from heat.

Spread vegetables on the hot tortillas, and top each with 1 tablespoon cottage cheese mixture. Garnish with remaining cilantro.

Per serving: Calories 268 (17% from fat), Fat 5 g (1 g saturated), Protein 11 g, Carbohydrate 49 g, Fiber 8 g, Cholesterol 0 mg, Iron 3 mg, Sodium 495 mg, Calcium 154 mg

Classic Stir-Fried Tofu and Vegetables
(For stir-fry technique, see page 159)

SERVES 4

SAUCE

1 cup fat-free, less-sodium chicken broth

2 tablespoons cornstarch

2 tablespoons water

2 tablespoons oyster sauce

2 tablespoons low-sodium soy sauce

1½ teaspoons sugar

½ teaspoon dark sesame oil

STIR-FRY

4 cups broccoli florets

⅔ cup red bell pepper strips

2 tablespoons vegetable oil, divided

1 package (about 12 ounces) reduced-fat extrafirm tofu, drained and cut into cubes

¾ cup diagonally sliced celery

3 cups 1-inch slices bok choy

1 cup sliced mushrooms

⅓ cup sliced green onions

2 cloves garlic, minced

1 cup canned whole baby corn, cut into 1-inch pieces

⅓ cup sliced water chestnuts

4 cups hot cooked rice

To prepare sauce, combine ingredients in a bowl; set aside.

To prepare stir-fry, steam broccoli and bell pepper, covered, 3 minutes; drain and set aside. Heat 1 tablespoon oil in a large nonstick skillet over medium-high heat. Add tofu; cook 9 minutes or until lightly browned. Remove from pan and set aside. Heat 1 tablespoon oil in pan. Add celery; stir-fry 2 minutes. Add bok choy, mushrooms, onions, and garlic; stir-fry 1 minute. Add broccoli, bell pepper, tofu, baby corn, and water chestnuts; stir in sauce. Stir-fry 3 minutes or until heated through. Serve over rice.

Per serving: Calories 456 (18% from fat), Fat 9 g (2 g saturated), Protein 17 g, Carbohydrate 79 g, Fiber 7 g, Cholesterol 0 mg, Iron 5 mg, Sodium 709 mg, Calcium 183 mg

Tomato and Potato Herb Frittata

SERVES 4

4 small red potatoes (about 10 ounces)

1 teaspoon olive oil, divided

½ cup diced red onion

2 cloves garlic, minced

KITCHEN TIP

Quick-cooking grains can help you pull together a meal when time is scarce. Bulgur and couscous, for example, cook in 10 to 15 minutes. For a fast tabbouleh, cook bulgur and mix with one fresh tomato, some chopped parsley and mint leaves. Dress with a mixture of olive oil and lemon juice.

3 large eggs

1 large egg white

3 tablespoons minced fresh basil, divided

3 tablespoons minced fresh parsley, divided

¼ teaspoon salt

⅛ teaspoon pepper

2 cups chopped seeded tomato, divided

½ cup shredded fontina cheese

Steam potatoes, covered, 15 minutes. Allow to cool slightly; cut into ¼-inch-thick slices.

Heat ½ teaspoon oil in a large nonstick skillet over medium-high heat. Add onion; sauté 2 minutes. Add potatoes and garlic; sauté 1 minute. Remove from heat.

Whisk together eggs, egg white, 1½ tablespoons basil, 1½ tablespoons parsley, salt, and pepper in a large bowl. Stir in potato mixture and 1 cup tomato.

Heat ½ teaspoon oil in large nonstick skillet over medium-high heat. Add egg mixture; lower heat to medium and cook 10 minutes or until set. Top with 1 cup tomato and cheese. Preheat broiler. Wrap skillet handle with foil; broil 5 minutes or until cheese melts. Sprinkle with 1½ tablespoons each basil and parsley.

Per serving: Calories 208 (42% from fat), Fat 10 g (4 g saturated), Protein 12 g, Carbohydrate 19 g, Fiber 3 g, Cholesterol 176 mg, Iron 2 mg, Sodium 223 mg, Calcium 122 mg

Portobello Mushrooms Stuffed With Spinach and Couscous

SERVES 4

4 large (6-inch) or 8 medium-size (3-inch) portobello mushrooms

nonstick cooking spray, preferably garlic-flavored

1 tablespoon rosemary- or basil-flavored or extra virgin olive oil

¾ cup diced red bell pepper

⅓ cup minced shallots or onion

3 cloves garlic, minced

1½ cups canned low-sodium chicken or vegetable broth

½ cup couscous, uncooked

2 teaspoons chopped fresh rosemary (or ½ teaspoon dried)

salt and pepper to taste

1 package (8 ounces) fresh baby spinach leaves

¼ cup grated parmesan cheese

Preheat oven to 450°. Clean mushrooms with a damp paper towel. Cut off stems and discard. Scrape out and discard mushroom gills. Place mushroom caps rounded side up on a baking sheet, and coat caps with cooking spray. Bake 5 minutes. Remove from oven; preheat broiler.

Meanwhile, heat oil in a large deep skillet over medium-high heat. Add bell pepper, shallots, and garlic; sauté 5 minutes. Add broth; bring to a boil. Stir in couscous, rosemary, salt, and pepper; simmer 1 minute. Add spinach; cover and cook until leaves wilt. Stir well, cover, and remove from heat. Let stand 5 minutes or until liquid is mostly absorbed.

Turn mushrooms over and fill with couscous mixture. Sprinkle cheese on top. Broil 4 inches from heat until cheese is golden brown.

Per serving: Calories 222 (27% from fat), Fat 8 g (2 g saturated), Protein 11 g, Carbohydrate 31 g, Fiber 5 g, Cholesterol 7 mg, Iron 4 mg, Sodium 543 mg, Calcium 162 mg

Meatless Chili

SERVES 4

2 tablespoons canola or olive oil

1 medium-size onion, chopped

1 large carrot, minced or grated

1 red bell pepper, chopped

salt to taste

¼ cup pure powdered chiles, ½ mild and ½ hot

2 teaspoons ground cumin

2 cloves garlic, minced or pressed

¾ cup water

1 can (28 ounces) crushed tomatoes

¾ teaspoon dried oregano

1 medium-size zucchini, diced

1½ cups pinto or red beans, cooked, or 15 ounces canned beans, drained

¼ cup chopped fresh cilantro

How to Stir-Fry Vegetables

Chinese-style sautéing has its own yin and yang. The first part of the process is relaxed and meditative, the second part fast and furious. The key to success is in the preparation.

1 Carefully cut the vegetables—for example, broccoli, bok choy, celery, peppers—and any meat or tofu into bite-size pieces. Mince the garlic, ginger, and other herbs. As you go, transfer the items into small bowls; this makes following the recipe a breeze. And mix the sauce so it's ready and waiting before you fire up the stove.

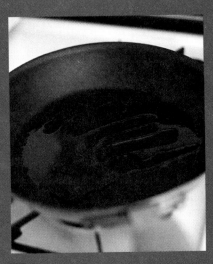

2 You don't need a wok to turn out great-textured vegetables; a large nonstick skillet serves equally well on standard kitchen stoves. Get the oil good and hot—peanut oil is popular for its high smoke point and pleasing flavor—swirling the pan so the oil coats the cooking surface.

3 Trust your senses as much as the clock to time the cooking. The ingredients should sizzle, not simmer, just long enough to soften slightly. With a wide spatula toss the mixture steadily to avoid burning. Add the sauce late so you don't boil away the veggies' freshness. Serve promptly.

Heat oil in a heavy soup pot or dutch oven over medium heat. Add onion and cook, stirring, until almost tender, 3 to 5 minutes. Add carrot, bell pepper, and some salt, and cook, stirring, about 5 minutes. Add powdered chiles and cumin, and cook, stirring, 2 to 3 minutes, until mixture begins to stick to pan. Add garlic and stir about 30 seconds. Add the water and stir 1 to 2 minutes, until mixture is thick. Stir in tomatoes, oregano, and zucchini. Add more salt to taste.

Bring to a simmer, reduce heat, cover, and simmer 45 to 60 minutes. Stir often to prevent sticking. Stir in beans, taste, and adjust seasonings. Set aside until ready to serve.

Just before serving, bring to a simmer and stir in cilantro. Accompany with cornbread or corn tortillas.

Per serving: Calories 275 (26% from fat), Fat 8 g (1 g saturated), Protein 11 g, Carbohydrate 42 g, Fiber 12 g, Cholesterol 0 mg, Iron 5 mg, Sodium 526 mg, Calcium 152 mg

Bell Peppers and Mirlitons With Creole Beans and Rice

SERVES 6

2 tablespoons olive oil, divided

1 large onion, chopped

½ cup thinly sliced celery

3 cloves garlic, minced

1½ cups converted white rice, uncooked

3 cups canned low-salt chicken or vegetable broth

½ teaspoon salt

1 can (16 ounces) red kidney beans, rinsed
  and drained

3 teaspoons blackened, cajun, or creole
  seasoning, divided

2 mirlitons or 3 medium-size zucchini, halved

3 yellow or red bell peppers

3 small leeks or bulb onions

⅓ cup chopped parsley

hot pepper sauce (optional)

Vegetable-Bean Ragout
With Polenta Triangles

Heat 1 tablespoon of the oil in a large saucepan over medium heat. Add onion, celery, and garlic; cook 5 minutes, stirring occasionally. Add rice; mix well. Add broth and salt; bring to a boil over high heat. Reduce heat, cover, and simmer 20 minutes. While rice is cooking, prepare charcoal grill. When rice is done, stir in beans and 1½ teaspoons seasoning mix; cover and simmer 5 minutes. (Mixture may be prepared up to 1 day ahead.)

Cut mirlitons lengthwise into ½-inch slices; discard pits. Cut bell peppers lengthwise into quarters; discard stems and seeds. Brush mirlitons, bell peppers, and leeks lightly with remaining 1 tablespoon olive oil; sprinkle with remaining 1½ teaspoons seasoning mix. Place vegetables on grid over medium-hot coals; grill 4 to 5 minutes per side or until vegetables are tender (mirlitons may take longer).

Spoon rice-and-bean mixture onto 6 dinner plates; top with grilled vegetables. Sprinkle with parsley and serve with hot pepper sauce, if desired.

Per serving: Calories 390 (15% from fat), Fat 6 g (1 g saturated), Protein 12 g, Carbohydrate 72 g, Fiber 11 g, Iron 4 mg, Cholesterol 2 mg, Sodium 717 mg, Calcium 82 mg

Vegetable-Bean Ragout With Polenta Triangles

SERVES 8

olive oil–flavored cooking spray
2 cups diced green bell peppers
1½ cups chopped onion
¼ teaspoon crushed red pepper
1 can (28 ounces) crushed tomatoes, with liquid
1 can (16 ounces) navy beans, rinsed and drained
1 can (15 ounces) no-salt-added chickpeas,
    rinsed and drained
¾ cup water
½ cup chopped fresh basil
1 teaspoon italian seasoning
½ teaspoon salt
¼ teaspoon freshly ground black pepper
2 teaspoons minced fresh flat-leaf parsley
1 clove garlic, minced
1 teaspoon grated lemon rind
Polenta Triangles (recipe follows)

RAGOUT

Coat a dutch oven with cooking spray; heat over medium-high heat. Add bell peppers, onion, and red pepper; cook 8 minutes or until tender. Stir in tomatoes and next 7 ingredients (through black pepper). Cover and cook over medium heat 15 minutes or until thoroughly heated.

Combine parsley, garlic, and lemon rind in a small bowl. Stir well and set aside.

Ladle ¾ cup ragout into bowls; top each with a polenta triangle and sprinkle with parsley mixture.

Per serving: Calories 256 (9% from fat), Fat 3 g (1 g saturated), Protein 10 g, Carbohydrate 46 g, Fiber 5 g, Cholesterol 0 mg, Iron 4 mg, Sodium 457 mg, Calcium 89 mg

POLENTA TRIANGLES

Place 1¼ cups yellow cornmeal and ½ teaspoon salt in a large saucepan. Gradually add 4 cups water, whisking constantly. Bring to a boil, then reduce heat to medium.

Cook 15 minutes, stirring frequently. Spoon polenta into a 9-inch square baking pan coated with cooking spray. Press plastic wrap onto surface of polenta; chill 2 hours or until firm.

Invert polenta onto a cutting board. Cut into 4 squares, then cut each square diagonally to make 2 triangles.

Heat 1½ teaspoons olive oil in a large nonstick skillet over medium-high heat. Add 4 polenta triangles and cook 3 minutes on each side or until lightly browned; remove from skillet. Set aside; keep warm.

Repeat procedure with 1½ teaspoons olive oil and remaining polenta triangles. Makes 8 triangles.

Per serving: Calories 95 (20% from fat), Fat 2 g (0 g saturated), Protein 2 g, Carbohydrate 17 g, Fiber 1 g, Cholesterol 0 mg, Iron 1 mg, Sodium 147 mg, Calcium 1 mg

Black Bean and Corn Burritos

SERVES 4

cooking spray

¾ cup chopped red onion

⅓ cup chopped green bell pepper

⅓ cup chopped red bell pepper

2 tablespoons minced jalapeño pepper

1 clove garlic, minced

1 can (15 ounces) black beans, drained and mashed

½ cup frozen whole-kernel corn, thawed

1 tablespoon chopped fresh cilantro

1 tablespoon fresh lime juice

1½ teaspoons chili powder

1 teaspoon ground cumin

⅛ teaspoon salt

⅛ teaspoon ground red pepper

4 6-inch flour tortillas

1 cup (4 ounces) shredded monterey jack cheese

2 cups shredded leaf lettuce

½ cup salsa

¼ cup nonfat sour cream

Preheat oven to 350°. Coat a large nonstick skillet with cooking spray; heat over medium-high heat. Add onion and next 4 ingredients (through garlic); sauté 3 minutes or until vegetables are tender. Remove from heat. Stir in beans and next 7 ingredients (through red pepper).

Spoon ½ cup bean mixture across center of each tortilla. Top each with 2 tablespoons cheese, and roll up.

Place burritos, seam side down, in a 9-inch square baking dish coated with cooking spray. Bake 15 minutes or until thoroughly heated.

Place burritos on individual lettuce-lined plates. Serve with salsa and sour cream.

Per serving: Calories 365 (30% from fat), Fat 12 g (6 g saturated), Protein 19 g, Carbohydrate 47 g, Fiber 7 g, Cholesterol 22 mg, Iron 4 mg, Sodium 667 mg, Calcium 312 mg

IN SEASON

September ends the peak season for sweet corn.

BEST BUYS

The natural sugar starts to fade soon after corn is picked. Hunt for bright green ears with silk that's still golden brown and soft. Kernels on fresh ears look plump and shiny.

COOKING TIPS

Serve corn the day you buy it, if possible. Plunge just-shucked ears into boiling unsalted water (salt toughens the kernels), and cook two minutes. To prepare for grilling, peel the husks back, pluck out the silks, then fold up the husks again. Place the ears over medium-hot coals, and cook 7 to 8 minutes, turning several times. Serve immediately.

HEALTH BONUS

Yellow corn is rich in two antioxidants, lutein and zeaxanthin. They help prevent macular degeneration, a major cause of blindness among older Americans.

Mediterranean Gyros

SERVES 8

1 can (15 ounces) no-salt-added chickpeas
    (garbanzo beans)

2 tablespoons lemon juice

2 cloves garlic

1 teaspoon olive oil

1½ cups thinly sliced onion

1½ cups red bell pepper strips

1½ cups green bell pepper strips

1 cup sliced mushrooms

8 8-inch pita bread rounds

1 cup chopped tomato

½ cup (2 ounces) crumbled feta cheese with basil
    and tomato

¼ cup chopped ripe olives

Drain beans through a sieve over a bowl, reserving 3 tablespoons liquid. Place beans, reserved liquid, lemon juice, and garlic in a food processor; process until smooth, scraping sides of processor bowl occasionally. Set aside.

Heat oil in a large nonstick skillet over medium-high heat. Add onion, bell peppers, and mushrooms; sauté 6 minutes or until vegetables are tender.

Wrap pitas in plastic wrap; microwave on high 45 seconds or until heated.

Spread about 2 tablespoons bean mixture over each pita round. Top each with ½ cup onion mixture, 2 tablespoons tomato, 1 tablespoon cheese, and 1½ teaspoons olive bits. Fold in half; secure each sandwich with a toothpick.

Per serving: Calories 264 (20% from fat), Fat 6 g (2 g saturated), Protein 10 g, Carbohydrate 44 g, Fiber 4 g, Cholesterol 8 mg, Iron 3 mg, Sodium 516 mg, Calcium 107 mg

heat through. (Mixture may be prepared up to 1 day ahead and reheated before serving.)

Prepare charcoal grill. Cut zucchini and squash in half lengthwise. Cut bell peppers into quarters lengthwise; discard stems and seeds. Place vegetables and corn cobs on a platter. Combine remaining 2 tablespoons salsa and barbecue sauce; mix well. Brush lightly over vegetables. Place on grid over medium-hot coals. Grill 5 minutes per side or until vegetables are crisp-tender, basting once with any sauce left on platter.

Transfer vegetables to cutting board. Cut kernels from corn; add to stew. Cut grilled vegetables into ¾-inch chunks; add to stew and simmer 5 minutes. Serve in shallow bowls; sprinkle with cilantro and add a lime slice to each bowl. Top with additional salsa, if desired.

Per serving: Calories 191 (16% from fat), Fat 3 g (0 g saturated), Protein 9 g, Carbohydrate 33 g, Fiber 8 g, Cholesterol 0 mg, Iron 2 mg, Sodium 528 mg, Calcium 50 mg

Posole Ahumado

SERVES 6

1 tablespoon vegetable or olive oil

3 cloves garlic, minced

2 cans (28 ounces) low-salt beef or vegetable broth

¼ cup plus 2 tablespoons tomatillo salsa, divided

1 can (16 ounces) white hominy, drained

1 can (16 ounces) pinto or black beans, rinsed
    and drained

2 medium-size zucchini

2 medium-size yellow summer squash

1 red bell pepper

1 green bell pepper

2 ears fresh corn, shucked

2 tablespoons hickory barbecue sauce

½ cup chopped cilantro

6 thin slices lime

Heat oil in a large saucepan over medium heat. Add garlic; cook 2 minutes, stirring. Add broth and ¼ cup salsa; bring to a boil. Reduce heat and simmer uncovered 5 minutes. Add hominy and beans;

Artichoke and Goat Cheese Wraps

SERVES 4

1 teaspoon olive oil

½ cup chopped red onion

1 cup cooked long-grain rice

¼ cup chopped fresh basil

2 teaspoons chopped fresh thyme

¼ teaspoon salt

⅛ teaspoon pepper

1 can (14 ounces) artichoke hearts, drained
    and chopped coarsely

1 bottle (7 ounces) roasted red bell peppers,
    drained and chopped

4 8-inch whole wheat tortillas

8 leaves spinach

¼ cup crumbled goat cheese

Heat oil in a nonstick skillet over medium heat. Add onion; sauté 5 minutes or until tender. Add rice and next 6 ingredients (through bell peppers); sauté 5 minutes or until thoroughly heated.

Warm tortillas according to package directions. Spoon about ¾ cup rice mixture down center of each tortilla. Top each with 2 spinach leaves and 1 tablespoon goat cheese; roll up.

Per serving: Calories 237 (14% from fat), Fat 4 g (1 g saturated), Protein 9 g, Carbohydrate 45 g, Fiber 3 g, Cholesterol 5 mg, Iron 3 mg, Sodium 334 mg, Calcium 73 mg

Warm "Texas Caviar"

SERVES 4

⅔ cup fat-free, less-sodium chicken broth

¼ cup uncooked long-grain rice

1 can (15.8 ounces) black-eyed peas, divided

½ cup frozen corn, thawed

½ teaspoon hot sauce

¼ teaspoon salt

⅛ teaspoon pepper

1 can (4.5 ounces) chopped green chiles

4 slices bacon

½ cup thinly sliced green onions

1 clove garlic, minced

1 package (10 ounces) thinly presliced green cabbage

2 tomatoes, each cut into 8 wedges

Bring broth to a boil in a small saucepan; add rice. Cover, reduce heat, and simmer 20 minutes or until tender.

Drain peas. In a large bowl, mash ¾ cup peas with a potato masher. Stir in remaining peas, cooked rice, corn, hot sauce, salt, pepper, and chiles.

In a large nonstick skillet, cook bacon over medium heat until crisp. Remove bacon from pan, reserving 2 teaspoons bacon drippings in pan and 2 teaspoons bacon drippings in a small bowl; crumble bacon and set aside. Add onions and garlic to skillet; sauté 2 minutes over medium heat. Stir onion mixture into pea mixture.

Heat reserved 2 teaspoons bacon drippings in skillet over medium heat. Add cabbage; sauté 4 minutes or until crisp-tender. Arrange ½ cup cabbage mixture on each of 4 plates; top each with 4 tomato wedges and ¾ cup pea mixture. Sprinkle with crumbled bacon.

Per serving: Calories 200 (22% from fat), Fat 5 g (2 g saturated), Protein 11 g, Carbohydrate 31 g, Fiber 5 g, Cholesterol 6 mg, Iron 2 mg, Sodium 593 mg, Calcium 74 mg

Savory Potato-Vegetable Medley

SERVES 6

5 cups (about 2 pounds) red potato, cut in 1-inch cubes

2 cups carrot, in 1-inch-long slices

1½ cups sliced celery

2 medium-size onions, each cut into 8 wedges

vegetable cooking spray

2 tablespoons olive oil

½ tablespoon dried basil

¼ teaspoon salt

¼ teaspoon pepper

1 clove garlic, minced

Preheat oven to 450°. Combine first 4 ingredients (through onions) in a jelly-roll pan coated with cooking spray. Combine oil and remaining ingredients in a bowl; stir well.

Drizzle over vegetables; toss to coat. Bake 1 hour or until tender, stirring every 15 minutes.

Per serving: Calories 154 (25% from fat), Fat 4 g (1 g saturated), Protein 3 g, Carbohydrate 27 g, Fiber 4 g, Cholesterol 0 mg, Iron 1 mg, Sodium 125 mg, Calcium 40 mg

Black Bean and Yellow Rice Torta

SERVES 6

1 package (5 ounces) saffron yellow rice

cooking spray

1 block (8 ounces) nonfat cream cheese, softened

1 carton (24 ounces) 1 percent cottage cheese

2 tablespoons packaged taco seasoning (such as McCormick's)

2 tablespoons chopped fresh cilantro

6 large eggs

Swiss chard is rich in lutein and zeaxanthin, antioxidants that help prevent macular degeneration, a leading cause of blindness.

2 cans (9 ounces) chopped green chiles

1 can (15 ounces) black beans, rinsed and drained

¾ cup diced seeded plum tomato

½ cup (2 ounces) shredded reduced-fat monterey
    jack cheese

Preheat oven to 350°. Cook rice according to package directions, omitting fat; allow to cool slightly. To prepare crust, spoon rice into a 9-inch springform pan coated with cooking spray. Cover surface with plastic wrap; firmly press rice into bottom and about 1 inch up sides of pan.

Place cream cheese in a food processor; process until smooth. Add cottage cheese, taco seasoning, and cilantro; process until smooth. Add eggs; pulse 12 times or until blended. Remove plastic wrap from crust. Pour 2½ cups egg mixture into prepared crust; sprinkle with chiles. Partially mash beans with a fork; crumble over chiles. Top with tomato, cheese, and remaining egg mixture. Bake 1 hour and 35 minutes. Let stand 15 minutes.

Per serving: Calories 376 (21% from fat), Fat 9 g (4 g saturated), Protein 35 g, Carbohydrate 37 g, Fiber 3 g, Cholesterol 238 mg, Iron 3 mg, Sodium 1,410 mg, Calcium 294 mg

Braised Greens With Porcini Mushrooms

SERVES 6

½ cup boiling water

½ ounce (about ½ cup) dried porcini mushrooms

1 pound swiss chard or turnip greens

1 teaspoon olive oil

¼ cup thinly sliced shallots

5 cloves garlic, minced

1 tablespoon chopped fresh sage

2½ cups (about 1 pound) chopped peeled turnip

¼ teaspoon salt

¼ teaspoon pepper

Combine boiling water and mushrooms in a bowl; cover and let stand 30 minutes.

Strain mixture through a sieve into a bowl, reserving ⅓ cup liquid. Chop mushrooms; set aside.

Remove stems and center ribs from swiss chard, and wash leaves thoroughly. Tear leaves; set aside.

Heat olive oil in a large nonstick skillet over medium heat. Add shallots and garlic; sauté 2 minutes. Add chopped mushrooms and sage; sauté 1 minute. Add reserved mushroom liquid and turnip; cover, reduce heat, and simmer 35 minutes. Stir in swiss chard, salt, and pepper; cover and simmer an additional 5 minutes.

Per serving: Calories 54 (17% from fat), Fat 1 g (0 g saturated), Protein 2 g, Carbohydrate 10 g, Fiber 2 g, Cholesterol 0 mg, Iron 2 mg, Sodium 297 mg, Calcium 64 mg

Sweet Potato Soufflé

SERVES 6

1 pound sweet potatoes

1 tablespoon butter

1 tablespoon sugar

3 tablespoons mild-flavored honey, such as
    clover or acacia

½ teaspoon ground cinnamon

¼ teaspoon ground nutmeg

⅛ teaspoon salt

¼ teaspoon ground ginger

¼ cup plain nonfat yogurt

5 egg whites, at room temperature

Preheat oven to 425°. Scrub sweet potatoes and pierce in several places with a sharp knife. Line a baking sheet with foil, and place potatoes on top. Bake 45 minutes to 1 hour, depending on size of potatoes, until thoroughly soft and beginning to ooze. Remove from heat, and allow to cool. Turn oven down to 400°.

Meanwhile, rub the inside of a 2-quart soufflé dish with butter and sprinkle with sugar, tilting dish to coat evenly.

Peel potatoes and put through a potato ricer, strainer, or food processor fitted with a steel blade. Add honey, cinnamon, nutmeg, salt, ginger, and yogurt; mix well.

Beat egg whites to stiff but not dry peaks. Stir ¼ of egg whites into potato mixture. Gently fold in remaining whites until thoroughly combined. Carefully pour into prepared soufflé dish. Bake 20 minutes, until puffed and just beginning to brown. Remove from heat and serve at once. The soufflé should be runny on the inside.

Per serving: Calories 139 (13% from fat), Fat 2 g (1 g saturated), Protein 5 g, Carbohydrate 26 g, Fiber 2 g, Cholesterol 6 mg, Iron 0 mg, Sodium 128 mg, Calcium 41 mg

Eggplant and Red Bell Pepper Panini

SERVES 6

2 small eggplants (about ¾ pound each)

3 red bell peppers

3 ¼-inch-thick slices red onion

12 slices vienna or italian bread, or
*   6 submarine rolls, split*

½ cup light or regular italian salad dressing

6 slices light or regular provolone cheese

12 large leaves spinach, stems removed

¼ cup sliced fresh basil leaves

Prepare charcoal grill. Cut eggplant lengthwise into ½-inch-thick slices, keeping 6 center pieces for the panini and reserving any leftovers for another use.

Cut bell peppers lengthwise into quarters; discard stems and seeds. Brush eggplant, bell peppers, onion slices, and one side of each slice of bread lightly with dressing.

Place vegetables on grid over medium-hot coals. Grill about 5 minutes per side or until tender. Lay cheese over eggplant slices during last minute of grilling to melt slightly. Remove vegetables.

Place bread on grid, dressing side down, and grill until lightly toasted. Remove bread. Arrange spinach leaves on 6 slices of grilled bread. Separate onion slices into rings; arrange over spinach. Top with grilled bell peppers and eggplant. Sprinkle basil over eggplant. Close sandwiches with remaining grilled bread.

Per serving: Calories 271 (21% from fat), Fat 7 g (2 g saturated), Protein 15 g, Carbohydrate 40 g, Fiber 6 g, Cholesterol 10 mg, Iron 2 mg, Sodium 579 mg, Calcium 63 mg

Roasted Vegetable Omelettes

SERVES 4

ROASTED VEGETABLES

1½ teaspoons balsamic vinegar

1 teaspoon olive oil

½ teaspoon dried rosemary, crushed

⅛ teaspoon salt

⅛ teaspoon pepper

1 cup diced red potato

½ cup sliced mushrooms

½ cup chopped plum tomato

⅓ cup chopped red onion

¼ cup chopped green bell pepper

¼ cup chopped red bell pepper

cooking spray

Preheat oven to 425°. Combine first 5 ingredients (through black pepper) in a large bowl; whisk well. Add potato and next 5 ingredients (through red bell pepper); stir well. Place vegetable mixture on a foil-lined jelly-roll pan coated with cooking spray. Bake 30 minutes or until tender, stirring occasionally. Keep warm.

TECHNIQUES

How to Fold Egg Whites Into Yolks

The fluffiest omelettes are made with whites and yolks that are separated, beaten, then put back together. The mixture will fall flat, though, if the whites are stirred too much while being blended with the yolks. The trick is to fold them together—gently. The best tool for the job is a rubber spatula.

1 Using a whisk or an electric mixer, beat egg whites with a pinch of cream of tartar in a glass, ceramic, or metal bowl. (Plastic may retain oil from earlier uses that will deflate whites.) A stiff glossy peak should form.

2 Beat yolks in separate bowl. Use a spatula to lightly stir ¼ of the whites into the yolks. Stir until barely combined. Then, with the spatula, scrape remaining whites into the bowl containing the yolk-white mixture.

3 Starting at the back of the bowl, cut down through the contents, then scrape across the bottom of the bowl and up the nearest side, turning (folding) some of the yolks over on top of the whites.

4 Rotate the bowl a quarter turn, and repeat the gentle folding motion. Repeat only as many times as is necessary to incorporate most of the yolk; stop before the mixture is completely blended.

Asian Braised Tilefish

OMELETTES

6 *large egg whites*

⅛ teaspoon cream of tartar

4 *large egg yolks*

¼ teaspoon salt

¼ teaspoon pepper

½ cup (2 ounces) shredded reduced-fat swiss
cheese, divided

In a bowl, beat egg whites and cream of tartar with
a mixer at high speed until stiff peaks form. Combine egg yolks, salt, and pepper in a large bowl;
whisk well. Gently stir ¼ of egg whites into egg
yolks; fold in remaining whites (see instructions on
preceding page).

Heat a medium-size nonstick skillet coated with
cooking spray over medium heat. Spread half of
egg mixture evenly in skillet; cover and
cook 6 minutes or until edges are set and bottom
is lightly browned. Spoon half of roasted vegetables
and ¼ cup cheese onto half of omelette. Carefully
loosen omelette with spatula and fold in half; gently

slide omelette onto a platter. Keep warm. Repeat
steps with remaining egg mixture, roasted vegetables, and cheese. To serve, cut each omelette in half.

Per serving: Calories 191 (44% from fat), Fat 9 g (3 g saturated),
Protein 14 g, Carbohydrate 13 g, Fiber 2 g, Cholesterol 227 mg,
Iron 1 mg, Sodium 333 mg, Calcium 203 mg

Huevos Rancheros

SERVES 6

2 *teaspoons olive oil*

1 *cup chopped onion*

1 *cup chopped green bell pepper*

2 *cloves garlic, minced*

2 *cans (14.5 ounces) mexican-style stewed tomatoes*
with jalapeños and spices, chopped, with liquid

1 *can (4.5 ounces) chopped green chiles*

1 *teaspoon chili powder*

½ teaspoon ground cumin

¼ teaspoon ground red pepper

6 corn tortillas

cooking spray

6 large eggs

½ cup (2 ounces) shredded reduced-fat sharp
  cheddar cheese

¼ cup sliced ripe black olives

Preheat oven to 350°. Heat oil in a large nonstick skillet over medium-high heat. Add onion, bell pepper, and garlic; sauté 5 minutes or until tender. Stir in tomatoes, green chiles, chili powder, cumin, and red pepper; bring to a boil. Reduce heat to medium; simmer 10 minutes or until thick, stirring frequently.

Heat tortillas according to package directions. Arrange tortillas in bottom and up sides of a 11" × 7" baking dish coated with cooking spray. Spread tomato mixture evenly over tortillas. Make 6 indentations in tomato mixture using a wooden spoon. Break 1 egg into each indentation. Bake 20 minutes. Sprinkle with cheese and olives; bake an additional 5 minutes or until cheese melts and eggs are set.

Per serving: Calories 249 (38% from fat), Fat 10 g (3 g saturated), Protein 13 g, Carbohydrate 28 g, Fiber 3 g, Cholesterol 227 mg, Iron 3 mg, Sodium 579 mg, Calcium 215 mg

Fontina Frittata

SERVES 2

2 teaspoons olive oil, divided

cooking spray

2 cups sliced zucchini

½ cup sliced onion

3 cloves garlic, minced

1 cup chopped seeded plum tomato

3 tablespoons minced fresh parsley, divided

½ teaspoon dried basil

¼ teaspoon dried thyme

¼ teaspoon salt

¼ teaspoon pepper

3 large egg whites, lightly beaten

2 large eggs, lightly beaten

1 cup thinly sliced plum tomato

2 ounces sliced fontina cheese or
  part-skim mozzarella

Heat 1 teaspoon oil in a large nonstick skillet coated with cooking spray over medium heat. Add zucchini, onion, and garlic; sauté 5 minutes or until tender. Combine zucchini mixture, chopped tomato, 1½ tablespoons parsley, basil, thyme, salt, pepper, egg whites, and eggs in a large bowl.

Heat 1 teaspoon oil in skillet coated with cooking spray over medium heat. Add egg mixture; cover and cook 5 minutes or until almost set.

Preheat broiler. Wrap handle of skillet with foil; broil 2 minutes or until set. Arrange sliced tomato and cheese on top; broil 1 minute or until cheese melts. Sprinkle with 1½ tablespoons parsley.

Per serving: Calories 331 (54% from fat), Fat 20 g (8 g saturated), Protein 23 g, Carbohydrate 18 g, Fiber 4 g, Cholesterol 254 mg, Iron 3 mg, Sodium 466 mg, Calcium 256 mg

Asian Braised Tilefish

SERVES 4

3 cups water

salt to taste

8 ounces (1¼ cups) red lentils

½ cup sweet white wine (such as riesling)

3 tablespoons soy sauce or tamari

1 teaspoon minced garlic

1 teaspoon minced fresh ginger

¼ teaspoon crushed red pepper flakes

4 skinless fillets tilefish or red snapper

1 package (10 ounces) fresh baby spinach leaves

1 teaspoon dark sesame oil

1 tablespoon minced chives or green onion tops

In a medium saucepan, bring water and salt to a simmer. Stir in lentils and simmer gently, uncovered, 12 minutes or until tender. (Do not overcook.)

Meanwhile, in a large skillet combine wine and next 4 ingredients (through pepper flakes); bring to a simmer over high heat. Add fish; reduce heat, cover and simmer, turning once, 6 minutes or until fish is opaque. Transfer fish to a plate; cover and keep warm.

Add spinach to skillet, cover and cook over medium-high heat 1 to 2 minutes or until wilted. Transfer with tongs to 4 dinner plates, leaving liquid in pan. Top spinach with drained lentils and fish. Boil juices in skillet over high heat until reduced to ½ cup, about 2 minutes. Stir in sesame oil and spoon over fish. Sprinkle with green onions.

Per serving: Calories 472 (20% from fat), Fat 8 g (1 g saturated), Protein 51 g, Carbohydrate 39 g, Fiber 10 g, Cholesterol 91 mg, Iron 3 mg, Sodium 916 mg, Calcium 126 mg

1½ tablespoons dijon mustard

2 teaspoons honey

cooking spray

Prepare grill. Sprinkle ¼ teaspoon salt and ¼ teaspoon pepper over both sides of steaks. Combine remaining salt and pepper, yogurt, and next 4 ingredients (through honey) in a small bowl. Stir well; set aside.

Place salmon on grill rack coated with cooking spray; grill 6 minutes on each side or until fish flakes easily when tested with a fork. Top with dill sauce.

Per serving: Calories 345 (42% from fat), Fat 16 g (3 g saturated), Protein 39 g, Carbohydrate 8 g, Fiber 0 g, Cholesterol 119 mg, Iron 1 mg, Sodium 590 mg, Calcium 131 mg

Grilled Salmon With Honey Mustard–Dill Sauce

SERVES **4**

½ teaspoon salt, divided

½ teaspoon pepper, divided

4 6-ounce salmon steaks (about 1 inch thick)

1 cup plain low-fat yogurt

¼ cup chopped fresh dill

2 tablespoons minced green onions

Shrimp and Lime Tacos

Shrimp and Lime Tacos

SERVES **4**

1 pound cooked miniature shrimp,
   rinsed and squeezed dry

¼ cup fresh lime juice

2 teaspoons finely minced lime zest

¼ cup chopped cilantro

1 teaspoon cumin seeds

salt to taste

8 corn tortillas

½ to 1 cup prepared red or
   green salsa

cilantro sprigs for garnish

Toss together shrimp, lime juice, zest, and cilantro. In a dry heavy skillet over medium heat, toast cumin seeds until they begin to pop and smell fragrant. Remove from heat and let cool. Lightly crush seeds in a spice mill or with a mortar and pestle, then stir into shrimp mixture. Add salt, if desired.

In skillet over medium heat, warm tortillas, turning once, until flexible. Wrap tightly in a clean kitchen towel or plastic bag until ready to use.

Place 2 tortillas on each of 4 plates and spread with shrimp mixture. Top each tortilla with a spoonful of salsa, and garnish with cilantro sprigs.

Per serving: Calories 262 (10% from fat), Fat 3 g (1 g saturated), Protein 27 g, Carbohydrate 31 g, Fiber 3 g, Cholesterol 221 mg, Iron 5 mg, Sodium 512 mg, Calcium 158 mg

Seafood Paella With Artichokes

Italian Fish Stew

SERVES 5

vegetable cooking spray

2 cups chopped onion

1 cup sliced celery

6 cloves garlic, minced

1 bottle (8 ounces) clam juice

1 pound sea bass or other firm white
    fish fillets,
    cut into 1-inch pieces

½ cup thinly sliced zucchini

½ cup thinly sliced carrot

½ cup water

1 teaspoon dried basil

¼ teaspoon crushed red pepper

2 cans (14½ ounces) no-salt-added stewed
    tomatoes, chopped, with liquid

¼ cup plus 1 tablespoon grated parmesan cheese

Coat a dutch oven with cooking spray; heat over medium heat. Add onion; sauté 3 minutes or until tender. Add celery, garlic, and clam juice; cook 5 minutes, stirring occasionally. Add fish and next 5 ingredients (through red pepper); cover, reduce heat to medium-low, and cook 10 minutes or until carrot is tender, stirring occasionally. Stir in tomatoes; cover and cook an additional 5 minutes, stirring occasionally. Ladle stew into serving bowls; sprinkle with cheese.

To freeze, spoon stew into airtight containers; store in freezer up to 2 months. To serve, thaw in refrigerator. Place in a saucepan; cover and cook over medium heat 8 to 10 minutes or until thoroughly heated.

Per serving: Calories 197 (14% from fat), Fat 3 g (1 g saturated), Protein 23 g, Carbohydrate 21 g, Fiber 2 g, Cholesterol 38 mg, Iron 2 mg, Sodium 296 mg, Calcium 187 mg

Seafood Paella With Artichokes

SERVES 4

2 tablespoons water

½ teaspoon saffron threads

2 teaspoons olive oil

1 cup diced onion

4 cloves garlic, crushed

1 cup water

½ cup diced peeled plum tomato

1 bottle (8 ounces) clam juice

dash crushed red pepper

dash freshly ground black pepper

¾ cup uncooked arborio rice or other short-
    grain rice

2 cups canned artichoke hearts, drained and
    quartered

⅓ cup dry vermouth

16 small mussels, scrubbed

8 medium (about ½ pound) shrimp, peeled and
    deveined

¼ cup minced fresh flat-leaf parsley

Combine 2 tablespoons water and saffron in a small bowl; let stand 10 minutes.

Heat oil in a dutch oven over medium-high heat. Add onion and garlic; sauté 2 minutes. Add saffron liquid, 1 cup water, tomato, clam juice, and red and black pepper; bring to a boil. Stir in rice; cover, reduce heat, and simmer 10 minutes.

Add artichokes, vermouth, mussels, and shrimp; cover and simmer 5 minutes or until mussel shells open. Discard any unopened shells. Sprinkle with parsley.

Per serving: Calories 290 (12% from fat), Fat 4 g (1 g saturated), Protein 18 g, Carbohydrate 47 g, Fiber 2 g, Cholesterol 70 mg, Iron 5 mg, Sodium 327 mg, Calcium 95 mg

Thai-Style Shrimp and Eggplant Wraps

SERVES **4**

1 teaspoon olive oil

1 tablespoon minced peeled fresh ginger

2 cups red bell pepper strips

2 cups julienned peeled eggplant

¾ pound medium shrimp, peeled and deveined

1 cup snow peas

4 cloves garlic, minced

⅓ cup sliced green onions

¼ cup chopped fresh basil

¼ cup low-sodium soy sauce

1 tablespoon brown sugar

1 teaspoon grated lemon rind

4 8-inch flour tortillas

Heat oil in a large nonstick skillet over medium-high heat. Add ginger; stir-fry 30 seconds. Add bell pepper and eggplant; stir-fry 4 minutes. Add shrimp, peas, and garlic; stir-fry 2 minutes. Add onions and next 4 ingredients (through lemon rind); stir-fry 2 minutes.

Warm tortillas. Spoon mixture onto tortillas and roll up.

Per serving: Calories 291 (18% from fat), Fat 6 g (1 g saturated), Protein 19 g, Carbohydrate 39 g, Fiber 4 g, Cholesterol 97 mg, Iron 5 mg, Sodium 714 mg, Calcium 143 mg

Salmon Provençale Wraps

SERVES **4**

1 ounce (about 12) sun-dried tomatoes

½ cup boiling water

1 8-ounce salmon fillet, skinned

cooking spray

1 tablespoon chopped pitted niçoise olives

1 tablespoon finely chopped fresh basil

1 teaspoon minced fresh thyme

2 cloves garlic, crushed

dash salt

dash pepper

4 8-inch flour tortillas

12 leaves arugula or spinach

Combine tomatoes and boiling water in a bowl; cover and let stand 15 minutes or until soft. Drain well; thinly slice.

While tomatoes soak, preheat broiler. Place fish on a broiler pan coated with cooking spray. Mix olives and next 5 ingredients (through pepper); spoon over fish. Broil 5 minutes or until fish flakes easily when tested with a fork.

Warm tortillas according to package directions. Divide salmon among tortillas. Sprinkle with tomatoes; top with arugula. Roll, then cut each tortilla crosswise.

Per serving: Calories 275 (29% from fat), Fat 9 g (1 g saturated), Protein 18 g, Carbohydrate 32 g, Fiber 2 g, Cholesterol 37 mg, Iron 2 mg, Sodium 425 mg, Calcium 116 mg

---

KITCHEN TIP

Looking to lighten up those old favorites? Log on to the Mayo Clinic's Web site, *www.mayohealth.org:* Click on Nutrition, then Virtual Cookbook. You'll find hundreds of dishes, including beef stroganoff and fettuccine alfredo, with the fat and calories trimmed. You can also submit recipes for revision.

Thai-Style Shrimp and Eggplant Wraps

Red Snapper Fillets With Tomatoes and Olives

SERVES 4

4 6-ounce red snapper or rockfish fillets

salt and freshly ground black pepper
    to taste

1 tablespoon olive oil

4 cloves garlic, minced or pressed

1 can (28 ounces) whole or chopped tomatoes,
    drained (or 1¾ pounds fresh peeled tomatoes),
    seeded, and crushed in a food processor

⅛ teaspoon sugar

½ to 1 teaspoon dried thyme

12 imported black olives (such as niçoise), pitted

Preheat oven to 425°. Oil a baking dish large enough to hold the fish fillets in one layer. Rinse fillets, pat dry, and lay in dish. Sprinkle lightly with salt and pepper. Set aside.

In a large heavy-bottomed nonstick skillet, heat oil over medium heat. Add garlic, and when it begins to color slightly add tomatoes, sugar, salt, and thyme. Cook, stirring often, 15 to 25 minutes, until tomatoes cook down and begin to stick to the pan. Stir in olives. Taste and adjust seasonings. Spread tomato-olive mixture over fish.

Tightly cover baking dish with aluminum foil and bake 10 to 20 minutes, until fish is opaque and comes apart easily when tested with a fork. Serve with rice or baked potatoes.

Per serving: Calories 241 (26% from fat), Fat 7 g (1 g saturated), Protein 34 g, Carbohydrate 10 g, Fiber 3 g, Cholesterol 58 mg, Iron 2 mg, Sodium 155 mg, Calcium 75 mg

Grilled Sea Bass Fillets With Tricolor Bell Pepper Salsa

SERVES **4**

cooking spray

1 tablespoon olive oil

1 cup diced green bell pepper

¾ cup diced red bell pepper

¾ cup diced yellow bell pepper

2 tablespoons capers

1 clove garlic, minced

3 tablespoons finely chopped fresh basil

1½ tablespoons red wine vinegar

¼ teaspoon salt

¼ teaspoon dried thyme

¼ teaspoon pepper

4 6-ounce sea bass fillets

Prepare grill. Coat a large nonstick skillet with cooking spray. Add oil; heat over medium-high heat. Add peppers, capers, and garlic; sauté 3 minutes or until peppers are tender. Remove from heat; stir in basil and vinegar. Set aside.

Sprinkle salt, thyme, and pepper over fillets. Place fillets on grill rack coated with cooking spray; cover and grill 6 minutes on each side or until fish flakes easily when tested with a fork. Top fish with bell pepper salsa.

Per serving: Calories 253 (36% from fat), Fat 10 g (2 g saturated), Protein 33 g, Carbohydrate 6 g, Fiber 2 g, Cholesterol 116 mg, Iron 4 mg, Sodium 604 mg, Calcium 149 mg

Orange Roughy With Parmesan Tomatoes

SERVES **4**

2 large lemons, thinly sliced

cooking spray

4 6-ounce orange roughy fillets (or other lean white fish fillets)

¼ teaspoon freshly ground black pepper

8 ¼-inch-thick slices tomato (about 2 tomatoes)

3 tablespoons grated parmesan cheese, divided

1 tablespoon capers

¼ teaspoon grated lemon rind

1 clove garlic, minced

2 tablespoons fresh lemon juice

Preheat oven to 425°. Arrange lemon slices in a single layer in a 9"×13" baking dish coated with cooking spray. Arrange fillets on lemon slices;

Grilled Tuna With Mango-Carrot Salsa

sprinkle with pepper. Top each fillet with 2 tomato slices. In a small bowl, combine 2 tablespoons cheese, capers, lemon rind, and garlic; sprinkle tomatoes with cheese mixture. Drizzle with lemon juice.

Bake 15 minutes or until fish flakes easily when tested with a fork.

Preheat broiler. Sprinkle tomatoes with 1 tablespoon cheese; broil 1 minute or until cheese is lightly browned. Serve immediately.

Per serving: Calories 147 (16% from fat), Fat 3 g (1 g saturated), Protein 27 g, Carbohydrate 3 g, Fiber 0 g, Cholesterol 37 mg, Iron 1 mg, Sodium 348 mg, Calcium 56 mg

Grilled Tuna With Mango-Carrot Salsa

SERVES **4**

1¼ cups diced peeled mango

1 cup grated carrot

3 tablespoons fresh lime juice

1 tablespoon minced fresh chives

¼ teaspoon crushed red pepper

⅛ teaspoon salt

⅛ teaspoon ground coriander

⅛ teaspoon ground cumin

¼ teaspoon salt

¼ teaspoon pepper

4 6-ounce yellowfin tuna steaks
    (about 1 inch thick)

cooking spray

Combine first 8 ingredients (through cumin) in a bowl. Stir well; set aside.

Prepare grill. Sprinkle ¼ teaspoon each salt and pepper over steaks. Place on grill rack coated with cooking spray; grill 4 minutes on each side or until done to desired degree.

Top with mango-carrot salsa.

Per serving: Calories 296 (26% from fat), Fat 9 g (2 g saturated), Protein 40 g, Carbohydrate 13 g, Fiber 2 g, Cholesterol 65 mg, Iron 2 mg, Sodium 298 mg, Calcium 16 mg

New Orleans-Style Shrimp Creole

SERVES **8**

1 tablespoon olive oil

2 cups fresh or frozen sliced okra

2 cups chopped green bell pepper

2 cups sliced mushrooms

1 cup chopped onion

1 cup chopped celery

2 cloves garlic, minced

¼ cup tomato paste

1 teaspoon dried oregano

1 teaspoon hot sauce

½ teaspoon sugar

½ teaspoon creole seasoning

1 can (28 ounces) whole tomatoes,
    chopped, with liquid

1 bay leaf

1½ pounds medium shrimp, peeled and deveined

8 cups hot cooked rice

½ cup chopped fresh parsley

Heat oil in a dutch oven over medium heat. Add okra, bell pepper, mushrooms, onion, celery, and garlic; sauté 10 minutes. Add tomato paste, oregano, hot sauce, sugar, creole seasoning, tomatoes, and bay leaf; bring mixture to a boil, stirring frequently.

Cover, reduce heat, and simmer 10 minutes. Stir in shrimp; simmer, uncovered, 3 minutes or until shrimp is done. Spoon mixture over rice and sprinkle with parsley.

Per serving: Calories 373 (8% from fat), Fat 3 g (1 g saturated), Protein 21 g, Carbohydrate 65 g, Fiber 4 g, Cholesterol 124 mg, Iron 6 mg, Sodium 504 mg, Calcium 119 mg

Peach-Blueberry Cobbler With Oatmeal Cookie Crust

SERVES 8

5 tablespoons butter or margarine, softened

1¾ cups sugar, divided

1 large egg white

1 teaspoon vanilla

1 cup all-purpose flour

½ cup regular rolled oats

1¼ teaspoons ground cinnamon, divided

3 pounds firm ripe peaches, peeled,
* pitted, and sliced*

2 cups blueberries

1 tablespoon lemon juice

3 tablespoons cornstarch

1 quart nonfat or low-fat vanilla
* frozen yogurt*

Preheat oven to 375°. In a bowl, combine butter and ¾ cup plus 2 tablespoons of the sugar; beat until fluffy. Add egg white and vanilla, and mix well. Stir in flour, oats, and ¾ teaspoon cinnamon, then pat mixture into a ball. If making ahead, wrap airtight and chill up to 1 day.

Pour peaches and blueberries into a shallow 3- to 3½-quart casserole; add lemon juice and stir to coat fruit. Mix remaining ¾ cup sugar with cornstarch; stir into fruit.

On a lightly floured board, roll oatmeal dough about ½ inch thick, and cut with floured cookie cutters. Lay cutout cookies on fruit filling; reroll dough scraps and cut more cookies until all dough is used. (Or break dough into small lumps, and scatter evenly over filling.) Mix remaining 2 tablespoons sugar and cinnamon; sprinkle over dessert. Bake until topping is richly browned and filling is bubbling in center, about 1 hour. Serve hot or cool with frozen yogurt.

Per serving: Calories 513 (14% from fat), Fat 8 g (5 g saturated), Protein 8 g, Carbohydrate 105 g, Fiber 6 g, Cholesterol 20 mg, Iron 1 mg, Sodium 153 mg, Calcium 108 mg

Creamy Vanilla Cheesecake With Fresh Strawberries

SERVES 12

CRUST

½ cup plus 2 tablespoons graham cracker crumbs

2 tablespoons granulated sugar

2 tablespoons butter or margarine, melted

cooking spray

FILLING

1 cup part-skim ricotta cheese

1 cup nonfat sour cream

8 ounces nonfat cream cheese, softened

2 egg whites

2 teaspoons vanilla extract

¾ cup granulated sugar

6 tablespoons all-purpose flour

TOPPING

2 cups fresh strawberries, hulled and sliced

2 tablespoons orange juice

Preheat oven to 300°. Coat bottom of a 9-inch springform pan with cooking spray and set aside.

To make crust, combine graham cracker crumbs, 2 tablespoons sugar and melted butter in a medium bowl, and mix well with a fork to combine. Press mixture into prepared pan and set aside.

To make filling, whisk together ricotta, sour cream, cream cheese, egg whites, and vanilla. Fold in sugar and flour. Pour filling into prepared pan. Bake 1 hour, until center is set. Turn off oven, prop open oven door, and allow cake to cool 15 minutes (to prevent cracking). Transfer cheesecake to a wire rack and cool completely. Cover with plastic, and chill until ready to serve.

Meanwhile, in a medium bowl, combine strawberries and orange juice. Let stand until ready to serve (at least 30 minutes). Just before serving, spoon strawberries over cheesecake.

Per serving: Calories 195 (21% from fat), Fat 5 g (3 g saturated), Protein 8 g, Carbohydrate 30 g, Fiber 1 g, Cholesterol 13 mg, Iron 1 mg, Sodium 217 mg, Calcium 126 mg

Super Moist Carrot Cake
With Cream Cheese Icing,
page 178

Super Moist Carrot Cake With Cream Cheese Icing

SERVES **12**

CAKE

cooking spray

1½ cups all-purpose flour

1½ teaspoons baking powder

1½ teaspoons ground cinnamon

1 teaspoon baking soda

½ teaspoon salt

2 tablespoons butter or margarine, softened

½ cup packed light brown sugar

2 egg whites

½ cup applesauce

1 teaspoon vanilla extract

1 cup grated fresh carrots

CREAM CHEESE ICING

2 tablespoons egg white powder
  (pasteurized, dried egg whites)

6 tablespoons warm water

4 ounces nonfat cream cheese

1½ cups confectioners sugar

1 teaspoon vanilla extract

Preheat oven to 350°. Coat a 9-inch round cake pan with cooking spray.

To make cake, combine flour, baking powder, cinnamon, baking soda, and salt in a medium-size bowl. Set aside. In a large mixing bowl, beat together butter and sugar until light and fluffy. Add egg whites, applesauce, and vanilla and mix well. Gradually add flour mixture and mix until just blended. Fold in carrots. Pour mixture into prepared cake pan and bake 25 minutes, until a wooden pick inserted in center comes out clean. Cool in pan, on a wire rack, 10 minutes. Invert cake, remove from pan and cool completely.

Meanwhile, to make icing, beat together egg white powder and water until stiff peaks form. Set aside. In a food processor or large mixing bowl, sift confectioners sugar over cream cheese. Process or mix until smooth and creamy. Fold in ¼ cup of egg whites. Fold in remaining egg whites and vanilla. Spread icing over top and sides of cake. Refrigerate until ready to serve.

Note: For a double-layer cake, when cake is cool, slice in half horizontally, like an english muffin. Spread ½ cup icing on bottom cake layer, top with second cake layer, and use remaining icing to coat top and sides.

Per serving: Calories 194 (10% from fat), Fat 2 g (1 g saturated), Protein 5 g, Carbohydrate 39 g, Fiber 1 g, Cholesterol 5 mg, Iron 1 mg, Sodium 359 mg, Calcium 72 mg

Chocolate Espresso Angel Food Cake

SERVES **12**

1¼ cups sugar, divided

¾ cup plus 1 tablespoon sifted cake flour

3 tablespoons unsweetened cocoa

2 teaspoons instant espresso granules

11 egg whites (at room temperature)

1½ teaspoons cream of tartar

½ teaspoon salt

1 teaspoon vanilla extract

1 tablespoon powdered sugar

Preheat oven to 375°. In a small bowl, sift together ½ cup sugar, flour, cocoa, and espresso granules; set aside. In a large bowl, beat egg whites until foamy. Add cream of tartar and salt; beat until soft peaks form. Add remaining ¾ cup sugar, 2 tablespoons at a time, beating until stiff peaks form. Sift flour mixture over egg white mixture, ¼ cup at a time; fold in after each addition. Fold in vanilla extract.

Pour batter into an ungreased 10-inch tube pan, spreading evenly. Break large air pockets by cutting through batter with a knife. Bake 35 minutes or until cake springs back when lightly touched. Invert pan; cool completely. Loosen cake from side of pan using a metal spatula; remove from pan. Sprinkle with powdered sugar.

Per serving: Calories 129 (0% from fat), Fat 0 g (0 g saturated), Protein 4 g, Carbohydrate 28 g, Fiber 0 g, Cholesterol 0 mg, Iron 1 mg, Sodium 174 mg, Calcium 6 mg

Apple-Cranberry Crisp

SERVES 6

4 granny smith apples, each cut into 8 wedges

½ cup dried cranberries

3 tablespoons apple juice

¼ cup all-purpose flour

¼ cup old-fashioned rolled oats

⅓ cup firmly packed brown sugar

¾ teaspoon ground cinnamon

¼ teaspoon ground nutmeg

1½ tablespoons chilled reduced-calorie
    stick margarine, cut into small pieces

cooking spray

Preheat oven to 375°. Combine first 3 ingredients in a bowl. Toss well and set aside. Combine flour and next 4 ingredients (through nutmeg) in another bowl. Cut in margarine with a pastry blender until the mixture resembles coarse meal.

Place apple mixture in an 8-inch square baking dish coated with cooking spray; sprinkle evenly with the flour mixture. Lightly coat top with cooking spray. Cover and bake 30 minutes. Uncover and bake an additional 20 minutes or until apples are tender.

Per serving: Calories 187 (13% from fat), Fat 3 g (1 g saturated), Protein 2 g, Carbohydrate 42 g, Fiber 5 g, Cholesterol 0 mg, Iron 1 mg, Sodium 33 mg, Calcium 27 mg

Bran-Apple Muffins

MAKES 1 DOZEN

1½ cups all-purpose flour

1¼ teaspoons baking soda

¼ teaspoon baking powder

½ teaspoon salt

¼ teaspoon ground allspice

⅓ cup currants

⅔ cup hot water

1¼ cups unprocessed wheat bran

¾ cup shredded unpeeled cooking apple

½ cup nonfat buttermilk

⅓ cup molasses

2 tablespoons vegetable oil

1 egg plus 1 egg white, beaten

cooking spray

Preheat oven to 400°. Combine first 5 ingredients (through allspice) in a large bowl; stir well. Make a well in center of mixture; set aside.

Combine currants and water in a medium-size bowl; let stand 2 minutes. Add bran; stir well. Add apple and next 4 ingredients (through eggs); stir well. Add to flour mixture, stirring just until dry ingredients are moistened.

Spoon batter evenly into muffin pan coated with cooking spray. Bake 20 minutes or until a toothpick inserted in center comes out clean. Remove from pan immediately.

Per muffin: Calories 128 (21% from fat), Fat 3 g (0 g saturated), Protein 4 g, Carbohydrate 23 g, Fiber 3 g, Cholesterol 18 mg, Iron 3 mg, Sodium 262 mg, Calcium 103 mg

Meringue Cloud With Strawberries

SERVES 8

5 large egg whites (about ⅔ cup)

½ teaspoon cream of tartar

1 to 1¼ cups sugar, divided

1 teaspoon vanilla

6 cups strawberries, divided

¼ cup orange-flavored liqueur

Preheat oven to 300°. In a deep bowl, combine egg whites and cream of tartar. Whip until whites are frothy. Gradually add 1 cup sugar, about 1 tablespoon per minute, beating until all the sugar is incorporated and whites hold stiff shiny peaks. Mix in vanilla.

Swirl meringue in an 8-inch-wide mound onto an oiled and flour-dusted ovenproof platter; don't smooth top. Bake until meringue is pale gold and surface no longer feels sticky, about 1¼ hours. Remove meringue from oven and let cool. If making ahead, cover airtight when cool and chill up to 1 day.

Rinse and hull berries. In a blender or food processor, smoothly puree half the berries with the orange liqueur; add sugar to taste. If making ahead, cover sauce and let stand up to 1 day.

Shortly before serving, slice remaining berries and scatter ¾ cup of them over meringue, then drizzle with about 1 cup strawberry sauce.

Cut meringue in wedges and accompany with remaining sauce and berries to taste.

Per serving: Calories 216 (0% from fat), Fat 0 g (0 g saturated), Protein 3 g, Carbohydrate 42 g, Fiber 2 g, Cholesterol 0 mg, Iron 0 mg, Sodium 36 mg, Calcium 17 mg

Banana-Poppyseed Bread

MAKES 16 ½-INCH SLICES

1 cup (about 2 medium) mashed ripe bananas

½ cup sugar

½ cup nonfat milk

3 tablespoons vegetable oil

1 egg, lightly beaten

1 cup all-purpose flour

1 cup whole wheat flour

2 teaspoons baking powder

2 tablespoons poppy seeds

½ teaspoon baking soda

½ teaspoon salt

½ teaspoon ground cinnamon

cooking spray

Preheat oven to 350°. Combine bananas and sugar in a bowl; stir well. Let stand 10 minutes, stirring occasionally. Stir in milk, oil, and egg; set aside. Combine all-purpose flour and next 6 ingredients (through cinnamon) in a large bowl and stir well. Make a well in center of dry mixture; add banana mixture, stirring until dry mixture is moistened.

Spoon batter into 8½" × 4½" × 3" loaf pan coated with cooking spray. Bake 1 hour or until a pick inserted in center comes out clean. Cool in pan 10 minutes. Remove from pan and cool on a rack.

Per slice: Calories 125 (27% from fat), Fat 4 g (1 g saturated), Protein 3 g, Carbohydrate 21 g, Fiber 2 g, Cholesterol 13 mg, Iron 1 mg, Sodium 145 mg, Calcium 62 mg

Ginger Cookies

MAKES 4 TO 5 DOZEN

¾ cup packed brown sugar

3 tablespoons margarine, softened

½ cup molasses

¼ cup water

2¾ cups all-purpose flour

1 tablespoon ginger

1 teaspoon baking soda

½ teaspoon salt

½ teaspoon ground cinnamon

¼ teaspoon ground cloves

vegetable cooking spray

2 tablespoons crystal sugar

Preheat oven to 350°. Cream brown sugar and margarine; add molasses and water, beating with an electric mixer set at medium speed until well

How to Cut Up a Pineapple

Fresh pineapples look fierce, but taming them is simple: Slice off the prickly peel and cut sections away from the core. Cubes of pineapple, with yogurt for dipping, make an easy dessert; for another way to put pineapple on your table, try Carribean Pork and Pineapple Kabobs (page 124).

1 Lay the pineapple on its side, and with a sharp knife slice off the bottom about ¾ inch from the end, leaving a flat surface. Stand the fruit on end.

2 Holding the leaves at the top to steady the fruit, slice down along the sides, removing all of the skin and the dark brown eyes that may still dot the surface. You'll make seven or eight main cuts.

3 Lay the pineapple on its side again, and slice off the top ¾ inch with the leaves. Trim any remaining eyes and bits of peel, then stand the peeled fruit on end.

4 At the edge of the core, slice straight down to remove a long slab. Turn the fruit, and slice off a second, smaller slab. Make two more cuts, leaving a column of core.

blended. Combine flour and next 5 ingredients (through cloves); gradually add to creamed mixture, beating well. Gently press mixture into a ball; wrap in heavy-duty plastic wrap, and freeze 30 minutes.

Roll dough to ⅛-inch thickness on a well-floured surface. Cut with cookie cutters.

Place dough on cookie sheets coated with cooking spray; sprinkle with crystal sugar. Bake 9 minutes. Cool on wire racks.

Per cookie: Calories 47 (13% from fat), Fat 1 g (0 g saturated), Protein 1 g, Carbohydrate 10 g, Fiber 0 g, Cholesterol 0 mg, Iron 1 mg, Sodium 44 mg, Calcium 12 mg

Poached Pears With Raspberry Coulis and Mint

SERVES 4

1 package (10 ounces) frozen raspberries in light
*   syrup, thawed overnight in refrigerator*
2 tablespoons powdered sugar
2 bosc or comice pears
½ cup riesling or rhine wine, or white grape juice
1½ teaspoons chopped fresh mint
mint sprigs

Place raspberries in a food processor or blender; add sugar. Process or blend until pureed; strain and discard seeds. In a small saucepan, bring puree to a boil, lower to a simmer, and cook gently until reduced to ½ cup, 8 to 10 minutes. Set aside.

Meanwhile, peel pears, cut in half lengthwise, and core with a melon baller or paring knife. Lay each pear half cut side down on a cutting board. Starting ¾ inch from the small end, cut pear lengthwise into ½-inch slices, leaving slices attached at small end. Place pears in a single layer in a microwave-safe dish. Pour wine over pears. Cover with vented plastic wrap. Cook in microwave oven on high 5 minutes. Baste pears with juices from dish, cover, and cook again on high until nearly tender, about 3 minutes. (For a warm dessert, proceed promptly to next steps.)

Spoon coulis onto 4 small plates. Using a spatula, place pears on coulis. Spread slices into fans, sprinkle with chopped mint, and top with mint sprigs.

Per serving: Calories 110 (4% from fat), Fat 1 g (0 g saturated), Protein 1 g, Carbohydrate 27 g, Fiber 4 g, Cholesterol 0 mg, Iron 0 mg, Sodium 2 mg, Calcium 19 mg

IN SEASON

For succulent fresh fruit in the dead of winter, look in your supermarket for bosc and anjou pears.

BEST BUYS

Choose pears that are unblemished and firm. Allow them to ripen at room temperature in a brown bag or other dark place. To gauge a pear's ripeness, apply gentle thumb pressure near its stem. If the flesh yields slightly, it's ripe.

COOKING TIP

For a fast flavorful salad to serve 4, peel and slice 2 ripe pears, then sprinkle lightly with lemon juice. Cut 2 large heads belgian endive into 1-inch pieces. In a salad bowl, toss pears and endive with 2 tablespoons raspberry vinegar and 1 tablespoon extra virgin olive oil. Season with salt and freshly ground black pepper, if desired.

HEALTH BONUS

One midsize pear delivers as much fiber as two slices of whole wheat bread (4 grams). Pears also offer potassium, which can help lower blood pressure.

KITCHEN TIP

Wondering when to retire that opened bottle of vanilla extract? The *Food Keeper* can help you figure out what's fresh and stale in your pantry. For your copy, call the Food Marketing Institute, 202/452-8444, or visit the Web site at *www.fmi.org*.

Raspberry Cream Angel Pie

SERVES 8

2 egg whites (at room temperature)

½ teaspoon vinegar

¼ teaspoon salt, divided

½ cup sugar

2 cups fresh raspberries, divided

⅓ cup sugar

2 tablespoons cornstarch

1½ teaspoons unflavored gelatin

1 cup nonfat milk

½ cup water

1 egg yolk

1 teaspoon almond extract

Preheat oven to 275°. Combine egg whites, vinegar, and ⅛ teaspoon salt in a bowl; beat until foamy. Add ½ cup sugar, 1 tablespoon at a time, beating until stiff peaks form. (Do not underbeat.)

Spoon egg white mixture into a 9-inch pie plate. Using the back of a spoon, spread and shape mixture against sides and bottom of pie plate.

Bake 1 hour. Turn oven off and let meringue cool for 2 hours before opening oven door. Let cool completely.

Place 1 cup raspberries in a small bowl; crush with the back of a spoon. Set aside.

Combine remaining ⅛ teaspoon salt, ⅓ cup sugar, cornstarch, and gelatin in a medium saucepan; stir in milk and water. Let stand 1 minute. Cook over medium heat, stirring frequently with a wire whisk, 8 minutes or until mixture comes to a boil and thickens.

Beat yolk in a small bowl; gradually stir ¼ of hot mixture into yolk. Add yolk mixture to remaining hot mixture, stirring constantly. Cook over medium heat 1 minute.

Remove from heat and pour into a medium-size bowl; stir in almond extract and crushed raspberries. Cover and chill 1 hour or until almost set.

Fold in remaining 1 cup raspberries; spoon into cooled meringue shell. Chill until set.

Per serving: Calories 128 (7% from fat), Fat 1 (0 g saturated), Protein 3 g, Carbohydrate 28 g, Fiber 2 g, Cholesterol 27 mg, Iron 0 mg, Sodium 104 mg, Calcium 49 mg

Summer Pudding

SERVES 4

5 cups strawberries, divided

1 cup blackberries, divided

¾ cup blueberries, divided

¾ cup raspberries, divided

½ cup sugar

⅓ cup water

about ⅔ loaf (1-pound size) firm-textured thin-sliced white bread

Rinse and drain strawberries, blackberries, blueberries, and raspberries; set aside 4 berries of each for garnish. Hull remaining strawberries; slice 2 cups and set aside.

In a blender, puree remaining strawberries; pour through fine strainer into bowl. Discard seeds. Cover puree and chill at least 4 hours, up to 1 day.

In a 2- to 3-quart pan over medium-high heat, bring blackberries, blueberries, sugar, and water to a boil; simmer 6 to 7 minutes. Remove from heat and stir in sliced strawberries and raspberries. Let cool, stirring occasionally.

Trim crusts from bread and discard or save for other uses. Cut bread to fit, with edges slightly overlapping, the bottoms, sides, and tops of 4 ramekins, 1- to 1¼-cup size; reserve any extra bread for other uses or discard. Snugly line bottoms and sides of ramekins with bread.

Pour off and save ½ cup cooked berry liquid; spoon remaining mixture into lined ramekins. Cover with bread tops and moisten evenly with all but 1 tablespoon fruit liquid. Cover ramekins with plastic wrap and set in a rimmed pan. Place a can of food (about 1-pound size) on top of each ramekin. Chill ramekins and remaining liquid at least 4 hours, up to 1 day.

Remove cans and unwrap ramekins. Invert each pudding onto a dessert plate. Moisten any white spots of bread with reserved berry liquid. Pour strawberry puree around puddings, and garnish tops with reserved berries.

Per serving: Calories 400 (9% from fat), Fat 4 g (1 g saturated), Protein 8 g, Carbohydrate 87 g, Fiber 9 g, Cholesterol 1 mg, Iron 3 mg, Sodium 409 mg, Calcium 126 mg

Cinnamon-Rice Stirred Custard

SERVES 5

1 cup nonfat milk

¾ cup evaporated nonfat milk

¼ cup sugar

¼ teaspoon ground cinnamon

2 eggs

1 cup cooked long-grain rice

½ teaspoon vanilla extract

Combine milks in a large saucepan; cook over medium-high heat to 180° or until tiny bubbles form at edges of pan. (Do not allow to boil.) Set aside.

Combine sugar and cinnamon in a medium-size bowl; add eggs and beat vigorously with a wire whisk until blended. Stir in cooked rice. Gradually stir about ¼ of hot milk into egg mixture; add egg mixture to remaining hot milk, stirring constantly.

Cook over low heat until mixture thickens enough to coat a metal spoon (about 30 minutes), stirring constantly with a wire whisk.

**Mixed Berry Tart
With Almond Cream**

LEIGH BEISCH

Pour custard into a large bowl; stir until cool. Stir in vanilla extract; cover and chill 2 hours.

Per serving: Calories 160 (11% from fat), Fat 2 g (0 saturated), Protein 8 g, Carbohydrate 26 g, Fiber 0 g, Cholesterol 85 mg, Iron 1 mg, Sodium 98 mg, Calcium 187 mg

Strawberries With Sour Cream–Mango Dip

SERVES 5

2 baskets (about 1 pound) fresh strawberries
1 small carton (8 ounces) low-fat vanilla yogurt
¾ cup cubed peeled mango
½ cup nonfat sour cream
1½ teaspoons honey

Spoon yogurt onto several layers of paper towels; spread to ½-inch thickness. Cover with additional paper towels; let stand 5 minutes. Scrape yogurt into a bowl and set aside.

Using a food processor, process mango until smooth. Add mango puree, sour cream, and honey to yogurt; stir well.

Cover and chill. Serve with whole, unhulled strawberries for dipping.

Per serving: Calories 124 (7% from fat), Fat 1 g (0 g saturated), Protein 4 g, Carbohydrate 25 g, Fiber 3 g, Cholesterol 3 mg, Iron 0 mg, Sodium 54 mg, Calcium 128 mg

Mixed Berry Tart With Almond Cream

SERVES 8

TART

1 cup all-purpose flour
1 tablespoon granulated sugar
¼ teaspoon salt
3 tablespoons butter or margarine, chilled and cut up
2 to 3 tablespoons cold water

FILLING

½ cup cold water
1 teaspoon unflavored gelatin
1 cup nonfat vanilla yogurt
½ teaspoon almond extract

TOPPING

½ cup each: raspberries, blackberries, and blueberries
2 tablespoons apricot preserves

Preheat oven to 400°. To make crust, in a large bowl or food processor fitted with metal blade, combine flour, sugar, and salt. Add butter and mix together with your fingers or process until mixture resembles coarse meal. Add cold water, one tablespoon at a time, and mix or process until a manageable dough forms. Turn dough to a lightly floured surface, roll into a 12-inch round and fit into a 9-inch, removable-bottom tart pan. Press dough into bottom and up sides of pan. Prick bottom all over with a fork and cover crust with foil or wax paper. Top foil with dried beans or rice.

Bake 10 minutes. Remove beans and foil and bake 15 to 20 more minutes, until crust is golden brown. Remove from oven and cool completely on a wire rack.

Meanwhile, to make almond cream, in a small saucepan, sprinkle gelatin over cold water. Let stand 1 minute. Place pan over low heat and simmer until gelatin is completely dissolved, 1 to 2 minutes, stirring constantly. Remove from heat and whisk in yogurt and almond extract. Pour mixture into cooled crust, cover with plastic and refrigerate until firm, 1 to 2 hours.

Top almond cream with fresh berries, alternating each to form decorative circles. Brush top with apricot preserves, until berries are glazed and shiny (if preserves are thick and unspreadable, warm slightly in microwave).

Per serving: Calories 170 (25% from fat), Fat 5 g (3 g saturated), Protein 4 g, Carbohydrate 29 g, Fiber 2 g, Cholesterol 12 mg, Iron 1 mg, Sodium 145 mg, Calcium 52 mg

Raspberry-Strawberry Granita

SERVES **4**

2 cups white grape juice

1 cup water

⅓ cup sugar

*1½ cups combination fresh raspberries and fresh
    strawberries, divided*

1 teaspoon fresh lemon juice

*mint sprigs or edible flowers such as pansies
    (optional)*

*½ cup vanilla yogurt, whipped cream, or crème
    fraîche (optional)*

Raspberry-Strawberry Granita

In a medium-size saucepan, bring grape juice,
water, and sugar to a boil. Boil 5 minutes, then
remove from heat. Meanwhile, place ½ cup berries
in a blender and whirl until smooth. (Reserve
remaining cup berries for garnish.) Add berries
and lemon juice to grape juice mixture. Let cool
at least 30 minutes.

Strain mixture into an 8-inch square glass baking
dish. Cover with plastic wrap, and place in freezer
until frozen.

Remove from freezer. Using a fork, break
mixture up into loose ice crystals. To serve, divide
among 4 martini glasses or wineglasses that have
been chilled in freezer. Sprinkle each serving
with reserved berries. If desired, garnish each with
a mint sprig, an edible flower, or a dollop of
yogurt, whipped cream, or crème fraîche.

Per serving: Calories 161 (1% from fat), Fat 0 g (0 g saturated),
Protein 1 g, Carbohydrate 40 g, Fiber 2 g, Cholesterol 0 mg,
Iron 1 mg, Sodium 4 mg, Calcium 21 mg

Cantaloupe Campari Sorbet

SERVES **8**

½ cup water

¾ cup sugar

5 cups diced cantaloupe

¼ cup orange juice

at least ¼ cup Campari, divided

orange slices for garnish

In a 1- to 1½-quart pan over high heat, bring water
and sugar to a boil and stir until sugar dissolves.
Let syrup cool.

In a blender, puree fruit with syrup, orange juice,
and 2 tablespoons of the Campari. Pour puree
into a shallow metal pan (at least 9 inches square).
Cover and freeze until solid, at least 4 hours, up
to 1 month.

Let sorbet stand at room temperature until
slightly softened, about 10 minutes, then break
into chunks and whirl in food processor or beat
with mixer to make a smooth slush. Serve sorbet at
once, or return to freezer up to 1 hour (it will get
very hard if frozen longer).

To serve, scoop sorbet into tall wineglasses,
and pour a little Campari around each scoop.
Garnish with orange slices.

Per serving: Calories 126 (0% from fat), Fat 0 g (0 g saturated),
Protein 1 g, Carbohydrate 28 g, Fiber 1 g, Cholesterol 0 mg,
Iron 0 mg, Sodium 10 mg, Calcium 14 mg

Strawberry-Banana Frozen Yogurt

SERVES 8

1 cup sliced fresh strawberries

¾ cup (about 1 medium) sliced banana

3 cups low-fat vanilla yogurt

Position knife blade in food processor bowl; add strawberries and banana. Process until smooth. Pour into a bowl; add yogurt and stir well.

Pour mixture into the freezer can of a hand-turned or electric frozen-dessert maker. Freeze according to manufacturer's instructions.

Per serving: Calories 91 (10% from fat), Fat 1 g (0 g saturated), Protein 4 g, Carbohydrate 16 g, Fiber 1 g, Cholesterol 4 mg, Iron 0 mg, Sodium 57 mg, Calcium 149 mg

Ginger-Berry Sorbet

SERVES 8

1½ cups fresh blackberries

2 tablespoons water

1½ cups sliced fresh strawberries

1½ cups fresh blueberries

¼ cup sugar

½ teaspoon grated peeled fresh ginger

1 bottle (10 ounces) lemon-lime sparkling water

Combine blackberries and 2 tablespoons water in a saucepan; place over medium heat and cook 5 minutes or until berries soften. Strain mixture and discard seeds.

Position knife blade in food processor bowl; add blackberry puree and remaining ingredients. Process 1 minute or until smooth. Pour mixture into the freezer can of a manual or electric frozen-dessert maker. Freeze according to manufacturer's instructions.

Per serving: Calories 75 (0% from fat), Fat 0 g (0 g saturated), Protein 1 g, Carbohydrate 19 g, Fiber 3 g, Cholesterol 0 mg, Iron 0 mg, Sodium 4 mg, Calcium 15 mg

Spiced Asian Pears With Chocolate Sauce

SERVES 4

3 cups water

1½ cups orange muscat wine, such as Essencia

½ cup sugar

2 sticks cinnamon, each about 3 inches long

about 1½ tablespoons finely shredded orange peel, divided

4 asian or other firm ripe pears, each about ½ pound, peeled, halved lengthwise, and cored

1 ounce unsweetened chocolate, chopped

1 teaspoon vanilla

mint sprigs for garnish

In a 3- to 4-quart, wide, shallow pan, combine water with wine, sugar, cinnamon sticks, and 1 tablespoon of the orange peel. Bring to a boil over high heat; cover and simmer 15 minutes; add pears. Cover and simmer until asian pears are crisp-tender when pierced (regular pears should be very tender), 15 to 25 minutes; turn fruit over occasionally. With a slotted spoon, set pears aside to use, either warm or at room temperature. If making ahead, cover and chill up to 1 day.

Discard cinnamon sticks. Boil liquid in pan, uncovered, over high heat until reduced to ¾ cup, about 20 minutes. Remove from heat and stir in chocolate and vanilla; mixture will look separated. Let stand until slightly cool, at least 5 minutes, then whisk to blend chocolate in smoothly. Use hot, warm, or cold. If making ahead, cover and chill up to 1 day.

Arrange pear halves on individual plates, and pour chocolate sauce around fruit. Sprinkle with remaining orange peel and garnish with mint.

Per serving: Calories 251 (14% from fat), Fat 4 g (2 g saturated), Protein 1 g, Carbohydrate 42 g, Fiber 6 g, Cholesterol 0 mg, Iron 1 mg, Sodium 6 mg, Calcium 23 mg

Chocolate-Almond Delight

SERVES 2

1 cup nonfat vanilla frozen yogurt

¾ cup nonfat milk

¼ cup chocolate syrup

¼ teaspoon almond extract

2 scoops plain, vanilla, or chocolate soy
   protein powder

Combine ingredients in blender. Cover and
blend at high speed about 1 minute. Pour into
frosted glasses.

Per serving: Calories 245 (4% from fat), Fat 1 g (0 g saturated),
Protein 17 g, Carbohydrate 47 g, Fiber 1 g, Cholesterol 2 mg, Iron
1 mg, Sodium 248 mg, Calcium 118 mg

Raspberry-Peach Spritzer

SERVES 8

3 cups sliced peeled fresh peaches

½ cup fresh raspberries

½ cup peach schnapps

¼ cup grenadine

3 cups sparkling water, chilled

3 cups sugar-free lemon-lime soda, chilled

1½ cups pineapple juice

1½ cups orange juice

Combine first 4 ingredients (through grenadine) in
a blender and process until smooth. Pour into a
large pitcher; cover and chill. Stir in remaining
ingredients just before serving.

Per serving: Calories 133 (0% from fat), Fat 0 g (0 g saturated),
Protein 1 g, Carbohydrate 25 g, Fiber 2 g, Cholesterol 0 mg, Iron
0 mg, Sodium 21 mg, Calcium 17 mg

Double Strawberry Shake

SERVES 2

2 cups strawberries

½ cup nonfat or 1 percent milk

3 tablespoons strawberry preserves

3 ice cubes

2 scoops plain, vanilla, or strawberry soy
   protein powder

Combine ingredients in blender. Cover and blend
at high speed about 1 minute.

Per serving: Calories 175 (5% from fat), Fat 1 g (0 g saturated),
Protein 13 g, Carbohydrate 30 g, Fiber 2 g, Cholesterol 1 mg, Iron
1 mg, Sodium 133 mg, Calcium 96 mg

Peach Smoothie

SERVES 4

3 cups sliced fresh peaches

¾ cup (about 4 ounces) cubed reduced-fat firm
   tofu, drained

½ cup orange juice

3 tablespoons honey or sugar

1 small carton (8 ounces) low-fat vanilla yogurt

5 ice cubes

In a blender, process first 5 ingredients (through
yogurt) until smooth. With blender on, add ice
cubes one at a time; process until smooth.

Per serving: Calories 166 (6% from fat), Fat 1 g (1 g saturated),
Protein 6 g, Carbohydrate 35 g, Fiber 3 g, Cholesterol 3 mg,
Iron 1 mg, Sodium 66 mg, Calcium 118 mg

Apricot-Mango Smoothie

SERVES 2

½ cup diced fresh apricots (unpeeled)

1 cup apricot nectar

½ cup plain nonfat yogurt

½ cup diced fresh mango, frozen at least
   30 minutes but no longer than 2 weeks

½ fresh banana, sliced and frozen

Combine all ingredients in a blender and whip until smooth.

Per serving: Calories 178 (3% from fat), Fat 1 g (0 g saturated), Protein 5 g, Carbohydrate 42 g, Fiber 3 g, Cholesterol 1 mg, Iron 1 mg, Sodium 50 mg, Calcium 134 mg

Watermelon Medley
With Yogurt Dressing

Tangy Tropical Smoothie

SERVES 2

1 cup unsweetened pineapple juice

⅓ cup frozen orange juice concentrate

1 large ripe banana

3 ice cubes

2 scoops plain or vanilla soy protein powder

Combine ingredients in blender. Cover and blend at high speed about 1 minute.

Per serving: Calories 247 (4% from fat), Fat 1 g (0 g saturated), Protein 12 g, Carbohydrate 51 g, Fiber 2 g, Cholesterol 0 mg, Iron 1 mg, Sodium 103 mg, Calcium 40 mg

Watermelon Medley With Yogurt Dressing

SERVES 4

YOGURT DRESSING

¾ cup nonfat or low-fat vanilla yogurt

1 tablespoon frozen orange juice concentrate

1 teaspoon fresh lime juice

1 teaspoon grated lime zest

WATERMELON MEDLEY

1 watermelon, cut into 20 equal-sided
   triangles (about ¼ inch thick)

4 chilled kiwis, sliced into ¼-inch-thick rounds

20 halved chilled green grapes

4 mint sprigs

Berry Blast

SERVES 2

2 cups fresh or frozen mixed berries

1 cup unsweetened apple juice

½ cup frozen cranberry cocktail concentrate

3 ice cubes

2 scoops plain, vanilla, or strawberry
   soy protein powder

Combine ingredients in blender. Cover and blend at high speed about 1 minute.

Per serving: Calories 313 (3% from fat), Fat 1 g (0 g saturated), Protein 11 g, Carbohydrate 67 g, Fiber 6 g, Cholesterol 0 mg, Iron 1 mg, Sodium 131 mg, Calcium 15 mg

For dressing, place all ingredients in a small bowl and stir. Chill in refrigerator.

   For salad, place 2 tablespoons dressing in center of each plate and spread out to form a large circle. On top of dressing, place 4 watermelon slices in pinwheel fashion. Top with 4 kiwi slices. Pile 10 grape halves at center of kiwis. Garnish with mint.

Per serving: Calories 187 (7% from fat), Fat 2 g (0 g saturated), Protein 5 g, Carbohydrate 41 g, Fiber 4 g, Cholesterol 0 mg, Iron 1 mg, Sodium 33 mg, Calcium 119 mg

RECIPE INDEX

COMMON MEASURES

1/2 teaspoon	=	30 drops
1 teaspoon	=	1/3 tablespoon or 60 drops
3 teaspoons	=	1 tablespoon
2 tablespoons	=	1/8 cup or 1 fluid ounce
4 tablespoons	=	1/4 cup or 2 fluid ounces
16 tablespoons	=	1 cup or 8 fluid ounces or 1/2 pint
2 cups	=	1 pint or 16 fluid ounces
1 quart	=	2 pints or 4 cups or 32 fluid ounces
1 gallon	=	4 quarts or 16 cups

METRIC EQUIVALENTS

1 teaspoon	=	5 milliliters
1 tablespoon	=	15 milliliters
1 cup	=	237 milliliters
2 cups or 1 pint	=	473 milliliters
4 cups or 1 quart	=	946 milliliters
4 quarts or 1 gallon	=	3.8 liters

MEAT TEMPERATURE GUIDE*

Hamburger	160°
Ground chicken or turkey	165°
Chicken: whole & pieces	180°
Turkey (unstuffed)	
whole	180°
breast	170°
dark meat	180°
Beef, veal, & lamb: roasts & steaks	
medium-rare	145°
medium	160°
well-done	170°
Pork: chops, roasts, ribs	
medium	160°
well-done	170°
Pork: ham & sausage (fresh)	160°

FOOD EQUIVALENTS

Beans, kidney (dried)
1 pound = 2 1/2 cups; 5 1/2 cups cooked

Broccoli (fresh)
1 pound = 2 cups chopped

Cheese (cheddar-style)
1 pound = 4 cups grated or shredded

Corn (fresh)
2 medium ears = 1 cup kernels

Noodles (1-inch pieces)
1 pound = 8 cups cooked

Oranges (fresh)
1 medium = 1/3 cup juice

Rice (regular white)
1 cup = 3 cups cooked

Rice (brown)
1 cup = 4 cups cooked

Spinach (fresh)
1 pound = 10 cups cut; 1 cup cooked

Strawberries (fresh)
1 pint = 1 1/2 to 2 cups sliced

Tomatoes (fresh)
1 pound = 3 medium; 1 1/2 cups chopped

* Cooking meats to these internal temperatures will kill harmful bacteria. For the most accurate reading, use an instant-read thermometer.